THE STATE *of* INDIAN AGRICULTURE

THE STATE *of* INDIAN AGRICULTURE

Agricultural Productivity, Food Security and Climate Change

SANJEEV KUMAR

Los Angeles | London | New Delhi
Singapore | Washington DC | Melbourne

First published in 2020 by

SAGE Publications India Pvt Ltd
B1/I-1 Mohan Cooperative Industrial Area
Mathura Road, New Delhi 110 044, India
www.sagepub.in

SAGE Publications Inc
2455 Teller Road
Thousand Oaks, California 91320, USA

SAGE Publications Ltd
1 Oliver's Yard, 55 City Road
London EC1Y 1SP, United Kingdom

SAGE Publications Asia-Pacific Pte Ltd
18 Cross Street #10-10/11/12
China Square Central
Singapore 048423

Published by Vivek Mehra for SAGE Publications India Pvt Ltd. Typeset in 10.5/13 pt Adobe Caslon Pro by Zaza Eunice, Hosur, Tamil Nadu, India.

Library of Congress Control Number: 2020940482

ISBN: 978-93-5388-334-8 (HB)

SAGE Team: Rajesh Dey, Syed Husain Naqvi, Mahira Chadha and Rajinder Kaur

This book is dedicated to my family and teachers for their unwavering support.

Thank you for choosing a SAGE product!
If you have any comment, observation or feedback,
I would like to personally hear from you.

Please write to me at **contactceo@sagepub.in**

Vivek Mehra, Managing Director and CEO, SAGE India.

Contents

List of Boxes

List of Figures

List of Tables

List of Abbreviations

ACZ	Agro-climatic zones
AER	Agro-ecological regions
CAGR	Compound annual growth rate
CMIE	Centre for Monitoring Indian Economy
CSO	Central Statistical Office
CSA	Climate-smart agriculture
CV	Coefficient of variation
EU	European Union
FAI	Food availability index
FAO	Food and Agriculture Organization
FSI	Food security index
FYP	Five-Year Plan
GCF	Gross capital formation
GDP	Gross domestic product
GHG	Greenhouse gas
GHI	Global Hunger Index
GoI	Government of India
GR	Green Revolution
GVA	Gross value added
HYV	High-yielding variety
IFA	Index of food accessibility
IFS	Index of food stability
IMD	Indian Meteorological Department
MT	Million tonnes
NARP	The National Agricultural Research Project
NFSA	National Food Security Act
NLPTP	Number of livestock per 1,000 population
PCFA	Per capita food grain availability
PMFBY	Pradhan Mantri Fasal Bima Yojana

PMKSY	Pradhan Mantri Krishi Sinchayee Yojana
PM-KSNY	Pradhan Mantri Kisan Samman Nidhi Yojana
RBI	Reserve Bank of India
RWBCIS	Restructured Weather Based Crop Insurance Scheme
SAD	Sustainable agricultural development
SDG	Sustainable Development Goals
SRES	Special Report on Emissions Scenarios
UNFCCC	United Nations Framework Convention on Climate Change
VIF	Variance inflation factor

Foreword

The agriculture sector is the most vibrant sector of Indian economy. It along with its allied sectors provides livelihood to approximately 70 per cent of India's households. It acts as an engine of growth for other sectors through its forward and backward linkages and has the potential to put the country on the global map in terms of quality and competitiveness of its produce. Technological change during the 1960s in the form of Green Revolution (GR) gave a big boost to Indian agriculture in terms of both production and productivity. Moreover, the benefits of GR also transformed India from an economy deficient in agricultural commodities into a self-sufficient one.

During the recent decades, however, the agriculture sector has been facing certain critical challenges reflected in an increase in the proportion of fragmented and marginal holdings of land, poor management of water use resulting in deteriorating water resources, worsening climate conditions, lack of rural and market infrastructure, price instability and rising cost of farm inputs. The performance of agriculture is mainly dependent on natural resources such as land, water, soil health and biodiversity. But these natural resources are rapidly shrinking due to increasing socio-economic and population pressure, climatic variability and natural disasters. It has resulted in declining productivity, leading to shortage of food grains and serious implications for food security in the long run. No wonder that despite having achieved an approximately 7.0 per cent annual growth rate from 1990–1991 to 2013–2014, the incidence of malnutrition has dropped only marginally from 210.1 million in 1990 to 194.6 million in 2014. It implies that Indian agriculture is engulfed by major crises.

It is in place to mention that climatic variability in the 21st century has become one of the major environmental challenges worldwide with debilitating consequences on the sustainability of food production mainly arising due to crop failure and productivity decline. The process of global warming through climate change shows no signs of reduction and it is predictable that it will bring long-term changes in weather conditions. Climate change has also been at the centre of scientific, economic and political debates with an undisputed consensus among scientists, policymakers, politicians, academicians, administrators and the common people for the fact that climate has changed and that it is still changing (IPCC, Synthesis Report, 2007). Moreover, it is also important to note that greenhouse gas emissions and concentrations are leading to a warming of 4°C by 2100 (IPCC, 2013). Owing to these enormous changes, there will be negative impact on food security and its four dimensions, namely food availability, food accessibility, food utilization and food system stability. Given that climate variability is already impacting agriculture and food security in India, it will make the challenge of ending hunger and malnutrition even more complicated. The effects of climate variability on our ecosystems are already severe and extensive, and in such scenarios, ensuring food security in the face of climate change is among the most daunting challenges faced by human race. There is a need of urgent action in order to build resilience into agricultural production systems through climate smart agriculture to overcome these problems.

This book *The State of Indian Agriculture: Agricultural Productivity, Food Security and Climate Change* is unique in the sense that it focuses on problems relating to low productivity, food security and climate change in Indian agriculture and makes policy descriptions on strategic intervention by the policymakers. It provides an overview of the impact of climatic variables and non-climatic variables on food security, keeping in mind four dimensions of food security, namely availability, accessibility, utilization and stability; and suggests that food security can be ensured through adoption of sustainable agricultural practices, crop diversification and long-term relief measures in the event of natural disasters. The agro-climatic zones and the trends of climatic factors in India and their impact on agricultural productivity are also discussed in the book on the basis of empirical analysis. Moreover, this study also presents the way forward and concluding synthesis drawn from the analysis. The conclusions arrived at by the author through research based on quantitative analysis of relevant data pertaining to trends of climate patterns, status of Indian agriculture, food security and agricultural productivity at aggregate as well as disaggregate levels are highly relevant.

I hope this book will be widely read and used by policymakers, academicians and researchers for developing strategies in the context of sustainable agriculture and food security.

N. K. Taneja
Vice Chancellor
Chaudhary Charan Singh University, Meerut

Preface

The agriculture sector of India contributes significantly to the national income and provides employment opportunities in rural areas. More than 50 per cent of the country's population still depends primarily on agriculture, and hence, it naturally plays a crucial role in the nation's development. As the demand for food increases, the agriculture sector of India needs to match the pace with other sectors and act as an engine of growth. However, farming is significantly affected by the variability in climatic change. Changes in climatic pattern affect the diversity and intensity of crops cultivated in any given region.

In spite of its importance, the agriculture sector is facing a dilemma. It is the tragedy of this sector that despite making large strides in achieving the agricultural development goals of food security, it is still being challenged by a frightening agrarian crisis. In this challenging scenario, a fresh approach for development of the agriculture sector is the need of the hour. The approach must be more focused on the welfare and prosperity of farmers. It is in this context that the honourable prime minister announced on Independence Day 2015 that the Ministry of Agriculture would be renamed as Ministry of Agriculture and Farmers Welfare. In this perspective, ecological sustainability of agriculture and allied sector, use of natural resources, water and forests as well as socio-economic sustainability of farmers in terms of prosperity, welfare and social security need to be prioritized. Innovating managerial solutions to maximize farmers' welfare—rather than relying solely on modern farming to raise productivity and production—is the clarion call of the day.

Climatic change is a serious concern for developing as well as developed countries as it significantly influences agriculture production in these economies. Research studies have argued that in mid-, high-latitude and higher-income countries, climate change has a positive impact on agricultural production and crop productivity/ yields; while lower-latitude and lower-income countries experience a negative effect on agricultural production (Lee, 2009). Climate is changing and a further change is inevitable. There is a close nexus between climate change, agriculture and food security. Agriculture is very sensitive to changes in rainfall and temperature, and change in climate will threaten agricultural production. Extreme climatic events such as droughts, heat waves, floods and cyclones cause considerable loss in production potential of agriculture and depress economic growth. Climate risks have always been a part of agriculture and farmers have adopted a number of ex ante and ex post technological, agronomic and institutional strategies. In the past five decades, India's surface temperature has increased by 0.3°C per decade. In recent years, climate change has been accompanied by increased incidence of natural calamities such as droughts, floods, cyclones and heat waves (Goswami et al., (2006). Such extreme events can cause a drastic decline in the agricultural output, exacerbating the problems of food insecurity and poverty.

Climate change affects the food grain production as well as productivity of crops in India directly or indirectly. Most studies empirically investigate the impact of climate change on agricultural productivity based on single crop or two to three crops and restrained to one state or region. But assessment of the overall effect of climate change on agriculture production and productivity are important empirical questions because food security directly depends on food grain as well as non-food grain production and some other additional factors. Thus, it can be said that climate change, agriculture productivity and food security are directly linked to each other. Against this backdrop, the present book gives the status of Indian agriculture in the context of agricultural productivity, food security and climate change. The overall objective of the proposed study is to analyse the impact of climate change on Indian agriculture and its implications for food security. The whole book has been divided into 12 chapters. Each chapter deals with a specific area of Indian agriculture.

With the hope that this book would contribute in enlightening the issues of Indian agriculture and serve as a benchmark in implementation of the policy, I present the book to the hands of the vigilant reader. Also this book could prove to be a useful reference for students, researchers, planning and development agencies.

Acknowledgements

Research is an activity in which lots of assistance, guidance, coordination and encouragement is required from academicians, seniors, colleagues, staff as well as family members. I have received a lot of assistance from all of the aforementioned and hence express my gratitude to all of them. First of all, I express my gratitude to my mentors Professor N. K. Taneja, Vice Chancellor, Chaudhary Charan Singh University, Meerut, and Professor Suresh Pal, Director, ICAR-NIAP, New Delhi, for their encouragement, continued guidance, constructive criticism and most valuable and inspiring suggestions. I also express my gratitude to the Vice Chancellor, University of Lucknow, for providing such a wonderful working environment which facilitated the completion of this report. I am highly grateful to Professor A. K. Singh, Former Director, GIDS, Lucknow; Professor V. K. Malhotra, Member Secretary, Indian Council of Social Science Research (ICSSR), New Delhi; Dr Shiv Kumar, Principal Scientist, ICAR-NIAP, New Delhi, and Professor Atvir Singh, Department of Economics, Chaudhary Charan Singh University, Meerut, for their most valuable and inspiring suggestions and constructive criticism throughout the course of this exploration. Some parts of this book are a modified and updated version of my research project work funded by ICSSR, New Delhi. It is my privilege to thank ICSSR, New Delhi, for their financial support.

I owe my special thanks to senior professors of the department—Professor Arvind Awasthi, Professor Arvind Mohan, Professor M. K. Agrawal, Professor Vinod Singh; and all my colleagues—Dr Roli Misra, Dr A. K. Kaithal, Ms Urvashi Sirohi and Shachi Rai for their kind support and valuable suggestions. I am also grateful to all staff of the Department of Economics, University of Lucknow for their kind cooperation in the completion of this book.

I am also thankful to my research team members, Dr Sanjay Kumar Upadhyay and Ms Devna Joshi for their untiring efforts and assistance. A thank you would not suffice to express my gratitude to my family members for their unfailing cooperation and affection, so I would prefer to share with them the sense of fulfilment that the work of such a kind necessarily produces. Most importantly, I wish to thank my loving and supportive wife, Priyanka, and my two wonderful children, Jayansh and Riddhima Singh, who provide unending inspiration.

All those authors, publications and agencies whose views, data and information have been used in the text of the book are gratefully acknowledged. Their contributions have been mentioned appropriately in the book in the reference section. Last but not the least, it is my privilege to thank SAGE Publications and their editorial team for their prompt and excellent job in producing this book.

CHAPTER 1

Introduction

We need a new vision for agriculture … to spread happiness among farm and rural families. Bio-happiness through the conversion of our bio-resources into wealth meaningful to our rural families should be the goal of our national policy for farmers.

—M. S. Swaminathan

Introduction

India is an agrarian economy. The agriculture sector has been dominating a major portion of the Indian economy since Independence. It contributes about 16 per cent in total gross domestic product (GDP) and 10 per cent in total exports besides being the largest employer in the country. However, with the other sectors rising, the share of agriculture in GDP has declined considerably, but even then agriculture plays an important role in the overall economy of the country. Its role in alleviating rural poverty and ensuring sustainable development is also well established. In India, agriculture is primarily practiced as subsistence agriculture and caters to the food requirements of the cultivator's family. Even traditionally, agriculture used to be the simplest method of feeding families. Hence, Indian agriculture is more of a 'way of life' than a 'mode of businesses.

However, despite making huge developments in achieving food security, still agrarian crises persist. Hence, a nuanced approach towards the development of the agriculture sector is the need of the hour. The approach must be more focused on the welfare and prosperity of farmers. Innovative solutions focusing on modern farming methods in order to raise productivity and production need to be the clarion call of the day. Also, ecological sustainability of agriculture and allied sector pertaining to the use of natural resources such as soil, water and forests as well as socio-economic sustainability of farmers in terms of prosperity, welfare and social security need to be prioritized (GOI: State of Indian Agriculture 2015–16). These priorities need to be in sync with the climate variable dynamics which can help the agriculture sector to flourish in a great way.

At present 11.0 per cent (1.5 billion hectare) of the global land surface (13.4 billion hectare) is used in crop production. This area represents slightly over a third (36%) of the land estimated to be to some degree suitable for crop production. Moreover, in lower-middle income countries, around 70 per cent of total population is dependent on agriculture. But certain climate variations such as droughts, floods, untimely rain, frost, hail, heat and cold waves, and severe storms are the prime reasons for the total annual crop losses in the world agriculture (Hay 2007). In order to avoid these kinds of unprecedented agriculture crises, sustainable development agricultural practices in the recent past have become prevalent. Sustainable development basically refers to natural resources usage patterns aiming to meet human needs while protecting the environment, besides ensuring that the need for resources can be met not only in the present but also in the indefinite future. It is a long-term activity involving the use of natural resources implying economic growth along with accommodating socio-economic content.

This concept of sustainable development has found its way in the domain of agriculture as well wherein sustainable agriculture is defined as the practice of cultivating food and other agricultural products to meet human needs indefinitely as well as having sustainable impacts on the environment at large. It further extends to avoiding severe or irreversible damage to the endogenous or external ecosystem services upon which it depends, notably soil fertility, irrigation water, genetic

---

Box 1.1 Definition of Sustainable Development

Sustainable Development: Sustainable development has been defined by the Food and Agricultural Organization (FAO, 1989) as follows:

> The management and conservation of the natural resources and the orientation of technological and institutional change in order to ensure the attainment and continued satisfaction of human needs for present and future generations. These types of sustainable development practices conserve land, water, plant and animal genetic resources. It is also environmentally non-degrading, technically appropriate, economically viable and socially acceptable.

---

variability, pollinators and so on, and having acceptable impacts on the broader environment (environmental stewardship). Moreover, sustainable agriculture further focuses on agricultural systems that maintain long-term economic, social and environmental viability. It also encompasses more than the agro-ecosystem's ability to maintain productivity and includes economic valuations, legal and social framework as well as environmental accounting and monitoring.

Sustainable agriculture has also been the agenda of the globalized world at various global platforms. For instance, alleviating absolute poverty, and ending hunger and malnutrition by 2030—the top most Sustainable Development Goals (SDGs)—are in the priority list of all nations. Agriculture seems to be a viable option in fulfilling these priorities and goals through multidimensional interventions aiming towards availability of and accessibility (both economic and physical) to diversified and balanced food. In the same direction, with focus on more climate friendly-sustainability paradigms, there is a need to incorporate a particular holistic developmental paradigm known as climate-smart agriculture (CSA). Food and Agriculture Organization (FAO) defines CSA as an approach that can contribute to the achievement of sustainable development goals as it combines the three dimensions of sustainable development, namely, economic, social and environmental by mutually addressing food security and climate challenges. It is primarily composed of three main pillars:

(a) augmenting agricultural productivity and incomes (b) enhancing resilience of livelihoods and ecosystem and (c) reducing and/or removing greenhouse gas (GHG) emissions, wherever possible. Under the climate change scenario, CSA is a method of developing the technical policy and investment conditions to achieve sustainable agricultural development (SAD) for food security. The magnitude, immediacy and broad scope of the effects of climate change on agricultural systems create a mandatory need to ensure holistic amalgamation of these effects into agricultural planning, investments and programmes at the national level. The CSA approach is primarily designed to identify and operationalize SAD within the explicit domains of climate change.

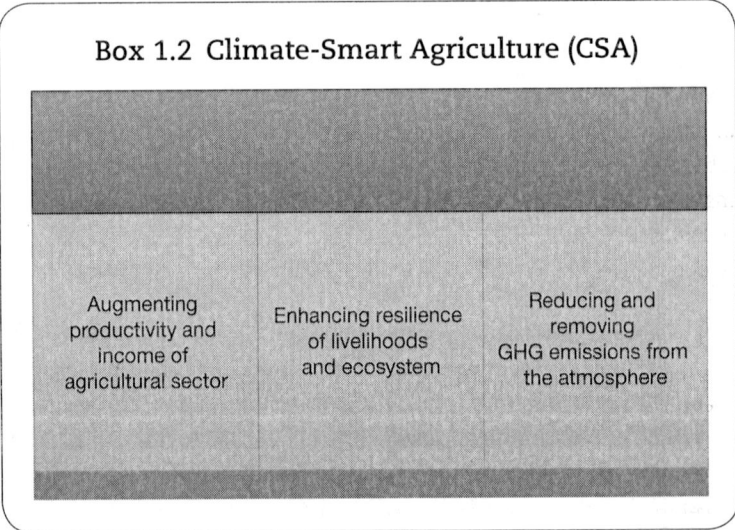

Box 1.2 Climate-Smart Agriculture (CSA)

Augmenting productivity and income of agricultural sector

Enhancing resilience of livelihoods and ecosystem

Reducing and removing GHG emissions from the atmosphere

Background of the Study

Change is the law of nature, and hence change in climatic factors is also inevitable. Climate, agriculture and food security are closely integrated. For instance, sensitivity of agriculture to changes in rainfall and temperature hampers agricultural production which in turn threatens food security. It has been witnessed that extreme climatic events such as droughts, heat waves, floods and cyclones result in significant loss of agriculture production, and ultimately depress economic growth. In this scenario, a number of ex ante and ex post technological, agronomic and institutional strategies such as borrowings, changes in production portfolio in favour of short-duration crops, use of climate-resilient crop varieties, conservation and judicious use of water, diversification into non-farm activities, mortgage or sale of productive assets and crop insurance are adopted by farmers to mitigate the impact of climate risks. However, at the broader level there is a need for greater efforts to develop a climate-resilient framework through a combination of mitigation and adaptation strategies, development of local governance and institutional structures, preference to agricultural research and development policy as suggested by emerging trends in agrarian structure, rainfall, temperature and demand for agricultural commodities.

Empirical studies reveal that climate change is a serious concern among developing as well as developed countries due to its significant impact on agriculture production. Further, studies suggest that in mid-latitude, high-latitude and higher-income countries, the impact of climate change on agricultural production or crop yields is positive, while in lower-latitude and lower-income countries, agricultural production is negatively affected by climate change (Lee 2009). Another study argues that climate change may increase the number of food-insecure children to 50 million by 2050 in south Asia (Greg et al. 2011). A study by Masters, Baker and Flood (2010) also revealed a similar argument stating that the problem of food insecurity becomes severe under changing climatic conditions and may threaten many millions of people in terms of increased disparities in cereal yields between developed and developing countries. Further, this study estimated that agriculture output and yield in lower developing countries may decline by 20 per cent and 15 per cent respectively in the presence of climate change.

Oluoko-Odingo (2009) observed that a rise in temperature would lead to either a drought or flood, a reason for the severe shortage of food availability and income of households, which would lead to poverty and food insecurity. Therefore, researchers took climatic change as one of the main reasons of food insecurity which means inability of a nation to feed its people through agriculture (Ahmad, Dastgir and

Haseen 2011). This is a very serious concern that presently more than 870 million people don't have secure resources to feed themselves at the global level.

Food demand is projected to increase by double by 2050 due to high population growth rate which will further augment the competition for resources such as land, water, capital and labour, and other precious natural resources (Ahmad, Dastgir and Haseen 2011). According to the Census, Government of India (2011), India accounts for 17.5 per cent of the global population, whereas in terms of the world's arable land this share is only 2.1 per cent. Therefore, in India, food security is a major concern in many perspectives such as increasing demand of food with growing population, poverty, declining arable land due to higher industrialization and urbanization, and declining agricultural productivity due to climate change or another reason. In reality, the list of factors affecting Indian agriculture due to climate change is quite long. Firstly, more than 60 per cent of India's total agricultural area is rainfed; secondly, more than 80 per cent of Indian farmers are small and marginal, thus, have less capacity to cope with climate change impacts (Ranuzzi and Srivastava 2012). Another very serious problem is that more than 52 per cent of the population depends on agriculture and allied sectors which are highly climate-sensitive. Also another very serious issue in India is that around 360 million undernourished people still reside in India. More than 40 per cent children in India suffer from malnutrition. (Dev and Sharma 2010).

Although these biophysical impacts vary according to time and place, the after-effects of the same hit the hardest in the agriculture and fisheries sectors especially among the already poor and vulnerable population as they possess marginal resources and live under stressful conditions. These impacts involve decline in crop productivities, heat stress for people, livestock and forest, changes related to the crops, varieties of animal species, races that thrive locally, stressed water resources and increases in price of agricultural commodities. In sum, for people whose livelihood depends on the agriculture sector, climate change alters what they can do as well as their ability to natural resource management and access to traditional safety nets. The impact of climate change also restricts access to basic resources, such as water and agrobiodiversity. The impacts of climate change on food security

Table 1.1 *Impacts of Climate Change on Food Security and Its Dimensions*

Availability	The pivotal impact of climate change on food security is via food production as well as yield changes. Short-term variations in climate are likely to be influenced by extreme weather events that upset production cycles and change seasonality. Climate change impacts on the availability of food grain will vary geographically—temperate regions in the high latitudes will see a slight increase in productivity. However, south Asia and southern Africa will suffer negative impacts on food crops, livestock, forest produce and fisheries.
Stability	Often extreme weather conditions along with climate variability becomes the main drivers of food production and productivity of crops instability. This specially happens in areas with limited irrigation facilities, especially in rainfed farming systems. More research is required to be undertaken along this domain
Utilization	It is witnessed that increases are projected in weather-related disasters, such as flooding, due to rising sea levels and increased precipitation especially for coastal settlements. This in turn result in increase in the number of men and women exposed to vector-borne (e.g., malaria) and water-borne (e.g., cholera) diseases, and ultimately, lower people's capacity to utilize food effectively, compromising with their food security status.
Accessibility	Food accessibility and food availability to all members of the population is arguably very pivotal. Food accessibility is often affected by complex secondary impacts of climate change including conflict, human insecurity, migration and soaring food prices.

Source: FAO (2008a) and Lambrou and Nelson (2010).

and its four dimensions are also potentially severe as adaptive capacity and resilience diminish (see Table 1.1).

Responding to climate change challenges has become a global priority. At the international policy level front, the major response has been institutionalized in the United Nations Framework Convention on Climate Change (UNFCCC). Within the UNFCCC, two major approaches to addressing climate change have been established, shaping the way climate change responses have been developed outside the UNFCCC. These two approaches are mitigation (by lowering GHG emissions) and adaptation (by reducing vulnerability). Moreover, the end result of climate change negotiations is not the main issue in the nexus between climate change, agriculture and food security. There is a need of producing food in a climate-friendly way, adopting practices that increase productivity on existing land areas, increasing robustness, reducing risks and GHG emissions despite the progress of the negotiations in order to achieve the global development goals of peace and prosperity.

Significance of the Book

Both climate change and agriculture are closely connected. The relationship between the two is depicted in Figure 1.1. The figure shows that on the one hand, agriculture, and changes in land cover and food systems emit GHGs that contribute to climate change, on the other hand, this climate change affects agriculture. In this regard, there are

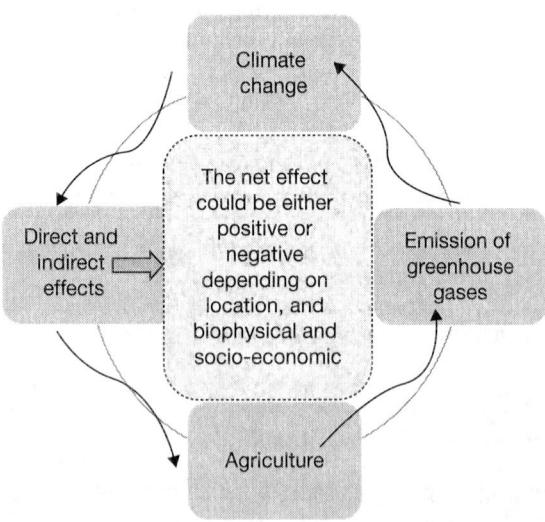

Figure 1.1 *Interrelationship between Climate Change and Agriculture*

numerous studies for example, EPA (2014), and Vermeulen, Campbell and Ingram (2012) argue that food systems lead to about 19 to 29 per cent of the total GHG emissions. Direct emissions emanating due to crop cultivation and livestock account for about 10 to 12 per cent of the total GHG emissions (Solomon et al. 2007). Not only the extent of agricultural emissions but also its trend is alarming. The recent data statistics of FAO indicate the doubling of emissions particularly from agriculture, forestry and fisheries over the past 50 years. The report further suggests an increase of additional 30 per cent by 2050 if necessary steps to reduce them are not undertaken timely.

The agriculture sector is affected directly and indirectly by climate change. The changes in climatic factors, namely, maximum temperature, minimum temperature and rainfall affect agricultural productivity through physiological changes in crops (Chakraborty, Tiedemann and Paul 2000).

In addition, climate change also affects other factors affecting agricultural production such as water availability, soil fertility and threat of pests (Porter 2014). In general, the effect of climate change could be positive or negative on agriculture; the extent of impact can also vary from very low to very high and it depends on geographical or regional location as well as status of socio-economic development (Mendelsohn, Dinar and Williams 2006; Tol et al. 2004; Tripathi 2016). These studies suggest that whether a little change in climate is bad or good depends on geographical and regional locations. For instance, Downing, Kuik and Smith (2004) found that a 1°C increase in temperature while a 20 centimetre rise in sea level had a positive impact on Organization for Economic Co-operation and Development (OECD) countries, Middle East countries and China, but a negative impact on other regions of the world.

High variation in climatic factors such as temperature and rainfall affects the crop productivity. Thus, these variations in climatic variables may have positive and negative impact on agricultural/crop productivity and food security situation in the economy (Greg et al. 2011). Agricultural productivity is an important part of food security which is an integral part of poverty eradication and hunger. It is further argued

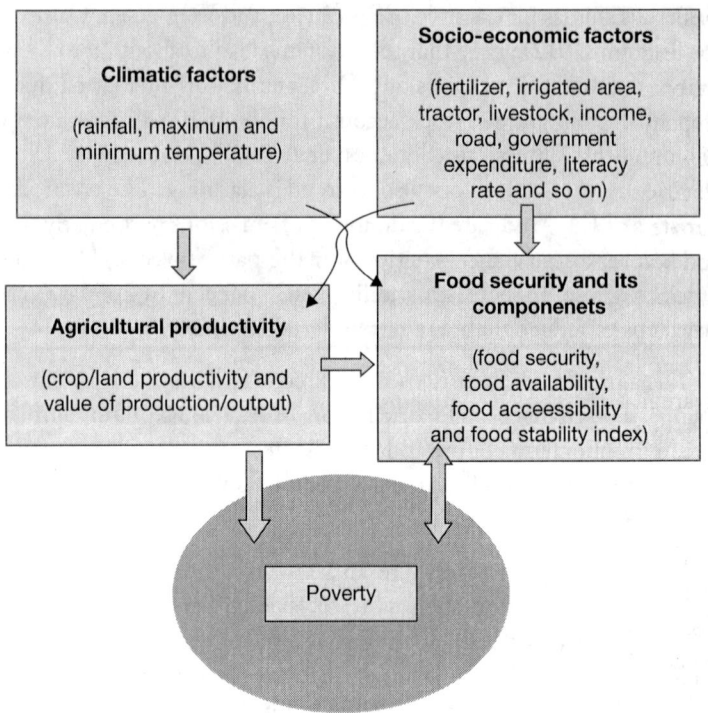

Figure 1.2 *Relationship among Climatic Factors, Socio-economic Factors, Agricultural Productivity and Food Security*

by Hollaender, (2010) that climate change, agricultural productivity, food security and poverty are inter-linked and strongly correlated.

Figure 1.2 shows the relationship among these broad aspects, namely, climatic factors, socio-economic factors, agricultural productivity and food security as well its components. There is a direct relationship between climatic factors and agricultural productivity. Furthermore, agricultural productivity has a direct impact on food security and its components. Socio-economic factors also influence agricultural productivity as well as food security and its components.

In the past five decades, India's surface temperature has increased by 0.3 °C per decade. Also, given that climate change accompanies increased incidence of natural calamities such as droughts, floods, cyclones and heat waves (Goswami et al. 2006), such extreme events can lead to a drastic decline in the agricultural output, exacerbating the problems of food insecurity and poverty. Bhandari et al. (2007) in their study conducted across some eastern states of India predicted a 24 to 58 per cent reduction in household incomes and 12 to 33 per cent increase in farm household poverty in a drought year. Moreover, climate change primarily affects small farmers, particularly those with land holdings measuring less than or equal to 1.0 hectare and comprising close to two-thirds of the total holdings. This is generally due to their lack of access to technologies, inputs, information and finances for mitigation and adaptation. Thus, against this backdrop, given the agrarian structure and potential threats of climate change to sustainable agricultural development and food security in the country, no other topic has attracted the attention of scientists and policymakers as climate change.

The above discussion shows that climate change affects food grain production as well as productivity of crops in India both ways, that is, positively and negatively. Most of the studies empirically examine the impact of climate change on agricultural productivity based on selected crops and are restricted to one state or region. But assessment of the overall impact of climate change on major food grain and non-food grain crops is important because food security is not only a function of food grain crop but a mix of several other additional factors also which may affect the level of food security including production of commercial crops, people's income, geographical region, availability of drinking water, level of education and employment, reduction in cultivated land, increasing population, urbanization and lack of food grain market number. Thus, it can be said that climate change, agricultural productivity and food security are interrelated.

Against this backdrop, the present book focuses on the status of Indian agriculture, agricultural productivity, scenario of food security and its components, and trends of climatic factors. The discussion of this book is based on national as well as state level analysis. Moreover, it makes an attempt to analyse the impact of climate change on agriculture/crop productivity and food security at aggregate level as well as disaggregate level in India. The book also constructs national and

state level food security index (FSI) by its components such as availability, stability and accessibility of food, and investigates the impact of
climate variables, socio-economic and policy variables on constructed
FSI. Finally, it suggests appropriate strategies and policies for climate-
resilient agriculture and its implications for food security

The main hypothesis of the proposed study is that climate change
directly affects agricultural productivity as well as food security. It is
assumed that severity of climatic effect in particular regions in India
caused drastic reduction in agriculture production and crop productivity, and shifting rainfall patterns will change the growing locations of
various crops. Some regions will be better suited for agriculture, while
others will experience decreased productivity. Food security is not
only related to agricultural performance of particular region or state
but also significantly influenced by the socio-economic and climatic
factors. It is also hypothesized that government policies mitigate the
effect of climate change on agricultural productivity and food security
as well as protect small farmers' interests in the market and the food
security of the people.

Agriculture, Food Security and Climate Change: Conceptual Framework

Climate change scenarios take into account higher temperatures,
changes in precipitation levels and high amounts of atmospheric
carbon dioxide (CO_2) concentrations which may impact yield (both
quality and quantity), growth rates, transpiration and photosynthesis
rates, availability of moisture through changes in water use (irrigation)
and agricultural inputs. Environmental impacts such as frequency and
intensity of soil drainage (leading to nitrogen leaching), soil erosion,
land availability and decline in crop diversity may also impact agricultural productivity. The flow of the impacts of climate change on
the agriculture sector as well food security can be illustrated as shown
in given Figure 1.3.

Food security and its components are both directly and indirectly
associated with climate change. Any change arising in the climatic
variables such as temperature and humidity influencing crop growth

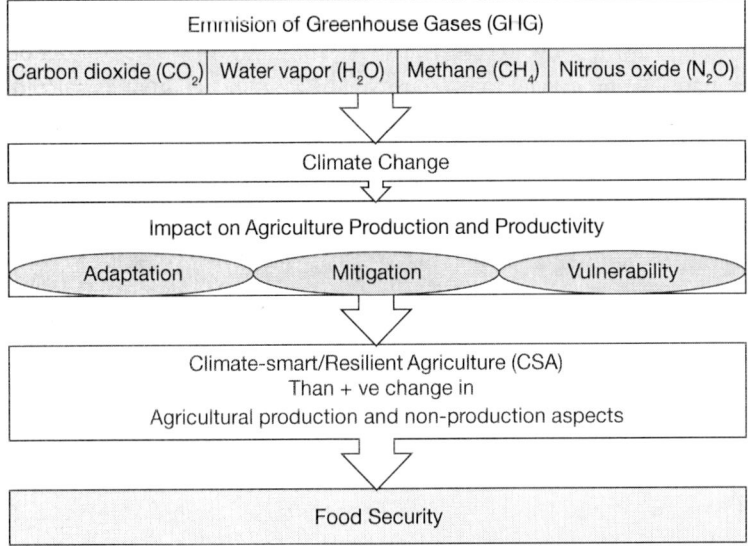

Figure 1.3 *Impacts of Climate Change on the Agriculture and Food Security*

will naturally have a direct impact on the quantity of food produced. Indirect linkage relates to catastrophic events such as flood and drought conditions which are projected to multiply as a result of climate change, leading to huge crop losses leaving large patches of arable land unfit for farming and hence threatening food security and its components. The overall impact of food security and its components will depend on the exposure to global environmental change and the capacity to cope with and recuperate from global environmental change. Globally, irregular weather patterns will result in fall in agricultural production and higher food prices, leading to food insecurity.

Climate change, agriculture and food security are complex and have a dynamic relationship. In the 21st century, agriculture food consumption systems are heavily influenced by socio-economic conditions, namely, changing patterns of consumption of food basket, macro-economic policies of the government, political conflict and the spread of disease. The report of the World Economic Forum (World Economic Forum 2008) warns, 'food security will become an increasingly complex political and economic problem in the near future.' It is therefore necessary to closely align the initiatives for better climate adaptation and food security. The agricultural production risks directly convert into additional risks for the food security and nutrition of a community that directly depends on agriculture for its food and livelihood. These risks can also have an impact on the food and nutrition security of distant communities through price volatility and disrupted trade. As shown in Figure 1.4, there is thus a cascade of risks from climate changes to agro-ecosystems, to agricultural production and post-harvest, to agricultural and other livelihoods and finally to food security and nutritionist components.

Organization of the Book

The present book looks at genesis of status of Indian agriculture along with trends of agricultural productivity, food security and components of food security at national as well as state level. The trends of climatic factors and their impact on agricultural productivity and food security are also discussed in the book. The book has been presented in 12 chapters. Each chapter delineates specific issues engulfing Indian agriculture. Chapter 1 describes the role of climate change in the area of agriculture sector and food security. Further, this chapter focuses on issues and challenges of climate change for agricultural productivity and food security. Significance, objectives, hypotheses and limitations of the present study are explained in this chapter. Chapter 2 presents the status of Indian agriculture at the globe and national levels. This chapter is also gives the current picture of Indian agriculture and new government initiatives to boost the agricultural system of India. Chapter 3 presents review of literature relating to the proposed research topic at international, national and state levels. Research gap is also discussed in this chapter. Research methodology and data sources with description are presented in Chapter 4. This chapter also provides descriptive method to construct FSI, comprehensive overview of various econometric models about impact of climatic and non-climatic variables on crop-wise productivity, value of agricultural output and food security at aggregate level as well as disaggregate level. Chapter 5 presents the agro-climatic zones in India and the trends of climatic variables at the national and state level. Chapter 6 focuses on national level analysis of climate change on Indian agriculture. Further, the trends of food security in India are discussed in Chapter 7. Chapter 8 delineates the impact of climate change on food security in India. Chapter 9 analyses the trends of agricultural productivity and value of output by the agriculture sector. Chapter 10 talks about the trends of food security at the national level. State level analysis of impact of climate change on agricultural productivity and food security is discussed in Chapter 11. Chapter 12 presents the conclusions and policy suggestions

Limitations of the Book

The present book/study has been analysed by using secondary data sources. Hence, all the limitations and drawbacks of a study while using secondary data can be seen in this study also. The time period covered in this study is limited in the sense that the impact of climate change on the agriculture sector is a long-term phenomenon. There are some major constraints which are affecting the climate change. The present study includes only three variables of climatic change, that is, annual rainfall, maximum temperature and minimum temperature due to the availability of data sources. Climate change is also influenced by exogenous factors. These factors are not taken into the study due to the wide coverage of those factors as well as resource constraints. In the present analysis, major crops are taken into consideration due to the non-availability of the data for other small crops. The role of the State in the changed scenario to mitigate climatic effect has not been analysed in the present study. The agro-climatic region-wise studies are also important to minimize the effects of climate change on the agriculture sector in India, which is also excluded in the present study. This can provide the basis for the future research work on this subject.

Implications of the Book

The present book study can be helpful in understanding the trends and impact of climate change on agricultural/crop productivity, value of output by agriculture and food security at national level as well as state level in India. Drivers of agriculture/crop productivity and food security, that is, climatic factors and socio-economic factors have been identified in the present study. The study will also be instrumental in building a climate-resilient framework through a combination of mitigation and adaptation strategies at various levels. It would also suggest appropriate strategies and policies for climate-resilient agriculture practices and their implications for food security. Thus, the study would be important both from methodological aspects as well as policy viewpoints.

CHAPTER 2

Overview of Indian Agriculture

We should look upon agriculture not just as a food-producing machine for the urban population, but as the major source of skilled and remunerative employment and a hub for global outsourcing.

—M. S. Swaminathan

Introduction

Agriculture is the backbone of the Indian economy and it is the most important sector not only because it contributes around 15 per cent towards net domestic product (NDP) but also provides employment to about 60 per cent of our population. This sector also accounts for a significant part of total exports and supplies raw material to a large number of rural and urban industries. Rural areas are goods markets for industrial goods and contribute a sizeable portion in household savings, which are very important source of resource mobilization. According to Professor Gunnar Myrdal, 'It is in the agriculture sector that the battle for long-term economic development of India will be won or lost.' Moreover, the primary role of agriculture sector in the process of transformation of developing economies like India was conceived as secondary to the main strategy aimed at achieving a high rate of industrial growth. It was viewed that the role of agriculture was ancillary to the main strategy of growth, which was accelerating industrialization.

In addition, India is the world's largest producer of milk, many fresh fruits and vegetables, major spices, fibrous crops and castor oil seed. India is also the second largest producer of fine cereal crops, that is, wheat and rice—the world's major food staples (FAO, World Agriculture Statistics 2014). The main focus of this chapter is to provide the status of Indian agriculture at national as well as international level. This chapter has also made a growth analysis of various aspects of the agriculture sector. The current scenario of the Indian agriculture and latest policies adopted by the government for the development of the agriculture sector are also discussed in this chapter.

After implementation of the Green Revolution (GR), India has made remarkable changes in the production of food grain crops, and recently it recorded food grain production of 275.11 Million tonnes (MT), along with 300MT of fruits and vegetables during 2016–2017. The main motivation for achieving such a huge growth rate in production of food grains, and vegetable, and fruits largely was a favourable monsoon. But there are also some limitations that should be borne in mind in order to maintain the momentum of the above mentioned growth rates as more than more than 17 per cent of the global population. Continuous growth in India's population is the major challenge for achieving food security. It also exerts pressure on the available resources. Figure 2.1 shows the population percentage and presence of natural resources.

World Scenario of Indian Agriculture Sector

India is one of the top producers of various crops, namely wheat, rice, pulses, sugarcane and cotton, and the highest producer of milk and milk products. It is the second highest producer of fruits and vegetables in the world due to the impressive growth of the agriculture sector. India also contributes around 25 per cent to the world's pulses production, which is the highest among countries, around 22 per cent to the rice production and around 13 per cent to the wheat production. Moreover, India also accounts for about 25 per cent of the total

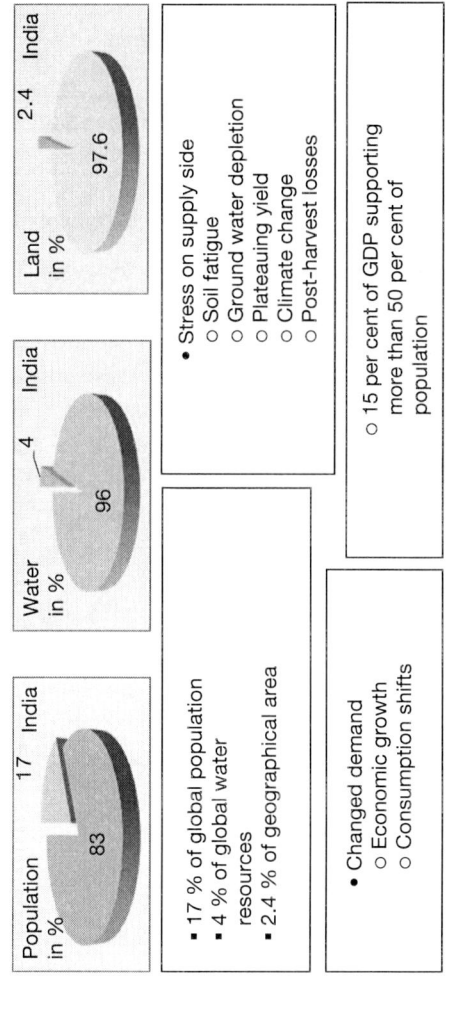

Population in %: 17 India, 83

Water in %: 4 India, 96

Land in %: 2.4 India, 97.6

- 17 % of global population
- 4 % of global water resources
- 2.4 % of geographical area

- Changed demand
  - Economic growth
  - Consumption shifts

- Stress on supply side
  - Soil fatigue
  - Ground water depletion
  - Plateauing yield
  - Climate change
  - Post-harvest losses

  - 15 per cent of GDP supporting more than 50 per cent of population

Figure 2.1 *Strain on Indian Agriculture System*

Source: Author's calculation based on RBI database, (https://www.rbi.org.in/).

Table 2.1 Status of Agriculture of Different Economies

	United States	EU–15	China	India
Agricultural GDP (%) in 2015	1.0	1.5	9.00	17.00
Population (%) in 2014–2015	>2.0	2.5	35.00	55.00
Average farm size (Hectare) in 2015	197.2	20.0	0.65	1.08

Source: Author's calculation based on FAO, World Agriculture Statistics 2016. (https://www.fao.org).

quantity of cotton produced and is the second highest exporter of cotton (FAO, World Agriculture Statistics 2014).

The contribution of the agriculture sector to the Indian economy is much better when compared to other developed countries, namely the United States, the European Union (EU)–15 area countries as well as developing countries like China. As shown in Table 2.1, in United States less than 2 per cent of population is dependent on agriculture and for EU–15 this percentage is 2.5 per cent. On the other hand, share of agricultural GDP of United States is 1.0 per cent while 1.5 per cent for EU–15. However, developing countries such as India and China show a different picture. The contribution of the agriculture sector towards GDP for India and China is around 17.0 per cent and 9.0 per cent respectively, and this sector engages more than 50 per cent population in India and more than 35 per cent population in China. This situation obviously reveals the fact that the agriculture sector has a leading role in the Indian economy as it provides livelihood support to mass rural population.

Global Trends of Agriculture Employment

The global trends of agriculture employment as a percentage of total employment from 1981 to 2011 are present in Table 2.2. From the table it can be witnessed that the share of employment in agriculture in total employment is the highest in China in 1981 at 68.1 per cent followed by India at 60.5 per cent. Pakistan, Egypt, Arab Republic and Brazil have the share at 52.6 per cent, 40.3 per cent and 29.3 per cent respectively.

Table 2.2 *Global Trend of Employment in Agriculture (% of Total Employment)*

	Years			
Country	1981	1991	2001	2011
Brazil	29.30	–	20.60	15.70
China	68.10	59.70	50.00	34.80
Egypt, Arab Republic	40.30	31.30	28.50	29.20
India	60.50	59.00	58.20	54.60
Pakistan	52.60	47.40	48.40	45.10
Russian Federation	–	14.20	12.00	7.70
United States	3.50	2.90	2.40	1.60

Source: Author's calculation based on World Bank database, (https://www.data.worldbank.org).

However, on an average over the years the share of employment in agriculture in total employment has declined across all the countries. The year 2011 shows a decline of almost 50 percentage points from 1981. The gradual decline in the share of employment in agriculture by almost 50 percentage points is observed in case of Brazil, that is, from 29.3 per cent in 1981 to 15.7 per cent in 2011, followed by China, that is, from 68.1 per cent in 1981 to 34.8 per cent in 2011 and further by United States, that is, from 3.5 per cent in 1981 to 1.6 per cent in 2011 respectively. In case of Egypt, Arab Republic, the decline is by 10 percentage points, that is, from 40.3 per cent in 1981 to 29.2 per cent in 2011.

Moreover, Pakistan followed by India show the least decline in the share of employment in agriculture in total employment—in the case of Pakistan the share was 52.6 per cent in 1981 and declined to 45.1 per cent in 2011. Similarly, in the case of India the share declined from 60.5 per cent in 1981 to 54.6 per cent in 2011. Hence, for India and Pakistan agriculture is still the major source of employment.

Global Trends of Share of Different Sectors

The global trends of share of different sectors as a percentage of GDP are presented in Table 2.3. In case of Bangladesh, it is observed that

Table 2.3 *Global Trends of Share of Different Sectors in Value Added (% of GDP)*

Country	Sector	1960	2000	2015
Bangladesh	Agriculture	61	26	16
	Industry	8	25	28
	Service	31	49	56
Brazil	Agriculture	16	6	5
	Industry	35	27	23
	Service	49	67	72
China	Agriculture	–	15	9
	Industry	–	46	41
	Service	–	39	50
Egypt	Agriculture	30	17	11
	Industry	24	33	36
	Service	46	50	52
India	Agriculture	50	23	17
	Industry	20	26	30
	Service	30	50	53
Pakistan	Agriculture	46	26	25
	Industry	16	23	20
	Service	38	51	55
Russian Federation	Agriculture	21	6	5
	Industry	62	38	33
	Service	17	56	63
Sri Lanka	Agriculture	34	20	9
	Industry	22	27	31
	Service	44	53	61
South Africa	Agriculture	12	3	2
	Industry	40	32	29
	Service	48	65	69
United Kingdom	Agriculture	4	1	1
	Industry	43	27	19
	Service	53	72	80

Country	Sector	1960	2000	2015
United States	**Agriculture**	4	1	1
	Industry	38	23	21
	Service	58	75	78

Note: The proposed book is based on agriculture sector, so the font of agriculture is bold.

Source: Author's calculation based on World Bank database, (https://www.data.worldbank.org).

in 1960, the share of the agriculture sector was the highest, that is, 61 per cent, followed by the share of the service sector at 31 per cent and the share of the industrial sector at 8 per cent respectively. However, in 2015, the sectoral shares reversed with service sector contributing the maximum share, that is, 56 per cent in GDP, followed by industrial sector at 28 per cent and the agriculture sector at 16 per cent respectively.

In the case of Brazil, the share of the agriculture, industry and service sector in 1960 was 16 per cent, 35 per cent and 49 per cent, respectively. However, in 2015, the share of the agriculture and industry sector decreased to 5 per cent and 23 per cent respectively. On the other hand, the share of service sector rose to 72 per cent.

In China, the share of the agriculture sector declined from 15 per cent in 2000 to 9 per cent in 2015. Also, the share of the industry sector in total GDP declined, but only at a modest rate. It was 46 per cent in 2000 and became 41 per cent in 2015. However, the share of the service sector raised from 39 per cent in 2000 to 50 per cent in 2015.

In Egypt, the share of the agriculture sector declined from 30 per cent in 1960 to 11 per cent in 2015. However, the shares of the industry and service sectors rose. Also, the rise in industry sector was more, that is, from 24 per cent in 1960 to 36 per cent in 2015 as compared to the service sector which grew from 46 per cent in 1960 to 52 per cent in 2015.

Moreover, in the cases of India, Pakistan and Sri Lanka, the shares of the agriculture sector fell from 1960 to 2015. For instance, in the case of India the share of the agriculture sector was 50 per cent in 1960 and declined to 17 per cent in 2015. Similarly, in Pakistan and Sri

Lanka, the sectoral shares of agriculture plummeted from 46 per cent and 34 per cent in 1960 to 25 per cent and 9 per cent, respectively in 2015. However, the shares of the industry sector and service sectors grew considerably. In the case of the industry sector, for instance, the share rose from 20 per cent to 30 per cent in the case of India, 16 per cent to 20 per cent for Pakistan and 22 per cent to 31 per cent in case of Sri Lanka. Moreover, the trend of the sectoral share of the service sector for India grew from 30 per cent in 1960 to 53 per cent in 2015, 38 per cent in 1960 to 55 per cent in 2015 for Pakistan and 44 per cent in 1960 to 61 per cent in 2015 in the case of Sri Lanka, respectively.

For other countries such as the Russian Federation, South Africa, United Kingdom and United States, the sectoral shares of both agriculture and industry sectors have declined over the years. However, the share of the service sector has increased. For instance, in the cases of Russian Federation, South Africa, United States and the United Kingdom, the share of the agriculture sector declined from 21 per cent in 1960 to 5 per cent in 2015, 12 per cent in 1960 to 2 per cent in 2015, 4 per cent in 1960 to 1 per cent in 2015 and again from 4 per cent in 1960 to 1 per cent in 2015, respectively. The share of the industry sector also declined considerably for the same set of countries. For instance, for Russian Federation it declined from 62 per cent in 1960 to 33 per cent in 2015, for South Africa it plummeted from 40 per cent in 1960 to 29 per cent in 2015, for United Kingdom it reduced from 43 per cent in 1960 to 19 per cent in 2015 while for the United States it declined from 38 per cent to 21 per cent, respectively.

The share of the service sector, however rose. In case of Russian Federation, the service sector grew from 17 per cent in 1960 to 63 per cent in 2015. For South Africa it rose from 48 per cent in 1960 to 69 per cent in 2015. In case of United Kingdom, it increased from 53 per cent in 1960 to 80 per cent in 2015 while for the United States it grew from 58 per cent to 78 per cent, respectively.

Global Trends of Production and Productivity of Wheat and Rice Crops

The trends of wheat production of wheat dominated countries, namely China, India, United States and Russia are presented in Figure 2.2.

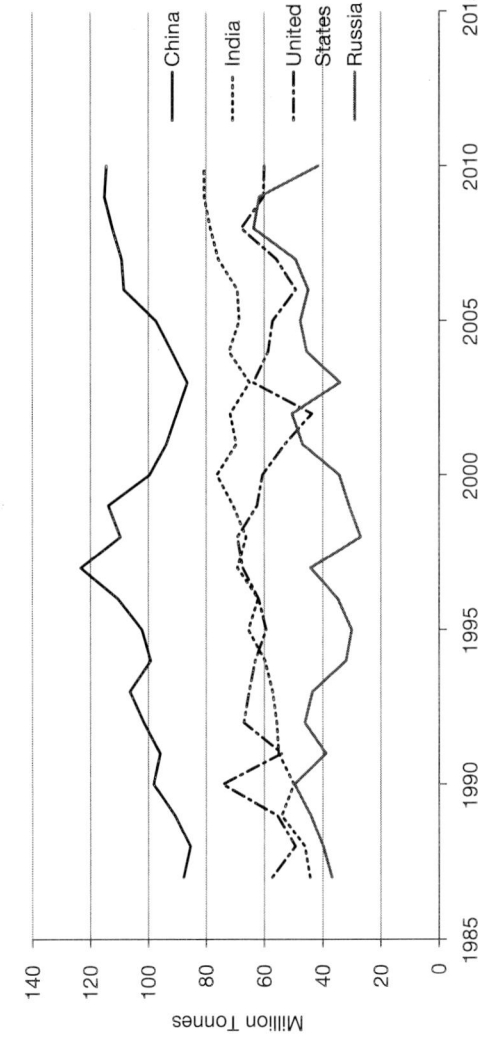

Figure 2.2 *Wheat Production in China, India, United States and Russia (1987–2010)*

Source: Author's calculation based on FAO, World Agriculture Statistics 2016. (https://www.fao.org).

Table 2.4 *Comparison of Productivity of Rice and Wheat in Various Countries*

| Country | Productivity (Yield) in Kg/Hectare | | | | | |
| | Rice (Paddy) | | | Wheat | | |
	1980	2000	2016	1980	2000	2016
Brazil	15,658	30,382	54,643	8,653	15,156	31,551
China	41,435	62,642	68,563	18,914	37,382	53,962
India	20,002	28,508	37,902	14,356	27,785	30,339
Pakistan	24,235	30,312	37,715	15,680	24,907	27,789
Russian Federation	–	34,863	53,031	16,144	26,835	58,782
United Kingdom	–	–	–	58,782	80,075	78,897
United States	49,461	70,397	81,121	22,513	28,238	35,408

Source: Author's calculation based on FAO, World Agriculture Statistics 2016. (https://www.fao.org).

The figure clearly indicates that the trend of wheat production has increased continuously with some fluctuations. The production of wheat is the highest in China followed by India, United States and Russia in that order. The growth rate of production of wheat crop was found highest in India. This is a good sign for the agriculture sector in India in achieving food security because wheat is the one of the main cereal food crops of the Indian population.

Table 2.4 shows the comparison of productivity of rice and wheat in various countries in 1980, 2000 and 2016, respectively. In the case of rice (paddy), the productivity rose the maximum in Brazil, China and United States, while it grew modestly in India and Pakistan. In the case of Brazil, the productivity rose from 15,658 kg/hectare in 1980 to 54,643 kg/hectare in 2016, while in China and the United States, it grew from 41,435 kg/hectare and 49,461 kg/hectare in 1980 to 68,563 kg/hectare and 81,121 kg/hectare respectively. In the case of India and Pakistan the productivity rose from 20,002 kg/hectare and 24,235 kg/hectare in 1980 to 37,902 kg/hectare and 37,715 kg/hectare in 2016 respectively.

In case of wheat, the productivity more than doubled in the cases of Brazil, China, India and Russian Federation, while increased modestly in the cases of Pakistan, United Kingdom and United Sates. For Brazil, the yield grew from 8,653 kg/hectare in 1980 to 31,551 kg/hectare in 2016. In the case of China, it rose from 18,914 kg/hectare in 1980 to 53,962 kg/hectare in 2016. Similarly, in the cases of India and Russian Federation, it rose from 14,356 kg/hectare and 16,144 kg/hectare in 1980 to 30,339 kg/hectare in 2016 and 58,782 kg/hectare in 2016. In the case of Pakistan the productivity rose from 15,680 kg/hectare to 27,789 kg/hectare in 2016. In United Kingdom and the United States, the productivity grew from 58,782 kg/hectare and 22,513 kg/hectare in 1960 to 78,897 kg/hectare and 35,408 kg/hectare in 2016, respectively. The same is also presented with a bar diagram (Figures 2.3 and 2.4) as well.

Although, India's rank in production of wheat and rice is second and third, respectively, in the world, the productivity of these crops is found to be much lower in India in comparison to other top producing countries such as China, Brazil, Russian Federation and United States. In sum, India's productivity (yield) is healthy but below the

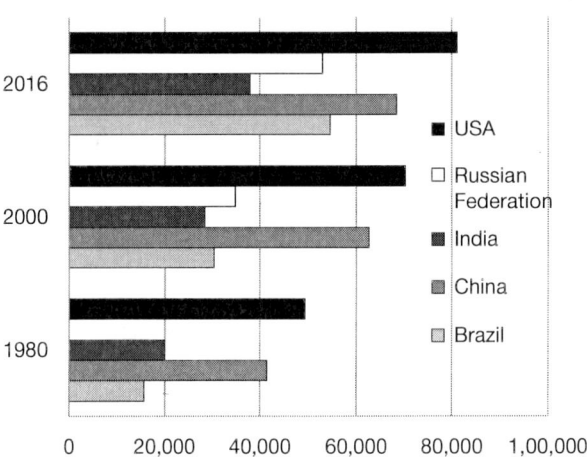

Figure 2.3 *Trends of Rice Productivity*

Source: Author's calculation based on FAO, World Agriculture Statistics. (https://www.fao.org).

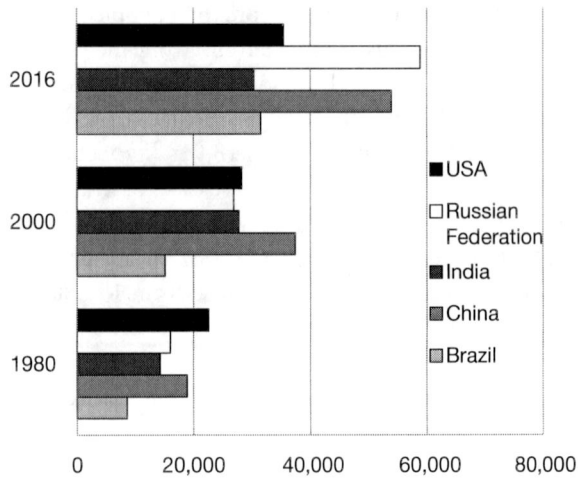

Figure 2.4 *Trends of Wheat Productivity*

Source: Author's calculation based on FAO, World Agriculture Statistics. (https://www.fao.org).

international norms. India could be a massive exporter of agricultural food only if we can put our 'house in order' to near world class standards. China has set an example for us because even with lesser cultivable land it has the capability to produce two-fold the food grains than us. God has been very kind to India for endowing it with a lot of natural resources such as availability of sunshine, rain, rivers, lakes, coastline and good, hard-working citizens. Therefore, the Indian government need to work for achieving higher growth rate of agricultural productivity in the world.

Performance of the Indian Agriculture

India is a developing country with its agriculture sector being an important pillar of its economy. The agriculture sector of India contributes around one-sixth to the nation's GDP and also provides employment to more than 50 per cent of the total workforce of India. This sector is the major source of livelihood for the majority of the rural population of India. The performance of agricultural sector has been impressive after the GR in the overall perspective of domestic and global economic scenarios. The challenge before this sector today is the absence of having a tight policy and regulatory framework that can plug loopholes in the farm input-side and at the same time address farm-produce side market imperfections so that the resources spent on agricultural development add to the farmers' welfare and prosperity. This can put the Indian economy on a higher agricultural development pedestal, supplementing sustainable and climate-smart agricultural practices.

Trends of GDP and Sectoral Share in India

Table 2.5 presents the trends of GDP and share of sectors in the Indian economy. The table indicates that the agriculture average GDP at 2004–2005 constant price was ₹1,636 billion during 1960–1961 to 1968–1969. It increased around four times, that is, to ₹5,771 billion during 2004–2005 to 2014–2015. But at the same time, average GDP by the service and industry sectors increased more than 12 times. It clearly indicates that the growth rate of the service and industry sectors has been found to be higher than the agriculture sector in India for the last 65 years. In the case of share in GDP, it is observed that the average shares of the agriculture sector and agricultural and allied activities in GDP during 1960–1961 to 1968–1969 were found to be 35.7 per cent and 43.7 per cent, respectively. There is a sharp and continuous decline in the share of the agriculture sector in GDP during the last 65 years. The average shares of agriculture and allied activities in GDP were found to be 12.7 per cent and 15.2 per cent, respectively during 2004–2005 to 2014–2015. During 1960–1961 to 1968–1969, the highest average share in GDP was of agriculture and allied activities was 43.7 per cent, followed by share of the service sector at 40.5 per cent, the share of agriculture sector at 35.7 per cent and the share of industry at 15.8 per cent respectively. However, during 2004–2005 to 2014–2015, the sectoral shares in GDP reversed with the service sector contributing the maximum share, that is, 63.9 per cent in GDP, followed by the industry sector at 20.9 per cent and the agriculture and allied activities at 15.2 per cent respectively. In sum, the share of agriculture sector in the Indian economy has sharply declined, but the dependence of population on this sector for their livelihood is declining at a very slow rate.

Table 2.5 *Trends of Average GDP and Sectorial Share in India*

Period	1960–1961/ 1968–1969	1968–1969/ 1975–1976	1975–1976/ 1988–1989	1988–1989/ 1995–1996	1995–1996/ 2004–2005	2004–2005/ 2014–2015
Average GDP at 2004–2005 Prices (₹Billion)						
Agriculture	1,636	1,955	2,547	3,473	4,358	5,771
Agriculture and Allied Activities	**2,004**	**2,401**	**3,047**	**4,116**	**5,174**	**6,911**
Industry	725	1,000	1,676	2,958	4,773	9,470
Service	1,859	2,517	4,078	7,286	13,083	28,991
Sectoral Shares as a Percentage of GDP						
Agriculture	35.7	33.0	28.9	24.2	18.9	12.7
Agriculture and Allied Activities	**43.7**	**40.6**	**34.6**	**28.7**	**22.5**	**15.2**
Industry	15.8	16.9	19.0	20.6	20.7	20.9
Service	40.5	42.5	46.3	50.7	56.8	63.9

Source: Author's calculation based on MOSPI database, (https://www.mospi.gov.in).

Sector-Wise Recent Growth Trends and Share of Gross Value Added in India

Figure 2.5 presents the recent trends of annual growth rate and sector-wise share of gross value added (GVA) statistics in Indian economy during 2011–2012 to 2017–2018 at constant prices. The figures indicate that the growth of the agriculture sector in terms of GVA at basic prices based on the year 2011–2012 witnessed high volatility from 2012–2013 onwards. After reaching a peak of 5.6 per cent in 2013–2014, the growth rate of GVA by the agriculture sector saw a sharp fall of –0.2 per cent and 0.6 per cent in 2014–2015 and 2015–2016, respectively. This low performance of the agriculture sector was mainly due to shortage of rainfall during these two years. However, with favourable monsoon and timely government policy interventions, the trend in growth overturned in 2016–2017, that is, 6.3 per cent. As per the first revised estimates of 2016–2017, GVA by agriculture and allied sector is estimated to grow around one trillion in 2016–2017 as compared to 2015–2016. The growth of agriculture and allied sector was found to be 6.3 per cent annually. The latest trends of share of different sectors of India economy are also illustrated in Figure 2.5.

Plan-Wise Growth Trends of the Agriculture Sector in India

The growth of the agriculture sector plays a very vital role in the overall economic development of the country. Plan-wise growth trends of the agriculture sector and the Indian economy are presented in Table 2.6 and Figure 2.6. During the plan periods, the growth rate of agriculture sector fluctuated between the ranges of 1.0 per cent to 4.0 per cent in India. On the other hand, the growth rate of the Indian economy was 3.6 per cent in the First Five-Year Plan (FYP), followed by 7.94 per cent in the Eleventh FYP and further declined to 7.04 per cent in the Twelfth FYP at national level. Similarly, the growth of agriculture and allied sector was above 4.0 per cent during the three annual plan

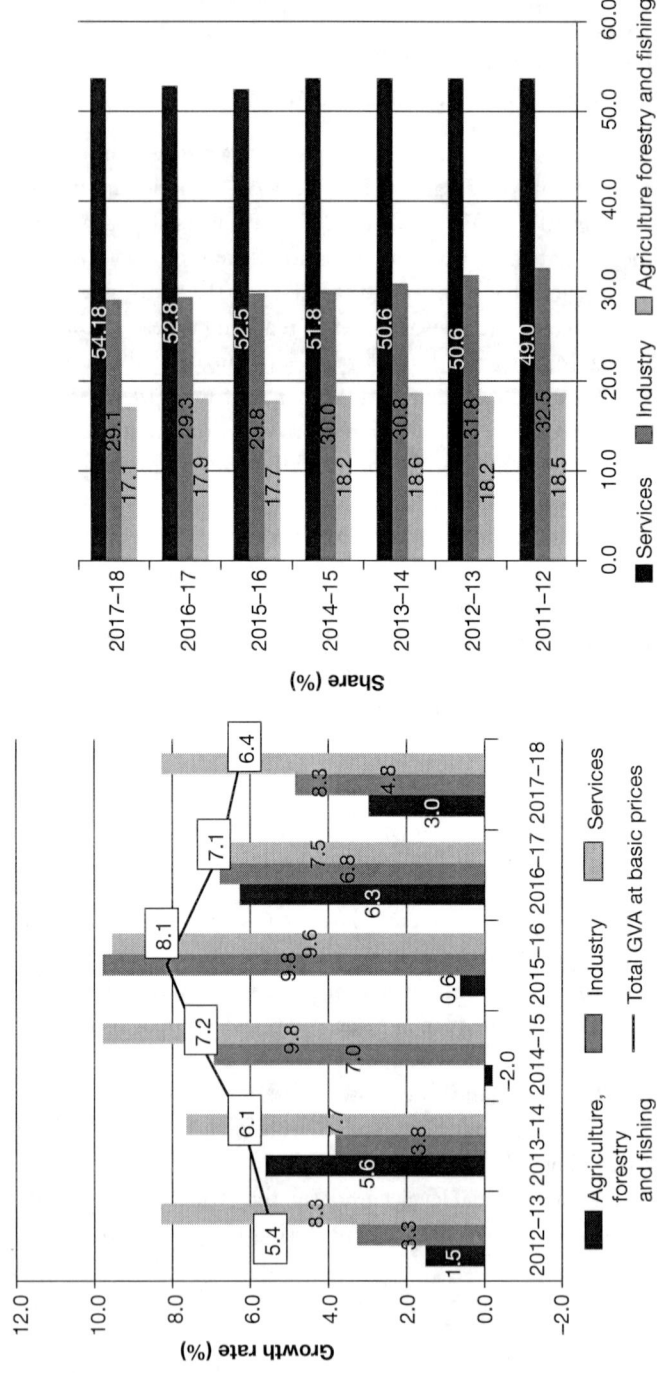

Figure 2.5 *Growth Rate and Share in GVA of Different Sectors at Constant 2011–2012 Prices*

Source: Author's calculation based on MOSPI database, (https://www.mospi.gov.in).

Table 2.6 *Plan-Wise Growth Trends of Agriculture Sector and Indian Economy*

| Five-Year Plan | Period | Growth Rate (%) | |
		Agriculture and Allied Sector	Overall Economy
First Five-Year Plan	1951–1956	2.71	3.60
Second Five-Year Plan	1956–1961	3.15	3.95
Third Five-Year Plan	1961–1966	–0.73	2.32
Annual Plans	1966–1969	4.16	3.69
Fourth Five-Year Plan	1969–1974	2.57	3.25
Fifth Five-Year Plan	1974–1979	3.28	5.30
Sixth Five-Year Plan	1981–1985	2.52	4.10
Seventh Five-Year Plan	1985–1990	3.47	5.80
Annual Plans	1990–1992	1.01	2.47
Eighth Five-Year Plan	1992–1997	3.90	6.80
Ninth Five-Year Plan	1997–2002	1.90	5.60
Tenth Five-Year Plan	2002–2007	1.10	7.70
Eleventh Five-Year Plan	2007–2012	3.20	7.94
Twelfth Five-Year Plan	2012–2017	2.21	7.04

Source: Author's calculation based on Planning Commission and NITI Aayog database (https://www.niti.gov.in).

period (1966–69) which was the highest as compared to all other plans in the country.

During the three annual plan periods, the Government of India as well as other agencies emphasized on various agricultural reforms such as high-yielding variety (HYV) seeds, and efficient use of agricultural resources, energy and modern technology. However, this plan also emphasized on agricultural credit, land reform, irrigation and high-value output to boost the agricultural growth and development at the national level. From the overall analysis, it is observed that there are huge gaps between the growth rates of both aspects.

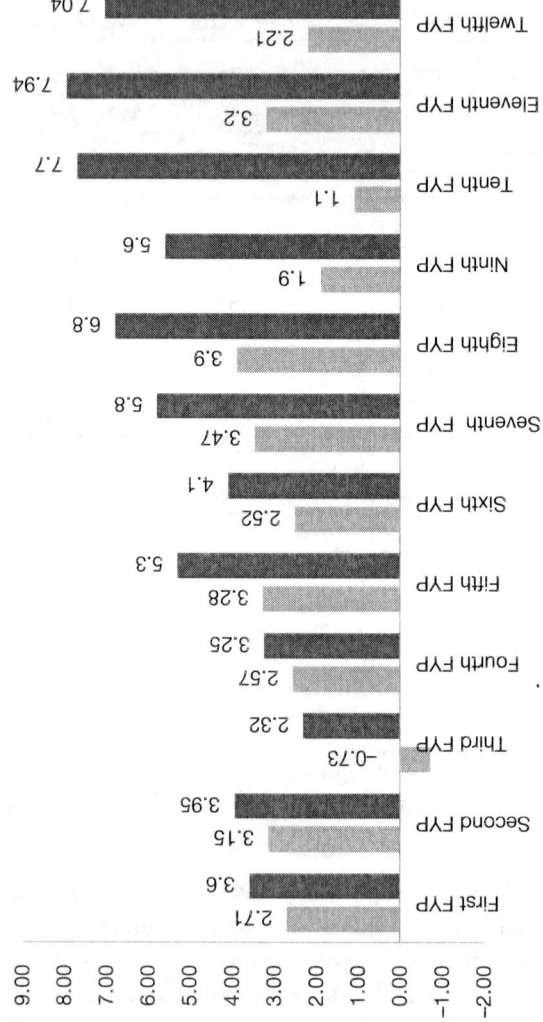

Figure 2.6 Plan-Wise Growth Rate Comparison between the Agriculture Sector and Indian Economy

Source: Author's calculation based on Planning Commission and NITI Aayog database (https://www.niti.gov.in).

Recent Trends of Share of Agriculture and Its Sub-sectors in the Indian Economy

The shares of GVA by agriculture and its sub-sectors in the Indian economy are presented in Table 2.7. It is found that the share of GVA by agriculture, forestry and fishing in the country has slightly decreased from 18.5 per cent in 2011–2012 to 17.9 per cent in 2016–2017. On the other hand, GVA by crops and livestock was 12.1 per cent and 4.0 per cent, respectively in 2011–2012 and came to 11.1 per cent and 4.6 per cent, respectively during the study period. In the case of forestry and logging, the share marginally dropped from 1.5 per cent in 2011–2012 to 1.3 per cent in 2016–2017. Similarly, the share of GVA by fishing and aquaculture has increased from 0.8 per cent in 2011–2012 to 1.0 per cent in 2016–2017.

Table 2.7 *Share of GVA of Agriculture and Its Sub-sector in Indian Economy (%)*

Year	Agriculture, Forestry and Fishing	Crops	Livestock	Forestry and Logging	Fishing and Aquaculture
2011–2012	18.5	12.1	4.0	1.5	0.8
2012–2013	18.2	11.8	4.0	1.5	0.9
2013–2014	18.6	12.1	4.1	1.5	0.9
2014–2015	18.2	11.2	4.4	1.5	1.0
2015–2016	17.7	10.6	4.6	1.5	1.0
2016–2017	17.9	11.1	4.6	1.3	1.0

Source: Author's calculation based on MOSPI database (https://www.mospi.gov.in).

Land Use and Agricultural Inputs Pattern

Trends of Land Use and Agricultural Inputs in India

The emerging trends of land use and selected inputs for the production of agriculture in India are given in Table 2.8. It is found that the net sown area in the country has marginally decreased from 1,402.7 lakh hectares in 1970–1971 to 1,401.3 lakh hectares in 2015–2016, whereas the gross sown area has increased from 1,657.9 lakh hectares in 1970–1971 to 1,983.6 lakh hectares in 2015–2016. On the other hand, the net irrigated area and gross irrigated area have slow increasing trends during 1970–1971 to 2015–2016 showing a compound annual growth rate (CAGR) of around 1.80 per cent and 2.13, respectively during the study period. The new agricultural policies have emphasized the development of widespread adoption of HYVs at the national level. As a result, the area under HYVs has continuously increased from 153.8 lakh hectares in 1970–1971 to 944.7 lakh hectares in 2015–2016 in India. In the case of consumption of fertilizers; Nitrogen, Phosphorus and Potassium (NPK), the use of these components was 21.8 lakh tonnes in 1970–1971 and sharply increased to 267.5 lakh tonnes in 2015–2016, but the consumption of pesticides has shown mixed trends during the overall period of time. In sum, it is quite clear that the inputs of agricultural development grew at a positive rate during the study period. The growth of fertilizers accounted for the highest among all the agricultural inputs. This shows that the excessive use of fertilizers may adversely affect the quality of soil, productivity, ecology and agricultural sustainability. There is a need to focus on new methods of land utilization, that is, towards organic fertilizers.

Emerging Trends of Population, Cultivators and Agricultural Labourers in India

The trends of total population, average annual growth rate of population, rural population, cultivators and agricultural labourers in India are given in Table 2.9. From the table, it is found that the population of the country was 361.1 million in the year 1951 and became 1,021.08

Table 2.8 Trends of Land Use and Selected Inputs for Agricultural Production in India

| Year | Area in Lakh Hectares [a] | | | | Consumption of Fertilizers (N+P+K) (lakh tonnes) | Consumption of Pesticides (T Grade Material) ('000 tonnes) |
	Net Sown Area	Gross Sown Area	Net Irrigated Area	Gross Irrigated Area	Area under HYVs		
1970–1971	1,402.7	1,657.9	311.0	382.0	153.8	21.8	24.3
1980–1981	1,400.0	1,726.3	387.2	497.8	430.8	55.2	45.0
1990–1991	1,430.0	1,857.4	480.2	632.0	649.8	125.5	75.0
2000–2001	1,413.4	1,853.4	552.0	761.9	798.4	167.0	43.6
2010–2011	1,415.6	1,976.8	636.7	889.4	895.9	281.2	55.5
2015–2016	1,401.3	1,983.6	683.8	964.6	944.7	267.5	54.1
CAGR	**0.0038**	**0.4111**	**1.7999**	**2.1293**	**5.0419**	**5.6689**	**0.3408**

Note: [a] 10 lakh = 1 million, 100 crores = 1 billion. (N + P + K) = sum of Nitrogen, Phosphorus and Potassium.

Source: Author's calculation based on Ministry of Agriculture & Farmers Welfare database, (https://eands.dacnet.nic.in/).

Table 2.9 *Trends of Population, Cultivators and Agricultural Labourers in India*

			Population in Million			
Year	Total Population	Average Annual Growth Rate (%)	Rural Population	Cultivators	Agricultural Labourers	Total
1951	361.1	1.25	298.6 (82.70%)	69.9 (71.90%)	27.3 (28.10%)	97.2 (100)
1961	439.2	1.96	360.3 (82.00%)	99.6 (76.00%)	31.5 (24.00%)	131.1 (100)
1971	548.2	2.22	439 (80.10%)	78.2 (62.20%)	47.5 (37.80%)	125.7 (100)
1981	683.3	2.20	523.9 (76.70%)	92.5 (62.50%)	55.5 (37.50%)	148 (100)
1991	846.4	2.14	628.9 (74.30%)	110.7 (59.70%)	74.6 (40.30%)	185.3 (100)
2001	1,028.70	1.95	742.6 (72.20%)	127.3 (54.40%)	106.8 (45.60%)	234.1 (100)
2011	1,021.08	1.77	833.0 (68.84%)	118.8 (45.20%)	144.3 (54.80%)	263.3 (100)

Source: www.censusindia.net

million in 2011. The annual growth rate of population increased from 1.25 per cent in 1951 to 2.22 per cent in 1971 and further continuously declined to 1.77 per cent in 2011. Similarly, the percentage of the rural population declined from 82.7 per cent in 1951 to 68.84 per cent in 2011. On the other hand, the percentage of cultivators decreased from 71.9 per cent in 1951 to 45.2 per cent in 2011, whereas the percentage of agricultural labourers increased from 28.1 per cent to 54.8 per cent in 2011.

From the overall analysis, it is observed that the growth of the population increased while the rural population declined during the study period. Although, the percentage of cultivators declined, agricultural labourers have increased during the same period.

Land Use Pattern in India

Land is a very important factor of production and economic development not only for acquiring higher growth but also for achieving maximum output in the country. Land has features of fixity in supply and scarcity so programme and policies must pay high attention for efficient allocation of land. According to Dr Marshal, 'By land is meant not merely land in the strict sense of the word, but entire of the materials and forces which nature gives freely for man's aid in land, water, in air and light and heat.'

Table 2.10 shows the pattern of land use in India during 2010–2011 and 2014–2015. The given Figure 2.7 shows that the net area sown

Table 2.10 *Pattern of Land Use in India during 2010–2011 and 2014–2015*

Pattern of Land Utilization	India (in '000 Hectare) 2010–2011	India (in '000 Hectare) 2014–2015
Reporting area	307,483	307,818
Forest	71,593	71,794
Non-agricultural use	26,400	26,883
Barren land	17,175	16,996
Pastures	10,305	10,258
Miscellaneous trees and so on	3,200	3,104
Cultivable waste	12,647	12,469
Other fallow	10,323	11,092
Current fallow	14,277	15,091
Net area sown	141,563	140,130
Total cropped area	197,683	198,360
Area sown more than once	56,120	58,230
Gross cropped area	197,563	198,360
Cropping intensity	140	142

Source: Author's calculation based on Land Utilization Statistics database (https://aps.dac.gov.in/LUS/Index.htm).

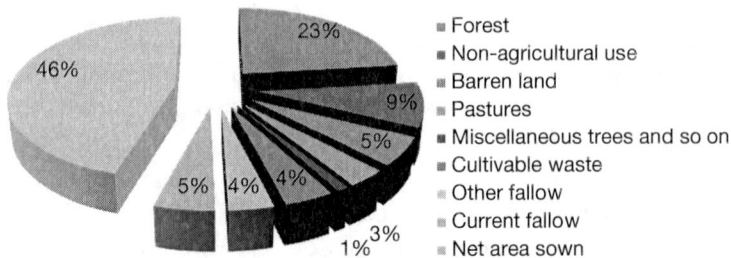

Figure 2.7 *Pattern of Land Use in India during 2014–2015*

Source: Author's calculation based on Land Utilization Statistics database (https://aps.dac.gov.in/LUS/Index.htm).

was 46 per cent and 23 per cent area is under forest of the total land in the country. The percentage of barren land and non-agricultural use is 5.0 per cent and 9.0 per cent whereas miscellaneous land and cultivable wasteland is 1.0 per cent and 4.0 per cent respectively in 2014–2015. Similarly, the percentage of pastureland is 3.0 per cent, followed by current fallow and other fallow land, that is, is 5.0 per cent and 4.0 per cent, respectively during 2014–2015. On the other hand, cropping intensity is 142 per cent in the year 2014–2015. It is found from the table that 81,900 thousand hectare area is under single cropping during the year 2014–2015.

From the above analysis, it is quite clear that there is a huge possibility of agricultural development through increase in net area sown and intensity because the country's major area is under fallow land and others. There is also huge scope of multiple cropping patterns to increase agricultural productivity. It is observed that the major area of the country either is degraded or not used for productive purpose. Therefore, there is a need to change the strategy of cultivation of agriculture and adopt modern technology for agriculture purposes in India.

The average size of land holdings in India during 2010–2011 and 2015–2016 (in hectares) have been shown in Table 2.11. It is found that the average size of land holdings of marginal, small, semi-medium, medium and large farmers was 0.39 hectares, 1.42 hectares, 2.71 hectares 5.76 hectares and 17.38 hectares respectively in 2010–2011. The average size of land holdings for marginal, small, semi-medium, medium and large farmers slightly declined during

Table 2.11 *Average Size of Land Holdings in India during 2010–2011 and 2015–2016 (in Hectares)*

Types of Land Holdings	Year 2010–2011	Year 2015–2016
Marginal holdings	0.39 (67.10%)	0.38 (68.45%)
Small holdings	1.42 (17.91%)	1.40 (17.62%)
Semi-medium holdings	2.71 (10.04%)	2.69 (9.85%)
Medium holdings	5.76 (4.25%)	5.72 (3.80%)
Large holdings	17.38 (0.70%)	17.07 (0.57%)
All holdings	1.15 (100%)	1.08 (100%)
Total Number of operational holdings	138.35 million	146.45 million

Source: Author's calculation based on Agriculture Census 2015–16 (http://agcensus.nic.in/document/agcen1516/T1_ac_2015_16.pdf).

2014–15 in the country. The average size of all holdings was 1.15 hectare in 2010–2011 and decreased to 1.08 hectare in 2015–2016 in India. On the other hand, the percentages of marginal, small, semi-medium, medium and large operational holdings were 67.10 per cent, 17.91 per cent, 10.04 per cent, 4.25 per cent and 0.70 per cent respectively in 2010–2011 which increased in the case of marginal operational holdings and declined for the other categories of land holdings in the year 2015–2016. The total numbers of operational holdings increased from 138.35 million in 2010–11 to 146.45 million in 2014–2015 showing an increase of 5.85 per cent from 2010–2011 to 2014–2015 in the country.

From the overall analysis, it is observed that the main reason for declining size of land holdings is sharp increment in population size, fragmentation of land holdings and inheritance laws of equal distribution of property leading to division of land into small blocks. Majority of farmers in India are small and marginal farmers. Their average sizes of land holdings are very small as compared to other categories of farmers in the country. Consequently, these small and marginal holdings increase disguised unemployment, decrease productivity and are operationally non-viable for modern technology in the agriculture sector. Apart from being characterized by the largest proportion of small and marginal land holdings among all size class, there is also high incidence of tenancy cultivation in the country dominated largely by large farmers. This has decreased the growth prospects of the country because such small segments of land remained out of investment. Moreover, there are also several tenancy restrictions in the country. There is a rapid need to improve the rule and regulation of tenancy in India.

Gross Capital Formation in Indian Agriculture

Gross capital formation (GCF) is a measure of investment by public and private sector and refers to the aggregate of gross additions to the fixed capital formation (FCF) and change in stocks during the orientation period. Machinery, farm equipment, irrigation, land improvement and so on are the fixed assets of the agriculture sector.

Emerging Trend of GCF in Agriculture

The recent growth trends and share of GVA by agriculture and GCF by private and public sector in India are given in Figure 2.8. In India, the share of private GCF in agriculture (i.e., farm households) in total investment has increased continuously and public sector GCF is mainly in major and medium irrigation systems and its share in total investment has consistently decreased.

As per the new series with base year 2011–2012 estimates by central statistics organization (CSO), the rate of growth of GCF in Indian agriculture, particularly private GCF, has shown a positive correlation with the agricultural GVA. Although the share of public sector GCF in total investment in agriculture and allied sector continues to be less than 20 per cent, its inducement effect on the private sector GCF makes it a vital policy variable.

Performance of Agricultural Production

In a developing country like India, optimum food grain production and agricultural production are the most important needs for achieving food security. Recently, government provided various facilities to

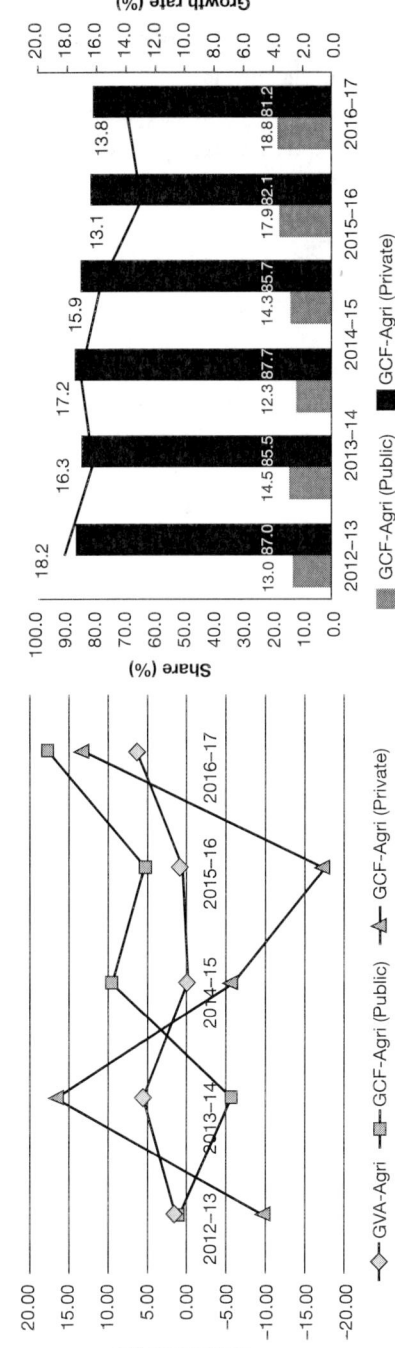

Figure 2.8 Trend in GVA in Agriculture and GCF at Constant Prices

Source: Author's calculation based on MOSPI database (https://www.mospi.gov.in).

the food grain cultivators in India through various policies. Because of this support, food grain production and agricultural production in India are increasing gradually, and play an important role in achieving food security.

Performance of Food Grains Production and Other Major Crops

The trends of production of food grains and other major crops from 1970–1971 to 2017–2018 in India are given in Table 2.12. The CAGR for the recent period, that is, 2000–2001 to 2017–2018 is also estimated for food and other major crops and presented in Table 2.12. The production of food grains in India has increased from 108.4MT in 1970–1971 to 285.0MT in 2017–2018, which indicates rapid growth rate in the production of wheat and rice crops. The government undertook several schemes and contingency measures as preparation of district-wise contingency plans, timely advisories and regular monitoring of the availability of seeds and fertilizers.

The total cereal production in 2017–2018 was found to be at 259.6MT as against 96.6MT in 1970–1971. It increased to around 163MT during the last 48 years. In the case of total production of pulses, it was estimated to be 25.4MT in 2017–2018 as against 11.8MT in 1970–1971.The production of pulses did not increase so high as compared to cereals production during the last 48 years. The CAGR from 2000–2001 to 2017–2018 for food grain and its components, that is, cereals and pulses was estimated to be 2.27, 2.16 and 3.80 respectively. Despite India being the highest producer and consumer of pulses in the world, our indigenous production of pulses is not adequate to meet the domestic requirements. Hence, this gap between the demand and supply of pulses is met through imports from other countries. The production of oilseeds in India increased from 9.6MT in 1970–1971 to 31.5MT in 2017–2018 with high fluctuations. The growth of oilseeds production during the last 48 years became almost five-fold. Moreover, the CAGR was found to be 2.72. Looking into the consequence of the problem, the government should emphasize to enhance the production and productivity of pulses and oilseeds.

Table 2.12 Trends of Production of Food Grains and Other Major Crops (in MT)

						Production in Million Tonnes (MT)					
Year	Rice	Wheat	Coarse Cereals	Total Cereals	Pulses	Food grains	Oilseeds	Cotton (in Million Bales of 170 Kg Each)	Jute & Mesta (in Million Bales of 180 Kg Each)	Sugarcane
1970–1971	42.2	23.8	30.6	96.6	11.8	108.4	9.6	4.8	6.2	126.4
1980–1981	53.6	36.3	29.0	119.0	10.6	129.6	9.4	7.0	8.2	154.3
1990–1991	74.3	55.1	32.7	162.1	14.3	176.4	18.6	9.8	9.2	241.1
2000–2001	85.0	69.7	31.1	185.7	11.1	196.8	18.4	9.5	10.6	296.0
2001–2002	93.3	72.8	33.4	199.5	13.4	212.9	20.7	10.0	11.7	297.2
2002–2003	71.8	65.8	26.1	163.7	11.1	174.8	14.8	8.6	11.3	287.4
2003–2004	88.5	72.2	37.6	198.3	14.9	213.2	25.2	13.7	11.2	233.9
2004–2005	83.1	68.6	33.5	185.2	13.1	198.4	24.4	16.4	10.3	237.1
2005–2006	91.8	69.4	34.1	195.2	13.4	208.6	28.0	18.5	10.8	281.2
2006–2007	93.4	75.8	33.9	203.1	14.2	217.3	24.3	22.6	11.3	355.5
2007–2008	96.7	78.6	40.8	216.0	14.8	230.8	29.8	25.9	11.2	348.2
2008–2009	99.2	80.7	40.0	219.9	14.6	234.5	27.7	22.3	10.4	285.0
2009–2010	89.1	80.8	33.6	203.5	14.7	218.1	24.9	24.0	11.8	292.3
2010–2011	96.0	86.9	43.4	226.3	18.2	244.5	32.5	33.0	10.6	342.4

(Continued)

Table 2.12 Continued

Year	Rice	Wheat	Coarse Cereals	Total Cereals	Pulses	Food grains	Oilseeds	Cotton (in Million Bales of 170 Kg Each)	Jute & Mesta (in Million Bales of 180 Kg Each)	Sugarcane
						Production in Million Tonnes (MT)				
2011–2012	105.3	94.9	42.0	242.2	17.1	259.3	29.8	35.2	11.4	361.0
2012–2013	105.2	93.5	40.0	238.8	18.3	257.1	30.9	34.2	10.9	341.2
2013–2014	106.7	95.9	43.3	245.8	19.3	265.0	32.8	35.9	11.7	352.1
2014–2015	105.5	86.5	42.9	234.9	17.2	252.0	27.5	34.8	11.1	362.3
2015–2016	104.4	92.3	38.5	235.2	16.4	251.6	22.1	30.0	10.5	348.4
2016–2017	109.7	98.5	43.8	252.0	23.1	275.1	31.3	32.6	11.0	306.1
2017–2018	112.8	99.9	47.0	259.6	25.4	285.0	31.5	32.8	10.0	379.9
CAGR (2000–2001 to 2017–2018)	**1.84**	**2.46**	**2.31**	**2.16**	**3.80**	**2.27**	**2.72**	**8.56**	**-0.16**	**1.77**

Source: Author's calculation based on Ministry of Agriculture & Farmers Welfare database (https://eands.dacnet.nic.in/).

As regards to other commercial crops, namely, sugarcane, cotton, and jute and mesta, the production of sugarcane was 126.4MT in 1970–1971 and grew to 379.9 in 2017–2018 with a CAGR of 1.77. In regards to production of cotton, it witnessed an eight-fold increase in the production from 4.8 million bales in 1970–1971 to 32.8 million bales in 2017–2018 with an impressive CAGR of 8.56. The production of jute and mesta was around 6.2 million bales of 180 kg in 1970–1971 and rose to a mere 10.0 million bales of 180 kg in 2017–2018 with a negative growth rate of –0.16 per cent.

Conclusion of the Chapter

After GR and second generation reforms, Indian agriculture has been developing rapidly especially in horticulture, fisheries and animal husbandry sub-sectors. This is because of diversification towards high-value crops. Moreover, food grain crops are the main drivers of food security in India. The results reveal that the production of food grains, oilseeds, pulses and other commercial crops, namely oilseeds, sugarcane, cotton, jute and mesta is also increasing continually in India. But capital formation level in the agriculture sector is decreasing due to the unfavourable policies regarding investment promotion and returns from investment. Recently, the production of high value crops such as fruits, vegetables and flowers in India increased sufficiently for higher growth in farmer's income. On the other hand, the production of oilseeds and pulses is not enough to satisfy the needs of domestic people. Hence, there is a need to change cropping patterns and enhance the productivity of these crops as per the needs of the domestic agricultural markets in India.

A list of several government initiatives have been added at the end of the chapter in the form of boxes. These boxes give the summarized, holistic picture of government initiatives towards boosting the agriculture sector in India. Box 2.1 talks about the productivity challenges of the Indian agriculture and government initiatives to boost agriculture, while Box 2.2 talks about the aspect of doubling farmers' income focusing particularly on concept, sources, strategies, road map and action plan. Recent government schemes for agricultural development are spelled out in Box 2.3, while Box 2.4 focuses on the government mission for promoting agricultural development in India.

Box 2.1 Productivity Challenges for Indian Agriculture and Government Initiatives to Boost Agriculture

At 169.6 million hectares, India's cultivated land mass is the largest in the world. The Government of India's top research institute reports that nearly 60% of agricultural land is at risk because of fertilizer misuse, poor cropping practices and soil nutrient deficiencies. India uses 13% of the world's extracted expanding irrigation which has been a key strategy for increasing productivity and proportion of arable land under irrigation increased from 20% to 35% from 1981 to 2013.

Irrigation water use efficiency is very low 35%–40% efficiency in surface irrigation such as flooding or canals, and 65%–75% efficiency when pumping groundwater. These unsustainable practices are depleting the countries aquifers. The country is faced with the prospect of declining rainfall during the monsoon, India's prime growing season for rainfed agriculture.

Nearly 55% of the population is engaged in agricultural production. As farms are divided among family members, average farm size today (1.16 hectares/2.87 acres) is half of what it was 40 years ago. Unemployment among agricultural workers rose from 9.5% in 1993–1994 to 15.3% in 2004–2005. Government subsidies to farmers for fertilizer, electricity and irrigation increased more than eight-fold between 1990–1991 and 2006–2007. Areas receiving the highest subsidies regularly underperform those with lower subsidies.

Productivity challenges

Government subsidies for buying and distributing foodgrains to low income and disadvantaged households grew from 2.2% of agricultural GDP during the 1990s to 5% in the 2000s, crowding out investments in agricultural education, research, technology and extension. India's Ministry of Agriculture reports that from 2005 to 2007, 30% of harvest and post-harvest economic losses came from the fruit and vegetable sectors, although that sector comprised only 13.6% of total production.

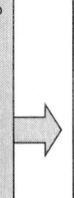

Government Initiatives to Boost Indian Agriculture

Government Initiatives

Financial Year			
FY 2014–2015	National adaptation fund for climate change established	Rural credit fund establishment	Soil health card and coil testing laboratories	Agri-tech infrastructure fund established
FY 2015–2016	More funds allocated to rural infrastructure development	Long-term rural credit fund for agriculture	Short-term cooperative rural credits refinance fund	Promotion of traditional agriculture systems
FY 2016–2017	Goal set to double farm incomes by 2022	Long-term irrigation fund for agriculture	Expansion of soil health card scheme	Organic value chain development programme in north-east India
FY 2017–2018	More credits earmarked for underserved areas and long-term irrigation fund doubled in size	Crop insurance coverage ex-paraded and micro irrigation fund establishment	Expansion of mini soil testing laboratories and contract farming for horticulture	Expansion of e-NAM coverage and dairy processing and infrastructure development fund established
FY 2018–2019	Exemption of income tax for FPO and MSP for unannounced kharif crops to be 1.5 times the cost of production	Organic farming by Village Producer Organizations (VPO) and FPOs	Operation greens on lines of operation flood. Total of ₹ 500 crore allocated.	Agri-market Infrastructure fund of ₹2,000 crore to set up 22,000 GrAMs

Box 2.2 Doubling Farmers Income: Concept, Sources, Strategies, Road Map and Action Plan

Doubling of Farmers' Income by 2022–2023

Background and Concept: The present government has redefined agricultural progress as measuring the real income of farmers rather than gross production of agricultural commodities which was recommended in a meeting at National Commission on Farmers under the chairmanship of Professor M. S. Swaminathan and co-chaired by the Secretary Agriculture, Government of India. Moreover, this vision got reverberated in Budget 2016when the finance minister mentioned about doubling farm incomes. Later, the same agenda of doubling farm incomes by 2022 was exhorted by the Prime Minister of India by spelling out 6 points strategy. Accordingly, a task group was formed under the aegis of Ministry of Agriculture to come out with detailed plans and its operationalization.

A nuanced analysis of the doubling farmers' income is portrayed in the report *Situational Assessment of Agricultural Households by the NSSO*, the average monthly per capita income from farming increased from ₹1,060 in 2003 to ₹ 3,844 in 2013, which is a compounded annual income growth rate (CAIGR) of 13.7%. To double the income of farmers by 2022, in nominal (numerical) terms—not considering the inflation factor—would require a 15% compounded income growth rate, which is a marginal increase over the achieved increase from 2003 to 2013. Moreover to increase the income in real terms would imply restructuring agriculture processes and policy interventions.

Current Status of Farmers' Income and Expenditure
Based on sample survey by NSSO (July 2012 to June 2013) @ 2011–2012 base prices

Average monthly income/agricultural household	₹6,426
Average monthly consumption expenditure/agricultural household	₹6,223

Division of Recommendations: A total of 40 recommendations for increasing farmers' income have been divided into five parts:

- Increasing incomes by improving productivity
- Water and agriculture-input policies
- Integrated farming system

- Better market price realization
- Special policy measures

Sources of Farmers' Income Growth: Doubling Farmers Income (DFI) Committee identified seven sources of income growth:

- Improvement in crop productivity
- Improvement in livestock productivity
- Resource use efficiency or savings in cost of production
- Increase in cropping intensity
- Diversification towards high value crops
- Improvement in real prices received by farmers
- Shift from farm to non-farm occupations

The Strategy of Improving Farmers' Income: The are four strategies identify to improve farmers' income:

- Development initiatives including infrastructure
- Enhancement in technology
- Policy reforms in agriculture through government interventions
- Institutional reforms

Road Map and Action Plan:

- Increase in productivity of crops and the production of livestock
- Improvement in efficiency of input use for cost saving
- Augmenting crop intensity
- Diversification towards high value crops
- Improved price realization by farmers

Box 2.3 Recent Government Schemes for Agricultural Development

Area of Scheme	Name of the Scheme	Assistance
Agricultural insurance	Pradhan Mantri Fasal Bima Yojana (PMFBY) (13 January 2016)	The purpose of the scheme is to adopt technology for yield estimation, providing financial support to farmers suffering crop loss/damage due to unforeseen events, ensuring flow of credit to the agriculture sector and insurance protection for food crops, oilseeds and annual horticultural/commercial crops notified by state government. The rate of premium payable by the farmer will be as per the following: • Kharif season: 2% of sum insured; Rabi season: 1.5% of sum insured • Annual commercial/horticultural crops: 5% of sum insured • The difference between actual premium and the rate of insurance payable by farmers shall be shared equally by the central government and state government
	Restructured Weather Based Crop Insurance Scheme (RWBCIS) (18 February 2016)	The aim of RWBCIS is to mitigate the hardship of the insured farmers against the likelihood of financial loss on account of anticipated crop loss resulting from adverse weather conditions namely abnormal rainfall, temperature, wind and humidity • Insurance protection for notified food crops, oilseeds and horticultural/commercial crops • Uniform maximum premium for all farmers like PMFBY • Kharif season: 2% of sum insured; Rabi Season: 1.5% of sum insured • Commercial/horticultural crops: 5% of sum insured

		• The difference between actual premium and the rate of Insurance payable by farmers shall be shared equally by the centre and state
National agricultural marketing	National Agriculture Market (e-NAM) (1 July 2015)	• The objective of this scheme is to usher reforms in the agri-marketing sector and promote online marketing of agri commodities across the country and to provide maximum benefit to the farmers. • Under the scheme, a web-based platform has been deployed across 585 regulated markets to promote online trading, digitalization of entire functioning of markets outline gate entry, lot making, bidding, generation of e-sale agreement and e-payment and so on, remove information asymmetry, increase transparency in the transaction process and enhance accessibility to markets across the country.
Irrigation	Pradhan Mantri Krishi Sinchayee Yojana (PMKSY) (1 July 2015)	• PMKSY was approved by the Cabinet Committee in 2015 with an outlay of ₹50,000 crore for a period of 5 years (2015–2016 to 2019–2020). • This yojana has been developed with the vision of extending the coverage of irrigation 'Har Khet Ko Pani' and improving water use efficiency 'More Crop Per Drop' in an efficient manner with end-to-end solution on source creation, distribution, management, field application and extension activities on extension services on new technologies and information and so on based on comprehensive planning process at district/state level.

Soil health	Soil Health Card (19 February 2015)	Under the scheme a soil health card will be provided to all farm holdings in the country at an interval of two years so as to enable the farmers to apply appropriate recommended dosages of nutrients for crop production and improving health and fertility of soil. The main objectives of the scheme are as follows: • Setting up of new soil testing laboratories and strengthening the existing labs • Training of lab staff/extension officers/farmers/field function on balanced use of fertilizer • Promotion and distribution of micro nutrients and issue of soil health cards
Agricultural credit	Interest Assistance and Collateral/ SF Loan (Oct 2006)	• This scheme provide crops loans up to Rs. three lakhs at 7% ROI • 3% waiver in interest rate for those farmers who repay crop loan on time • There is no requirement of collateral security for farm loan up to ₹1.6 lakh
	Kisan Credit Card (August 1998)	• Farmers can avail crop loan through Kisan Credit Card • Loan/credit limit is fixed on the basis of crop sown and area under cultivation. Kisan Credit Cards are valid for three to five years • Farmers are also provided risk coverage in the event of accidental death/ disability. Crop coverage loans are covered under the crop insurance scheme

Organic farming	Paramparagt Krishi Vikas Yojna (PKVY) 2015	PKVY a sub-component of Soil Health Management (SHM) scheme under National Mission of Sustainable Agriculture (NMSA) aims at development of models of excellence in organic farming
		• Promotes different crop/cropping system suitable to agro climatic conditions • In organic farming use more bio-chemicals, bio-pesticides and bio-fertilizers
Direct benefit to farmers	Pradhan Mantri Kisan Samman Nidhi Yojana (PM-KSNY) (December 2018)	• Under the PM-KSNY scheme an income support of ₹6000/per year in three equal instalments will be provided to small and marginal farmer families who have combined land holding of up to 2 hectares • State government and union territory (UT) administration will identify the farmer families which are eligible for support as per scheme guidelines and fund will be directly transferred to the bank accounts
Agricultural development	Rashtriya Krishi Vikas Yojana (RKVY RAFTAAR, 2007)	• Ensuring holistic development of agriculture and allied sectors at state and district level • Strengthening farmers by making farming a remunerative economic activity • Creating required pre- and post-harvest agri-infrastructure to strengthen the farmers • Providing autonomy and flexibility to states to plan and execute schemes as per local/farmers' needs

Box 2.4 Government Mission for Agricultural Development

Mission for Agricultural Development	Details of Mission
Sustainable agriculture	• Quality and availability of natural resources such as soil and water are necessary for sustaining agricultural productivity • 'Water use efficiency', 'nutrient management' and 'livelihood diversification' through adoption of sustainable development ways by progressively shifting to environmental friendly technologies, adopting efficient equipment of energy, conserving of natural resources and integrated farming • Aims at promoting soil health management, enhanced water use efficiency, judicious use of chemicals, crop diversification, progressive adoption of crop-livestock farming systems and integrated approaches such as crop-sericulture, agro-forestry and fish farming
National Mission for Sustainable Agriculture (NMSA)	• Aims at promoting sustainable agriculture practices through a series of adaptation measures emphasizing on 10 major dimensions covering Indian agriculture 'water use efficiency', 'pest management', 'enhance farm practices', 'nutrient management', 'insurance of agriculture', 'credit support', 'agriculture markets', 'access to information' and 'livelihood diversification
Water management mission	• **Drip irrigation:** Financial assistance up to 55% for small and marginal farmers and 45% for other farmers • **Sprinkler irrigation** (Portable, mini, micro, semi, permanent and large volume/rain gun). Financial assistance up to 55% for small and marginal farmers and 45% for other farmers

Sub-mission on agro-forestry	• Tree plantation drives on cultivated land 'HarMedh Par Ped', along with crops/cropping system • Multipurpose tree species with short-, medium- and long-term returns be planted, which is a source of farmers getting additional income at regular intervals. These can include fruits, fodder, medicinal, timber and aromatic tree species
Integrated farming: Assistance under National Mission for Sustainable Agriculture	• Focus on crop/cropping system suitable for agro-climatic conditions • Diversify crop/cropping system incorporating livestock, fisheries, horticulture, dairy and agro-forestry
Mission for Integrated Development of Horticulture (MIDH)	• A centrally sponsored scheme for the comprehensive development of the horticulture sector covering fruits, vegetables, root and tuber crops, mushrooms, spices, flowers, aromatic plants, coconut, cashew, cocoa and bamboo • Includes supply of quality planting material, technology promotion, productivity improvement, human resource development, creation of post-harvest management infrastructure
National Food Security Mission (NFSM)	• Promotes and extends improved technologies, that is, seed, micro nutrient, soil amendments, integrated pest management, farm machinery & implements, irrigation devices, and capacity building of farmers. • Cluster developments of rice, wheat, pulses and nutri-cereals, distribution of improved seeds/need based inputs, resource and energy conservation techniques, efficient water application tools, cropping system-based training and local initiatives.

CHAPTER 3

Past Inferences on Agriculture, Food Security and Climate

The subjects of every state ought to contribute towards the support of the government, as nearly as possible, in proportion to their respective abilities.

—Adam Smith

A study of the history of opinion is a necessary preliminary to the emancipation of the mind.

—John Maynard Keynes

Introduction

Review of literature plays an important role in research work in social science. It is a justification of the present study which can be clarified by reviewing the available literature on the subject. It demonstrates the nature and scope of climate change, agricultural yields and food security in India, laying the foundation for analysing the interrelationships among them. Analysing the literature in context of the present study will help us in displaying the effect of climate change on agricultural productivity and food security at the state as well as national levels. For rationality and convenience, the review is organized according to their themes and year-wise. Therefore, an attempt has been made to review the available literature on the subjects to find out research gaps.

Literature Related to Climate Change and Agriculture

Decker (1975) has revealed his views on the impact of climate on world food production. Agriculture production depends on many factors such as climate change, soil, availability of water for irrigation, technological development of the regional agriculture, management skills of the farmers and capital. He has found that the grains produced in small areas of the world meet the abundance of the world market and supply of food for trade for deficient region. In the United States, the central and plains areas are one of the granaries which are dependent on rainfall. In the subtropical border of the equatorial region, production depends on the strength of the monsoon. It is observed that the impact of climate change on food production is worldwide. It is also found that an increase in the variability in the year-to-year weather of the mid-latitudes will decline the food production in the region.

    Reilly (1995) has examined climate change and its impact on the agriculture sector. He found that the overall impact of change on global agricultural production, prices and economic welfare was relatively small (less than 0.3% of global gross national product). The direct effect of CO_2 fertilization was very important in reducing the negative effect of climate change. It was worth between US$115 and US$190 billion in 1990. The direct adaption was way less important and adaptation declined losses by between US$7 and US$24 billion. It is also found that low-income countries overall were more severely affected as compared to high-income countries. The study concluded that climate change impacted global agriculture but uncertainties remain. There is a need to minimize the cost and increase benefits from climate change.

    Futang and Zong-ci (1995) have highlighted their views on the impact of climate change on natural vegetation in China and its implications for agriculture. The study found that the temperature in east Asia and China will be increased by 0.88°C in 2030, 1.40°C in 2050 and 2.95°C in 2100 respectively. The precipitation will also be increased by 2.6 per cent in 2030 to 4.2 per cent in 2050 and further increase by 8.9 per cent in 2100 respectively. It is clear that various changes would occur in the cropping pattern in the year 2050. The current area of single cropping would be decreased to 23.1 per cent and the triple cropping would become 22.4 per cent, while the double cropping area would remain the same.

Mendelsohn and Dinar (2001) have shown their views on the effect of development on the climate responsiveness of agriculture. The objective of the study was to examine the link between development and climate sensitivity. The climate sensitivity of agriculture in the United States, Brazil and India is measured using the Ricardian approach. The study has found that development has increased and climate sensitivity has reduced in countries such as India and Brazil. It is observed that development may reduce climate sensitivity. On the other hand, it is clear that the Ricardian function for Indian agriculture is far more climate sensitive than the American Ricardian function. Development has been affecting climate responsiveness. Farmers in less developed countries are currently more climate sensitive than the farmers in more developed countries. The government should develop research and development technology for handling climate change and encourage farmers to adjust to the new market and ecological conditions.

Chang (2002) has highlighted his view on the impact of climate change on Taiwan's agriculture. The aim of the research was to estimate the potential impact of climate change on Taiwan's agriculture sector. The pooling data on crop yields, and climate and non-climatic variables are used to estimate yield. The study found that climatic variables such as temperature and precipitation have a significant and non-monotonic impact on crop productivity. Climate changes also have a significant impact on many crop yields and their impacts on welfare are mostly positive. The impacts of climate change on producers are much more significant than on consumers. It is observed that temperature rise is not stressful for Taiwan farmers. However, the upwards shift in rainfall could be affecting the farmers of Taiwan.

Beg et al. (2002) have studied the linkages between climate change and sustainable development. They found that climate change has the most adverse impact in developing countries because populations of these countries are most vulnerable and least to easily adapt to climate change. On the other hand, the slow process of mitigating global GHG emissions implies that climate change will decrease the potential for economic development in some of the poorest of developing countries. Therefore, countries should make the commitment to mitigate targets for long-term stabilization of GHG concentrations in the atmosphere. There is also a need to participate in the public and private sectors to fight for retaining biodiversity and combat climate changes.

Mall and Aggarwal (2002) have presented their views on climate change and rice yields in diverse agro-environments of India. The objective of the study was to estimate the impact of climate change on crop production. The study found that the impact of various climate change scenarios on the yield of rice crop with two popular crop simulation models at a different level of management. The effect of climate change on rice crops in different agro-climatic regions in India would always be positive irrespective of the various uncertainties. Rice yield increased between 1.0 per cent and 16.8 per cent in the pessimistic scenario of changing climate depending upon the level of management and model used. This increase was between 3.5 per cent and 33.8 per cent in an optimistic scenario. The southern and western parts of India which currently have relatively lower temperatures as compared to northern and eastern regions are likely to show greater sensitivity in rice yield under climate change.

Parry, Rosenzweig, Iglesias, Livermore and Fischer (2004) have conducted their study on the effect of climate change on global food production under *Special Report on Emissions Scenarios* (SRES) emissions and socio-economic scenarios. The impacts of climate change are estimated for climate change scenarios developed from the HADCM3 global climate model under the IPCC's SRES A1F1, A2 and B2 scenarios. The change in yield is calculated using transfer functions derived from crop model with observed climate data and climate change scenarios. The basic linked system (BLS) was developed to evaluate consequent changes in global cereal production, cereal prices and the number of people at risk from hunger. The model shows that most parts of the world would be able to continue to feed themselves under the SRES scenarios during the rest of the country. However, the outcome is achieved through production in developed countries compensating for declines for most parts of developing nations. While global production seems to be stable, the regional variations in crop production are likely to grow stronger with time, leading to a significant polarization of effects, with a substantial increase in prices and risk of hunger among the poorest nations. The SRES scenarios reveal several non-linear aspects in the food supply system in the biophysical sense, where changes in population, and economic and political structure complicate the translation of biophysical climate change impacts into social indices like the number of people at risk of hunger.

Slingo et al. (2005) have revealed their views on food crops in a changing climate. The aim of the paper was to analyse the mean and variability of climate change. Crop yields and quality are more sensitive to the impact of climate change and gases in the atmosphere. The variability of climate change, associated with El Nino events, has larger impacts on crop production. Africa is the most vulnerable to climate variability and change. The study suggested that there is a need to know the knowledge of crop yields in the conditions of rainfall and temperature. There is also a need to use the climate information and regional impact of climate variability. The proper and appropriate adaptation strategies of climate change should be developed globally to predict the quantity and quality of food crops.

Kumar (2007) has highlighted his views on climate change studies in Indian agriculture. Agriculture is a climate-sensitive sector that provides for 60 per cent of India's population. The aim of the study was to estimate the macro-level impact of climate change. He has shown that under double CO_2 concentration level, in the latter half of the 21st century, GDP would decline by 1.4 per cent to 3.0 per cent due to climate change. The study has also shown the Ricardian approach, which is based on Hedonic pricing theory. He argues that by examining two agricultural areas that are similar in all respects except that one has temperature on average 3 °C warmer than the other, one would be able to infer the willingness to pay in agriculture to avoid a 3 °C temperature rise. Rising 5.0 per cent of climate variation would result in an almost 10 per cent drop in the farm net revenue. There is a need to develop improved technological to measures climate change in India.

Srinivasan (2008) estimated that the surface temperature of the Earth is controlled by the balance between the observed solar radiation and the emitted infrared radiation. It is found that in the past 15 years the amount of CO_2 in the Earth's atmosphere has increased from 280PPM to more than 380PPM due to burning of fossil fuels. The Earth's temperature is increasing due to the higher absorption of infrared radiation by the atmosphere. The burning of fossil fuels has also caused an increase in sulphate and soot aerosols in the atmosphere. These two aerosols are reducing the solar radiation incident at the Earth's surface. So the surface of the Earth has cooled on account of an increase in aerosols. The net impact of an increase in CO_2 and aerosols has been increasing the surface of the earth by 0.7 °C since the past 100 years.

Rajeevan, Bhate and Jaswal (2008) have revealed their views on the analysis of variability and trends of extreme rainfall events over India by using 104 years of gridded daily rainfall data. They have estimated the high resolution daily gridded rainfall data, variability and long-term trends of extreme rainfall over central India with the help of using 104 years (1901–2004) data. The frequency of extreme rainfall events shows significant annual and inter-decadal variations in addition to a statistically significant long-term trend of 6 per cent per decade. They have also shown that the long-term trends of extreme rainfall events are modulated by sea surface temperatures (SST) variations over the tropical Indian Ocean. It is estimated that the increasing trend of extreme rainfall events in the last five decades could be associated with the increasing trends of SST and surface latent heat flux over the tropical Indian Ocean. The coherent relationship among Indian Ocean, SST and extreme rainfall events suggests an increase in the risk of major floods in central India.

Wang et al. (2009) have stated their view on the impact of climate change on China's agriculture. The objective of the study was to examine the effect of changes in climate on agriculture in China. Cross-sectional data on rainfed and irrigated farms have been taken to the effects of temperature and precipitation on net crop revenue. The study is based on empirical survey data collected from 8,405 households across 28 provinces of China. They found that the average impact of higher temperatures has a negative effect and average impact of precipitation has a positive effect. Rising temperature and rainfall have different effects on different farm types in different regions. Warming is beneficial to irrigated farms in China, and rainfed farms are quite vulnerable to warming and suffer reductions in net revenue. Climate change has been affecting net revenue and a higher temperature increases the net revenue of irrigated farms.

Felkner, Tazhibayeva and Townsend (2009) have put their views on the impact of climate change on rice production in Thailand. The objective of the paper was to evaluate the impact of climate change on crop yield of south-east Asia. They revealed that high emission scenario is more extreme. The daily temperatures increase under both high emission scenario and low emissions scenario, the magnitude of increase under high emissions climate relative to low emissions is about 40 per cent higher. On the other hand, a decrease in aggregate yields is predicted compared to the neutral climate simulations for both high and low emissions scenarios by 3.53 per cent and 13.79 per cent respectively. Lower aggregate yields under low emissions scenario compared to high emission scenario, despite the fact that the low-emissions scenarios is the less extreme of the two.

Guiteras (2009) has revealed his views on the impact of climate change on Indian agriculture by using 40 years' district-level panel data set covering over 200 Indian districts. The study estimated the effect of random year-to-year variation in weather on agricultural output. These panel estimates incorporate farmers within year adaptations to annual weather shocks. These estimates, derived from short-run weather effects, are relevant for predicting the medium-run economic impact of climate change if farmers are unable to adapt quickly. It was also argued that projected climate change over the period 2010–2039 reduces major crop yields by 4.5 per cent to 9.0 per cent. The long-run (2070–2099) impact is dramatic, reducing yields by 25 per cent or more in the absence of long-run adaptation. This indicates that climate change is likely to put significant costs on the Indian economy unless farmers can quickly recognize and adapt to increasing temperatures. Such quick adaptation may be less feasible in a developing country like India, where access to information and capital is limited.

Kaul and Ram (2009) have pointed on the impact of global warming on production of jowar in India. The aim of the study was to examine the effect of fertilizer and labour inputs on productivity of jowar, and also investigate the impact of climate variables such as rainfall and temperature on production of jowar. It found that excessive rains and extreme variation in temperature has adversely affected the productivity of jowar crop, and thereby has affected the incomes as well as food security of farming families in Karnataka. The study suggested that improved irrigation facilities are adopted by farmers for reducing the harmful effect of global warming on agricultural productivity and minimizing the global food crisis.

Food Agriculture Organization's (2010) report focused on climate change mitigation and adaptation in agriculture, forestry and fisheries. The report concluded that the poor people of rural and urban areas are the most affected as they depend on climate-sensitive activities and have a low capacity to adapt. Changes in temperature and precipitation are the major causes of crop failure. Agriculture is not only the victim of climate change but is also a source of GHG. However, agricultural and deforestation account for about one-third of global GHG emissions from human activities such as 25 per cent of carbon, 50 per cent of methane and over 75 per cent of nitrous oxide. About, 80 per cent of total emissions from agriculture, including deforestation are from the developing countries. It is observed that half of all agricultural land in Latin America is likely to be affected by dissertation and salinization by 2050.

Srivastava, Kumar and Aggarwal (2010) have presented their views on the assessment on the vulnerability of sorghum to climate changes in India. The objectives of the study were to analyse the impacts of climate change on sorghum production system in India by using InfoCrop—sorghum simulation model. The study argued that climate change will reduce monsoon sorghum productivity up to

14.0 per cent in central zone and up to 2.0 per cent in south central zone by 2020, and the model of the study also suggested that yields are likely to be affected even more in 2050 and 2080 scenarios; climate change impacts on winter crop are projected to reduce yields up to 7.0 per cent, 11.0 per cent and 32.0 per cent by 2020, 2050 and 2080 respectively in India. The study suggested that by adapting strategies such as changing variety and sowing date can reduce the vulnerability of monsoon sorghum to about 10 per cent, 2.0 per cent and 3.0 per cent in central zone, south central zone and south west zone regions in 2020. Adaptation strategies will reduce the climate change impacts and vulnerability of winter crop to 1–2 per cent in 2020, 3–8 per cent in 2050 and 4–9 per cent in 2080. There is a need to explore low-cost adaptation strategies to reduce the net vulnerability of the sorghum production system in India.

Auffhammer, Ramanathan and Vincent (2011) have revealed their views on the impact of climate change on rice yield in India. The study is based on secondary data from 1966–2002. They found that lower rainfall or drought has a negative impact, whereas higher rainfall has a positive impact on rice yield. Extreme rainfall has a negative impact, but non-linearity related to drought is more important than then the related extreme rainfall. The study concluded that drought and extreme rainfall negatively affected rice yield in the main rainfed areas during 1966 to 2002, and drought has a greater impact than extreme rainfall. The Monte Carlo simulation reveals that yield is 1.7 per cent higher on average if monsoon had not changed since 1960. The productivity would be higher by 4 per cent if warmer nights and lower rainfall at the end of the growing season had not occurred. Climate change has already negatively affected India's hundreds of millions of rice producers and consumers.

Iqbal and Siddique (2012) studied the impact of climate change on agricultural productivity in Bangladesh from 1975 to 2008 for 23 regions. Firstly, the study explored the long-term changes at both the country and local levels in climatic variables such as temperature, rainfall, humidity and sunshine using descriptive statistics and maps. Secondly, it used regression models to study the causal relation-ship between climate changes on agricultural productivity. Unlike the existing literature, the study exploited within-region time series variations (regional fixed effect) to estimate the impact of long-term changes in climatic variables on the productivity of agriculture in order to control for regional differences. Moreover, the results indicate that long-term changes in means and standard deviations of the climatic variables have different impacts on rice productivity and thus the entire impact of climate change on agriculture is not unambiguous. The paper suggested that scientists and policymakers should strongly predict of the impact of climate change on agricultural productivity in different climatic scenarios of the country.

Mahmood (2012) in his study examined the impact of temperature and precipitation on rice productivity in rice–wheat cropping system of Punjab province. The objective of this study was to estimate the impact of climatic variables on rice productivity in the rice–wheat cropping system. The study observed that temperature and precipitation variables have a significant effect on rice. It is clear that an increase in the temperature by 1.5°C and 3°C would increase productivity by 2.09 per cent and 4.33 per cent respectively. However, an increase in precipitation by 5.0 per cent and 15 per cent during September to October adversely affected rice productivity by 5.71 per cent and 15.26 per cent respectively. The study suggested that some measures such as research and development, improved farm management practices and creation of awareness among farmers about climate change should be taken to protect the impact of climate change on rice yield.

Lobell and Gourdji (2012) have studied the influence of climate change on global crop productivity. The study has found that technological and agronomic development will increase the growth rate of aggregate crop productivity until 2050. Climate change would result in a net decline in global yields. The net effect of climate change and CO_2 on the global average supply of calories will be close to zero over the next few decades, but it could be large as 20 per cent to 30 per cent of overall yield. The impact of CO_2 and ozone (O_3) is significant at the global level. Global food production has been changing due to the effect of changes in climate such as CO_2 and O_3. The increased investment in climate science and crop physiology will help to sustain yield growth over the next few decades.

Asha latha, Gopinath and Bhat (2012) have revealed their views on the impact of climate change on rainfed agriculture in India: a case study of Dharwad. The study has selected Dharwad district of Karnataka to assess the impact of climate change. The total sample constitutes 250 sample respondents. The climate variation such as occurrence of drought has a high impact on the yield of a rainfed condition such as yield reduction and reduction in net revenue. The small and medium rainfed farmers are highly vulnerable to climate change and to a larger extent they have adopted a copping mechanism for climate change compared to large farmers. The farmers are adapting to the changes in the climate both by adopting the technological coping mechanism on the positive side and on the negative side through shifting to other professions. The impact of climate change should be intensifying day by day. There is a need to make effective policies to avoid short-term effects such as yield and income loss and long-term effects such as quitting agricultural profession by the rainfed farmers.

Dagar et al. (2012) have pointed out their views on climate change on Indian agriculture. Climate change has been effecting huge population and cropping patterns in the agriculture sector. Climate change is a serious problem influencing the performance of the Indian agriculture. The study found that rising temperatures increased climate variability and extreme weather conditions are effecting food production and livelihoods of millions of people in India. Climate events such as cold waves, heat waves, drought and floods have increased the weather factor to effect the production of food crops. Modern science and indigenous wisdom of the farmers should increase the resilience of Indian agriculture to climate change. There is a need to improve efficient cropping systems, resources conservation technologies, water harvesting and water management technologies to mitigate the adverse impact of climate change and variability. The agro-forestry system and biological carbon capture system technologies should be adopted for the mitigation of climate variability.

World Bank (2013) highlighted the obvious risks posed by the warming climate of India to agriculture, water resources and health. With over 60 per cent of crops being rainfed, agricultural areas are very vulnerable to changes in precipitation arising due to climate change.

With 15 per cent of India's groundwater tables already overexploited, changes in precipitation will further affect the water supply. Research argues that the mean temperature will rise by 2 °C globally by 2040; and if this happens, crop production in south Asia is expected to drop by 12 per cent. This will ultimately cause a reduction in food availability, which will lead to severe health problems, including increase in childhood stunting by 35 per cent by 2050. Consequently, the World Bank is supporting projects to assist communities to utilize their watersheds better, and is sponsoring groups that are developing environmentally sustainable hydropower in India. Moreover, if warming levels are held below 2 °C, it is highly likely that the worst effects stemming out from climate change can be avoided. It is thus pivotal that action on climate change happens fast as the window of opportunity to balance global warming is closing rapidly.

Neenu, Biswas and Subba Rao (2013) have discussed their views on the impact of climate factors on crop production. Climate effects crop productivity in terms of quality and quantity. The precipitation conditions and CO_2 contents are rapidly increasing in the atmosphere due to increasing temperature, which is affecting crop productivity. Rising temperature has decreased the soil moisture and increased the demand of crops for water. The study also found that solar radiation also effects photosynthesis and crop yield. They suggested that the effect of interrelationship between the climatic factors such as temperature, rainfall, solar radiation, CO_2 concentration and crop yield needs to be understood to take necessary adaptation measures to maintain crop yield.

Joshi and Chaturvedi (2013) have focused on the impact of climate change on agriculture. Climate change is one of the most crucial challenges facing the world. It is known that this global conversion leads to environmental deprivation and demographic stress which displace millions of inhabitants. The study found that global temperature is rising and climate conditions become a more erratic threat to vegetation and biodiversity progression, and have an enduring effect on food security as well as human health. The variation in climate change in terms of a high level of CO_2 and other gases brings about a hidden hunger crisis among individuals by decreasing vital nutrient content in food crops.

Javeed and Manuhaar (2013) have stated their views on climate change and its impact on the productivity of Indian agriculture. The aim of the paper was to analyse the impact of climate changes on the productivity of Indian agriculture. Agriculture depends on the weather and climate change is responsible for the decrease in the agricultural productivity. Cereal crops such as rice and wheat are the most vulnerable to impact of climate change. Small and marginal farmers are the most vulnerable groups because these people have small farm sizes, and low capital and technological development. The agriculture sector has been suffering from climate change in terms of floods and droughts. The Government of India should develop adaptation and mitigation strategies to combat the effects of climate change. It is crucial for India to make effective climatic programmes and policies at regional and national levels.

Wagh (2013) has revealed his views on global warming and its impact on agriculture. The objective of his research was to discuss the impact of climate change and solutions for minimizing global warming. This paper is based on secondary data. The impact of climate change is a worldwide phenomenon. The growth of agricultural productivity is directly and indirectly dependent on climate. But climate change has a direct impact on food production across the globe. The agriculture sector is the most sensitive to the climate change. However, the increase in the mean seasonal temperature has been reducing the duration of the crops and productivity. Food production is also sensitive to climate changes such as changes in the temperature and precipitation, which may lead to an outbreak of pests and disease, reducing harvest and affecting the food security of the country. There is need to carefully manage resources such as soil, water and biodiversity to protect agriculture from the impact of climate change. There is also need to act at the global, regional, national and local levels to cope with the impact of climate on agriculture and food production.

Kumar and Gautam (2014) have analysed the impact of climate change on agricultural productivity in India. The main objective of the study was to analyse the factors of the climate change which are affecting the agricultural productivity in India. They argued that changes in climate have a grave impact on the availability of various resources on Earth, especially water. They also analysed that human health and quality of life are directly affected by the changes in the biosphere, biodiversity and natural resources. According to them, India in the 21st century will also begin to experience more seasonal deviation in temperature with more warming in the winters than summers. During the recent years, longevity of heat waves across India has extended with warmer nights and hotter days, and this trend is expected to continue in the future. The mean of temperature change is predicted to be 2.33 °C to 4.78 °C with a doubling in CO_2 concentrations.

Banday and Ranjan (2014) have analysed the deterioration of agricultural productivity due to climate change in Haryana. The study concluded that climate change is adversely impacting the agriculture in Haryana. There is a significant impact of temperature on wheat production in Haryana. Rainfall has significant impact on wheat production as 1 per cent decrease in rainfall will lead to −1.25 per cent decreases in production. They suggested that crop insurance for climate variability, and new varieties and certified seeds are necessary to overcome the impact of climate change. To control the emission of atmospheric gases, there is also need to adopt organic farming and use fertilizer less.

Kumar and Sharma (2014) have conducted a study on climate change and sugarcane productivity in India. The aim of the study was to assess the impact of climatic and non-climatic factors on sugarcane productivity in different weather seasons. The panel data has been taken of 13 states during 1980 to 2009. To show empirical results, simple regression model (L–R model), Ricardian productivity regression non-linear model (R–P model) and C–D production function model are used and the regression results based on Prais–Winsten model with panels corrected standard errors. The study found that average maximum and minimum temperature in summer and rainy season negatively impact sugarcane productivity. Rising average minimum temperature in winter and summer seasons have positive and statistically significant impact on sugarcane productivity. The study concluded that climatic factors have a negative impact on sugarcane productivity. They suggested that a policy maker is needed to improve irrigation facilities and prices to farmers for sugarcane production.

Chaturvedi (2015) has analysed the cost loss in agriculture productivity as well as health. The paper found that climate change causes significant economic losses in India. It is found that the production loss in rice, wheat and maize could become US$208 billion and US$366 billion in 2050 and 2100 respectively. The capital investment for additional power generation could be US$33 billion and US$123 billion in 2050 and 2100 respectively to meet higher cooling energy demand of India. On the other hand, deaths due to malaria will increase to 5,000 in 2050 to 19,500 in 2100. Deaths due to dengue will also increase. If deaths are at life time earnings, then loss of economic output will be US$2.5 billion and US$21 billion in 2050 and 2100 respectively. The cost will be in a range of 0.45 per cent to 1.19 per cent of India's GDP and 0.59 per cent −1.17 per cent of India's GDP in 2050 and 2100.

Prajapati, Singh and Gangwar (2015) have revealed their views on effect of climate change on plant diseases in Bundelkhand zone leading to changing cropping pattern. The paper has analysed the two major indicators of climate change, that is, rainfall and temperature. The paper has highlighted the trends of climate variability from 1980 to 2005. It is observed that there is an increase in the mean maximum temperature in Bundelkhand region by 0.28 °C as compared to the baseline period of 1960–1990. The rainfall trends show declining trends of rainfall in Bundelkhand. The monsoon season has been shifted from the month July to August. As a result, there is a delay in sowing and harvesting which decreases the productivity of agricultural crops. The variation in temperature and wet weather are causing diseases in crops. The high temperature and high humidity also extend the viral disease. The climate change increases moisture content and warmer temperatures in the region; which is lead to the possibility of aggravate epidemics.

Literature Related to Climate Change and Food Security

There are number of studies at national as well as international level that analyse the relationship between climate change and food security. These are summed up in the following paragraphs.

Sinha and Swaminathan (1991) have presented their views on deforestation, climate change and sustainable nutrition security in India. They have analysed that an increase of 2 °C of the mean temperature could decrease the rice yield by about 0.75 tonnes/hectare in the high-yield areas, whereas only by 0.06 tonnes/hectare in the low-yield rice coastal regions. They have also observed that a 0.5 °C increase in the winter temperature would reduce wheat crop duration by seven days and reduce yield by 0.45 tonnes/hectare. An increase of 0.5 °C in mean temperature in the high yield states of Punjab, Haryana and Uttar Pradesh will decrease the wheat production by 10 per cent.

Hadke and Jichkar (2006) have presented their views on food security in the Indian scenario. The study found that there is direct relationship between food consumption and poverty. It is seen that poor families not only suffer from chronic hunger but are also the segment of the population most at risk during food shortages and famines. The problem of food security could be improved in developing countries by improving profit maximization, food justice and food sovereignty. Moreover they highlighted that a proper balanced diet is still a far cry for millions of poor families; their present income levels are too low to register their demands in agriculture and further that sector to propel, which still has tremendous unused potential.

Pathania and Vashis (2006) have focused on the present scenario and future strategies of food security. The main objective of the study was to analyse the availability and requirement of food grains and to suggest ways and means for improving the food security in Himachal Pradesh state by using secondary data. The study found that the population in Himachal Pradesh has increased by 76 per cent over the years and the reduction in poverty has resulted in increased demand for food grins as well as quality food. Due to the pressure of human labour on agriculture, the size of land holdings has decreased over the years. These results not only call for the reduction of the increased population dependent on agriculture but also creates the problem of food insecurity in the state of Himachal Pradesh.

Khatkar and Singh (2006) have analysed the consumption pattern and food security in Haryana and Rajasthan, and analysed the status of consumption pattern in relation to food security in arid regions of these states by using primary data of 200 respondents drawn from two selected districts from each state. It was observed that consumption of cereals in both the categories, that is, irrigated and un-irrigated farms is less than the suggested level. The consumption of cereals in un-irrigated farms is more than the irrigated farms in the selected areas, which is an indicator of prosperity because income and consumption of cereals have negative relationship in case of both selected districts. In the case per capita consumption of pulses in all the farms, that is, irrigated and un-irrigated, it was found that it was less than the recommended quantity. The recommended quantity of consumption of pulses is 50 gm/capita/day, while in this study it ranged from 12 gm/capita/day in Jaisalmer (un-irrigated) to 0.26 gm in Hanumangarh (un-irrigated). Also, the consumption of coarse cereals and pulses in selected districts was found to be higher in un-irrigated farms owing to more production of these commodities on such farms and that of rice, wheat, vegetables and fruits was found higher in irrigated farms due to superior income on the latter category of farms.

Varghese and Mordia (2006) have made an attempt on inter-state assessment of food security in India and the main objective of the study was to analyse the inter-state disparities of food security in the major states of India. It was found that there is direct link of food grain production, poverty and food security. The CAGR of food grains during the new economic regime in different states revealed that the growth rate of food grain production has been higher than population growth in the states. In India, the inter-state variability within a year in the per capita production remained very high during the recent past; the inter-year variability within the states in per capita production has been high for states. The rank correlation between overall development indices and food security indices turned out to be non-significant for Indian states.

Sinha (2006) has analysed the trends in food consumption and nutrition of food security concerns. The study found that India was the most populous country in south-east Asia. It is observed that the country has achieved significant progress in term of social-economic indicators such as life expectancy, infant mortality rate, maternal mortality rate and literacy rate. However, the poor section of the society has been suffering from the lack of availability of nutritional food. It was also observed that the population of India doubled between 1960 and 1992, but the impressive food grain production nearly kept pace with population growth.

World Bank (2007) examined that sustainable food security in a world of growing population and changing diets is a major challenge under climate change. As per the estimation of the World Bank, there is a need to increase food production to 70 per cent by the year 2050 when the global population will be 9 billion. Food security depends on both gross production of staples and agriculture's ability to provide income for its practitioners. In developing countries, diverse and balanced food basket and socio-economic factors determine whether poor people, particularly women are able to acquire and consume sufficient food.

Brown and Funk (2008) have discussed their views on food security under climate change. According to them, the impact of climate change on farmers varies from region to region, depending upon the use of technology. Climate change will reduce the agricultural production and food availability. The impact of this reduced production includes other changes such as rising oil price, the globalization of the grain market and a structural change in demand for food supplies due to increasing demand for bio-fuels and rising over capita consumption. These changes have pushed up supply costs for main foods by 40 per cent or more in many other areas. The study suggested that there is need of transformation of agricultural systems through improved seeds, fertilizers, land use and governance.

Charles (2011) has highlighted his views on climate change and its impacts on food safety. Climate change has been impacting food security. The changes in temperature and precipitation in regions with many of the industrialized countries, including the United States, will be less severe and will have less of an impact on agricultural practices than in region such as sub-Saharan Africa and Asia. It is seen that in Africa, climate change is reducing the length of the growing season and forcing large areas of marginal agriculture out of production. And, in many other countries, it is projected 50 per cent fall of the yield by 2020. There is a need to develop effective policies and capacity building programmes for adaptation to climate change.

Rukhsana (2011) has analysed dimension of food security in a selected state—Uttar Pradesh. The study found that poverty is the major determinant of food insecurity. It was observed that the poor people do not have adequate nutritional food quantities for a healthy life, hence food security is an absolute necessity for development. The results also show western Uttar Pradesh (WUP) as the highest food secure region and the northern portion as a low food secure region due to lack of agricultural markets and low purchasing level. Food security is positively correlated to its components, namely, food availability, stability and accessibility. The study found that food availability is reducing mainly due to the transformation of cereal crop cultivation into commercial cropping and food stability may be reduced due to changing land use pattern associated with industrialization, commercialization and globalization. On the other hand, food accessibility depends on the purchasing power of people and is different from food availability and stability.

Kumar et al. (2012) have observed the trends of food security in India with the latest available evidences in terms of availability, accessibility, utilization and absorption and has observed that they are interrelated. They found that availability is a necessary condition for food security and its components. The per capita availability (PCA) of food grains is hovering around 200 kg per annum. The availability of non-food-grain food commodities has depicted an inspiring trend. However, it was found that hugeness has almost vanished in most of the states but the nutritional deficiency continues to persist among the poor households across different states. On the other hand, it was found that utilization of public distribution system (PDS) has improved nutritional deficiency, though the picture is still not very bright and has shown declining trends. The study suggested that there is a need to develop the long-term strategies for augmenting food production and agricultural productivity.

Shakeel, Jamal and Zaidy (2012) have highlighted their views on regional analysis of food security in Bundelkhand region. The main aim of the study was to analyse the condition of food security in the Bundelkhand region of Uttar Pradesh. It was found that agriculture is the mainstay of the economy and mostly dependent on monsoonal rainfall and the region is continuously facing drought since last few years and people are migrating for employment. The study concluded that the condition of food security is unfavourable and majority of the districts are moderate and low food secure due to insufficient purchasing power of the people. On the other hand, irrigation facilities are also not well developed, leading to low consumption of fertilizer and low productivity of crops. Employment rate, rate of urbanization, storage capacity and agriculture markets are also unsatisfactory which lead to deplorable food security condition. They suggested that the government should increase literacy and employment through various schemes so that the problems of food security can be removed.

Brahmanand et al. (2013) have focused on challenges of food security in India. With the enormous pressure from the ever-increasing population in India, the need for achieving food security is felt significantly in the recent years. Also, due to the change in preferences in crop production techniques over the years have drawn attention to several new challenges pertaining to food security. Critical analysis of the article relates to challenges such as crop diversification, issues related to bio-fuel and medicinal plant cultivation, climate change, mismatch between water demand and availability, recent status in production of high-yielding crop varieties, agricultural crop pricing and insurance, and new trends in globalization and urban encroachments. In sum, it may be concluded that India's food security can be achieved by paying higher attention to issues such as mitigation of climate, integrated water management, agricultural crop pricing and crop insurance. The impact of openness of agriculture has been both positive and negative in terms of agricultural prosperity and the need of the hour is to regulate the policies related to globalization for reducing its negative effects on food security in India.

Jaswal (2014) has studied on the challenges to food security in India. Food security means to access enough food by all people at all times for an active and healthy life. It was seen that India is developing in terms of income generation, infrastructure development and per capita income (PCI). But the food management and its distribution are the major problem faced by India. Agriculture sector of India is not only providing employment to 55 per cent of its population but also is contributing 16.5 per cent to the annual GDP, and ranks second worldwide in farm output. Existence of food insecurity at the micro-level in the country like India has remained an alarming challenge for India. In the recently released Global Hunger Index (GHI) of 2013, India ranked 63rd out of 120 countries and this GHI report is quite worrying because India is one of the largest producers of food grain in the world. It also covered the several development schemes taken up by the Government of India to counter various food insecurity issues. Still India's biggest challenge remains ensuring food security and nutritional security to its mass population.

Literature Related to Climate Change, Agriculture and Food Security

There are few numbers of studies that shown the interrelationship among climate change, agriculture and food security at aggregate as well as disaggregate level. These are summed up in the following paragraphs.

Breisinger et al. (2011) have given their views on climate change, agricultural production and food security. The aim of the paper was to develop a model to assess local and global climate change impacts in the case of Yemen, focusing on agricultural production, household incomes and food security. It was found that global climate change was mainly transmitted through rising world food prices. Climate change-induced price increases for food will raise agricultural GDP while decrease real household incomes and food security. On the other hand, rural non-farm sector are knocked the hardest as they tend to be net food consumers with high share of food budget, but households of farm sector also experience real income losses given that many of them are net buyers of food. Local climate change impacts obvious itself in long-term productivity changes, which differ between the two alternative climate scenarios considered. Agricultural GDP under MIR scenario is somewhat higher than with perfect mitigation of climate changes and rural incomes augment due to higher crop productivity and lower prices for coarse cereals. The positive and negative yield changes cancel each other out under the CSI scenario. As a result, agricultural GDP and household incomes hardly change compared to perfect mitigation of climate changes.

Ranuzzi and Srivastava (2012) have studied the impact of climate change on agriculture and food security. The aim of the paper was to explore the effects of global warming and climate change on food security and food production. This paper has highlighted that climate change has been affecting the productivity of agriculture and food security in India. It is observed that if the temperature goes up to 20 °C, then rice production will be decreased by almost one tonne/hectare. Similarly, 10 °C rise in mean temperature would decrease wheat yield by 7 million tonnes or around US$1.5 billion at current prices per year in India. There is a need to improve several factors such as soil health, water conservation and management, and pest management, which make agriculture and food production more sustainable and ecologically friendly so as to better adapt to climate change effects. There is also a need to promote farm ponds, fertilizers trees and biogas plants in semi-arid rain-fed areas.

Kumar and Sharma (2013) have focused on the impact of climate variation on agricultural productivity and food security in rural areas of India. The main objectives of the study were to analyse the association between climate change and agriculture in terms of crop productivity in quantity terms, value of production in monetary terms and food security in rural India. The study was based on state-wise analysis with secondary data from 1980 to 2009. It was found that climate variability affects food grain and non-food grain productivity. These factors and other socio-economic and government policy variables affect food security. On the other hand, the results show that climate variation had negative impact on production and value of output from the agriculture sector. The adverse impact of climate change on the value of output from agriculture and food grain production indicates food security threat to small and marginal farming households. FSI also gets adversely affected due to climatic fluctuations.

Birthal et al. (2014) have highlighted their views on the impact of climate change on yields of major food crops and food security in India during the period 1969–2005. The study found that increasing temperature has an adverse impact on yield of most crops and pigeon pea, rice, chickpea and wheat were the most vulnerable to rise in temperature. Rainfall had a positive effect on most crops. It is estimated that the impact of temperature and rainfall will decrease rice yield by 15 per cent, wheat yield by 22 per cent and coarse cereals will be less affected, while pulses will be affected more than cereals.

Mahato (2014) has studied climate change and its impact on agriculture. In the world, climate is one of the most important factors that affect the agricultural productivity. In the long term, climatic change affects agriculture in several ways such as quantity and quality of crops in terms of productivity, growth rates, photosynthesis, transpiration rates and moisture availability. Climate change has been affecting food security across the globe. The climatic parameters such as temperature and humidity are affecting crop growth and quantity of food produced. Indirect linkage relates to catastrophic events such as floods and drought which are consequences of climate change. These events are leading to huge crop loss and leaving large patches of arable land unfit for cultivation. On the other hand, increase in the mean seasonal temperature is reducing the duration of many crops and final yield. The study suggested that coping with the impact of climate change on agriculture will require management of resources such as soil, water and biodiversity. The government will also need to act at global, regional, national and local levels.

Singh (2016) has given his views on how achieving food and nutritional security in the backdrop of degrading natural resources (water, soil, biodiversity) and climate vulnerabilities is a big challenge. As it is well known, global warming has already triggered the melting of icebergs, rising of sea levels and submergence of islands/coastal areas, along with changes in rainfall and temperature patterns. This is predicted to continue over the next century as well. In such a situation, water, land and biodiversity patterns demanding a new set of land-use patterns including enterprises, commodities, crops and varieties will be severely affected. Effects of climate change have already started affecting productivity of agriculture in several agro-climatic regions and sub-regions of India. These kinds of predicted scenarios of climate change on agriculture, location-specific case studies showing climate change impacts such as drought, cold and heat waves and required adaptation and mitigation strategies are discussed elaborately in his research paper. He further argued that adaptations of agriculture to climate change will call upon active involvement of researchers in the field of enterprises, commodities, crops, varieties and farming systems resilient to cold, heat and moisture stresses.

Bocchiola et al. (2017) have examined the impact of climate change on agriculture and food security in Nepal. It is observed that Nepal is amongst the poorest countries and its varied topography and social vulnerability make the country particularly susceptible to climate change. It is found that the country has low adaptive capacity to respond to the variability of climate change. Agriculture is the mainstay of Nepal's economy, employs 78 per cent of the workforce, and contributes nearly 36 per cent to Nepal's GDP. It is found that about 27 per cent of agricultural land has access to irrigation, whereas the greater part of arable land is rainfed. The study concluded that recently climate change in Nepal has demonstrably impacted crop productivity, food security at national level.

The main findings of the related literature reviewed above can be summarized as follows:

- Climate change is expected to affect crop sector, livestock sector, fisheries and aquaculture adversely. There is strong evidence of negative impacts of climate change on the performance of crop sector but much less evidence is available for livestock, fisheries and aquaculture sectors.

- The impact of climate change is worldwide on food production, productivity and farm income. Climate variations such as occurrence of droughts and floods have a high level of impact on the productivity and net revenue from the farm sector at aggregate and disaggregate levels.

- Small and marginal farmers are the most vulnerable groups because these people have small farm sizes, low capital and technological development in India. Farmers in less developed countries like India are currently more climate sensitive than the farmers in more developed countries.

- An increase in the mean seasonal temperature has reduced the duration of crops and productivity in the world. Half of all agricultural land in Latin America is likely to be affected by dissertation and salinization by 2050.

- Climate events such as cold waves, heat waves, droughts and floods have increased the weather factors to effect the production of food crops and soil health and it has a negative impact on food security. The effects of climate change vary according to region and country.

Box 3.1   Gaps in Existing Literature

There are numerous studies looking into climate impacts on soils but most overlook linkages of agriculture and food security. Although very few studies have been carried out to study major aspect of impact of climate change on agricultural productivity in India and its implication for food security for the nation, not many attempts have been made to study the symmetrically impact of climate change on agricultural productivity at aggregate as well as disaggregate level and also identify its determinants. There are huge variations from state to state in India at the agricultural productivity level as well as the food security level. Hence, the present study entitled 'Impact of climate change on

Indian agricultural productivity and its implication for food security' has been taken to analyse at the national level as well as state level and also identify the major drivers of both aspects, that is, productivity and food security. The present study fills the gap of literature by evaluating the impact of climate change on agricultural productivity and food security at both levels. In the up-coming chapters we would be analysing the same in greater detail.

CHAPTER 4

Research Methods and Techniques for the Analysis

Introduction

In the 21st century, climate change is one of the main determinants of agricultural production and productivity. Throughout the world there is significant concern about the effects of climate change and its variability on agricultural performance and its implication for food security. Academicians, administrators and researchers are concerned with the possible damages and benefits that may arise in future from climate change impacts on the agriculture sectors and will affect domestic and international policies, trading patterns, resource use, and food and nutrition security. Climate change refers to a change in climate over a period of time which is linked directly or indirectly to human activity that changes the composition of the global atmosphere in addition to natural climate variability observed over comparable time periods (IPCC 2007).

The main objective of the present study is to analyse the impact of climate change on Indian agricultural productivity and its implication for food security. Various research methods have been used for this study in order to obtain results for the achieved objectives at state and national level. Research methodology is the most important tool for achieving the research objectives. This chapter focuses on the research design and includes data base and research methodology. There are various methodological limitations with the ethical aspects. The present chapter can be divided into various sections, namely, area of study, time period of the study, data base of the study, methods of data analysis which include estimation of food security and its components at national and state-level as well as regression analysis. To identify the missing values, interpolation has been used.

Area of Study

The present study is based on aggregate (national) as well as disag-gregate (states) level analysis. At the disaggregate level, 16 major agriculturally intensive states, namely Andhra Pradesh, Assam, Bihar, Gujarat, Kerala, Madhya Pradesh, Maharashtra, Haryana, Himachal Pradesh, Karnataka, Orissa, Punjab, Rajasthan, Tamil Nadu, Uttar Pradesh and West Bengal have been taken with different climate conditions. All these states are major food grain and non-food grain producers, and contributes more than 90 per cent to the total agricul-tural production of the country. Figure 4.1 shows the selected states for the study marked in dark colour and these selected states cover majority of the agro-climatic zone of India.

Data Base for the Study

The present study is based on secondary data taken from various state and national level government sources such as government departments/agencies/publications relating to different variables/ parameters to analyse the objectives. To estimate the missing values, interpolation and graphical methods have been used. The data for agricultural, socio-economic and climatic variables have been taken from the following sources.

1. **Agricultural data:** Data for crop-wise production, area and pro-ductivity as well as gross and net irrigated area, crop-wise farm harvest price, state-wise gross sown area, gross irrigated area, net

Figure 4.1 *Selected States for Study in India*
This figure has been redrawn by Sanjeev Kumar and is not to scale. It does not represent any authentic national or international boundaries and is used for illustrative purposes only.

sown area, forest area, tractor and consumption of fertilizers at national level as well as state level has been taken from *Agricultural Statistics at a Glance*, Ministry of Agriculture, Government of India and Centre for Monitoring Indian Economy (CMIE). Data relating to other aspects on food grain and non-food grain has also been taken from *Handbook of Statistics on Indian Economy*, Reserve Bank of India (RBI), GoI. Data on fellow land and arable land has been taken *Land Use Statistics* (LUS) prepared by the Department of Agriculture and Co-operation Network (DACNET), Ministry of Agriculture, GoI. Data on GCF in agriculture at national as well as state-level has been collected from *Economic Survey*, Ministry of Finance, GoI. Values of agricultural food grain and non-food grain output, per capita income and number of agricultural labour at both levels, that is, national and state levels, have been taken from CSO, GoI.

2. **Demographic data:** Population characteristics-related data at state as well as national level, that is, literacy rate, population density and infant mortality rate (IMR) has been taken from Census of India,

Government of India. Urbanization, rural population and poverty data has been taken from Planning Commission, Government of India.

3. **Climatic variables**: The climatic variables are very important for the present study. In the present study, we have taken three climatic variables, namely, annual rainfall, average maximum temperature and average minimum temperature to identify the impact of climate change on agricultural productivity and food security at national as well as state level. The trends of these variables in the last 60 years are shown in Figure 4.2.

   Minimum and maximum temperature data has been taken from the Indian Meteorological Department (IMD), GoI which is available on a daily basis with regard to latitude and longitude information of monitoring stations. Information pertaining to stations has been identified in the situation of unavailability of city-wise data of temperature. Based on this information so generated, geographical regions have been identified. The different geographical regions are then linked to arrive at the state-level data points to group such region. Monthly district-wise rainfall information has also been taken from Hydromet Division, IMD, GoI. Annual average minimum temperature, average maximum temperature and annual rainfall have been taken for analysing the impact of climatic factors on agricultural productivity (crop sectors/specific crops) and food at national level as well as state level during the study period.

4. **Livestock and food availability**: The data information of the livestock sector has been taken from the Department of Animal Husbandry Dairy and Fisheries, GoI. Information regarding storage capacity has been collected from the Department of Food and Public Distribution, Ministry of Consumer Affairs, GoI and Rural Development Statistics, National Institute of Rural Development (NIRD), Hyderabad. Per capita calorie intake per day and per capita consumption expenditure (PCCE) has taken from National Sample Survey Organization (NSSO), Department of Statistics, Government of India (GoI).

5. **Infrastructure:** The data on road length and number of buffer stocks has been taken from CMIE, India during the study period.

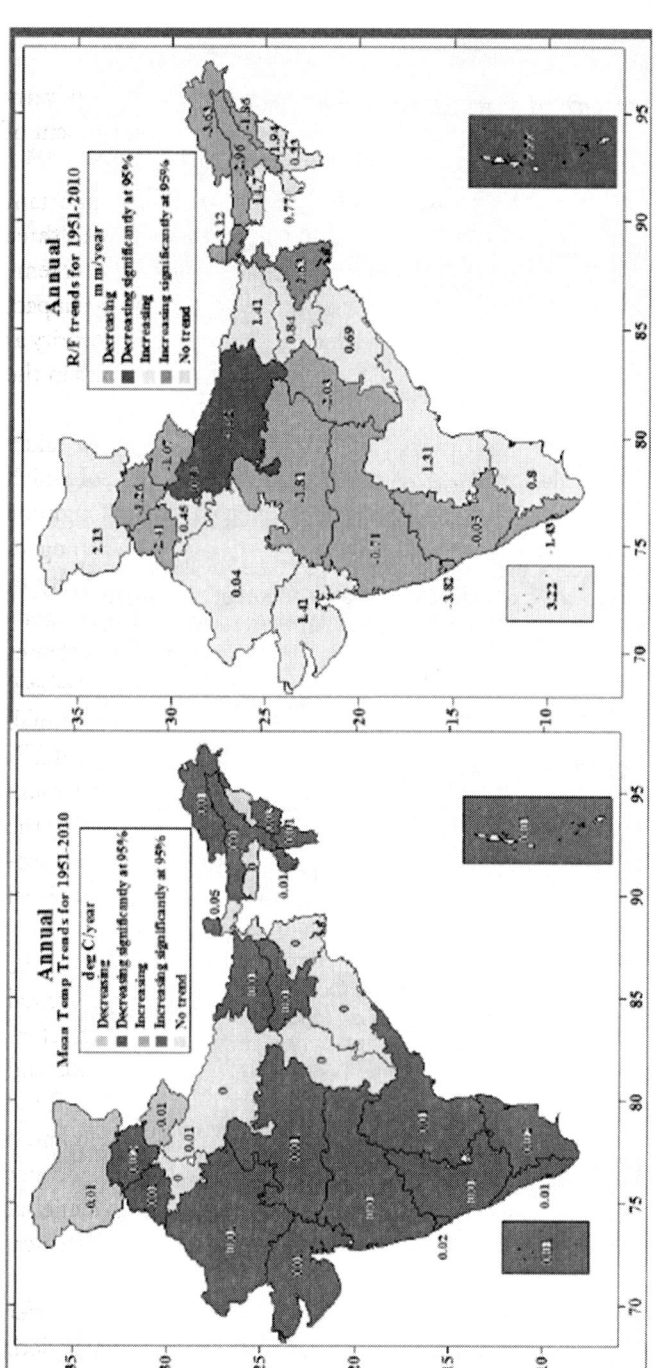

Figure 4.2 Trends of Climatic Variable during 1951–2010

Source: India Meteorological Department (IMD), New Delhi.

Time Period of the Study

The time periods of the study has been taken broadly from 1950–1951 to 2014–2015 at the national level and 1980–1981 to 2014–2015 at the state level. The time periods are different for the different levels of analysis. The analysis of national level as well as state level is given in Boxes 4.1 and 4.2.

Box 4.1 Time Period of Study for National-Level Analysis

- Performance of the agricultural sector , that is, food grain and non-food grain crops of India as well value of output form agriculture
    - Study period: From 1950–1951 to 2014–2015 and its sub periods, that is, pre-GR period (1950–1951 to 1965–1966), GR period (1966–1967 to 2014–2015), before economic reform (1950–1951 to 1989–1990) and after economic reform (1990–1991 to 2014–2015)
- Performance of climatic variables, that is, rainfall, maximum and minimum temperature
    - Study period: From 1950–1951 to 2014–2015
- Performance of food security and its dimensions
    Study period: From 1980–1981 to 2014–2015 and its sub periods, that is, before economic reform (1950–1951 to 1989–1990) and after economic reform (1990–1991 to 2014–2015)
- For regression results of impact of climate change on agriculture productivity, value of output and food security
    Impact of climatic variables on food grain and non-food grain Productivity: Period for study (1950–1951 to 2014–2015), before economic reform (1950–1951 to 1989–1990) and after economic reform (1990–1991 to 2014–2015)
    - Impact of climatic variables and non-climatic variables on food grain, non-food grain productivity and value of output from agriculture: Period for study (1950–1951 to 2014–2015)
    - Impact of climatic variables and non-climatic variables on food security and its components: Period for study (1980–1981 to 2014–2015) and its sub-periods

---

Box 4.2 Time Period of Study for State-Level Analysis

- Performance of agriculture sector at state level , that is, productivity of food grain and non-food grain crops as well value of output form agriculture
  - Study period: From 1980–1981 to 2014–2015 and its sub-periods
- Performance of climatic variables, that is, rainfall, maximum and minimum temperature
  - Study period: From 1980–1981 to 2014–2015
- Performance of food security and its dimensions
  - Study period: From 1980–1981 to 2014–2015 and its sub-periods
- For regression results of impact of climate change on agriculture productivity, value of output and food security
  - Impact of climatic variables and non-climatic variables on food grain and non-food grain productivity: Period for study from 1980–1981 to 2014–2015
  - Impact of climatic variables and non-climatic variables on value of output from agriculture: Period for study from 1990–1991 to 2014–2015
  - Impact of climatic variables and non-climatic variables on food security and its components: period for study from 1980–1981 to 2014–2015

Methods of Data Analysis

Growth Estimation

A widely accepted exponential model, $y = ab^t e^u$, has been fitted to the time series data for estimating the CAGR of different variables such as agriculture-related variables, climatic and non-climatic variables during the study period as well as its sub-periods. The logarithmic form of exponential model is given by

$$\ln(y) = \ln(a) + t \ln(b) + u,$$

where y is the dependent variable whose growth rate is to be estimated, that is, agriculture-related variables, climatic and non-climatic variables; t is the independent variable (time); and u is the disturbance or error term; a and b are the parameters to be estimated from sample observations. The regression coefficient b of exponential model is estimated by ordinary least squares (OLS) technique.

The CAGR in percentage term is estimated as follows:

$$CAGR = \{antilog(b) - 1\} \times 100$$

Estimation of Food Security and Its Components at National Level

To calculate FSI and its components index, namely, food availability index (FAI), index of food stability (IFS) and index of food accessibility (IFA), the technique of Z-score has used (http://www.foodsecurityindex.eiu.com/). If the parameters/indicators are favourable for food security and its components, then the following formula has been used to estimates the Z-score for various indicators of food security and its components:

$$CI_i = \frac{\{(xi - Min\,(x)\}}{\{Max(x) - Min(x)\}},$$

where CI is composite Z-score (Z-index); Min (x) and Max (x) are lowest and highest value in each indicators/parameters during the study period for food security or its components.

If the parameters are the unfavourable for food security and its components, then the following formula has been used to estimates the Z-score:

$$CI_i = \frac{\{(xi - Max\,(x)\}}{\{Max(x) - Min(x)\}}.$$

With the help of composite Z-score (CI), we have calculated FAI, IFS and IFA with their respected indicators/parameters by the following manner:

$$\text{FAI or IFS or IFA} = \frac{\sum \text{CI}_i}{n}.$$

Finally, FSI is based on the simple average of food availability, food stability and food accessibility Z-score and it is calculated by the following formula:

$$\text{FSI} = \frac{\text{FAI} + IFS + IFA}{n = 3},$$

where FSI is food security index; CI_i is the composite Z-value of the components of food security, that is, food availability, food stability and food accessibility; and n is the number of components of food security.

It is clear that the high values of variables indicate more favourable conditions of environment for food security, while the low values indicate an unfavourable environment for food security of the nation. Further, the normalized value of Z-score is then transformed from a 0–1 value to a 0–100 score to make it directly comparable with other indicators. This in fact means that the year with the highest raw data value will score 100, while the lowest will score 0. The indicators of food security and its components can be explained with the help of Figure 4.3.

Estimation of Food Security and Its Components at State Level

To calculate FSI and its components index, namely, FAI, IFS and IFA, the technique of Z-score has been used during the study period. This approach of estimating FSI and its components has been already discussed in the previous section. Due to the non-availability of data at state level, there has been made some changes in the indicators of food security and its components. The state level indicators of food security index and its components, namely, FAI, IFS and IFA, have been given in the following Figure 4.4.

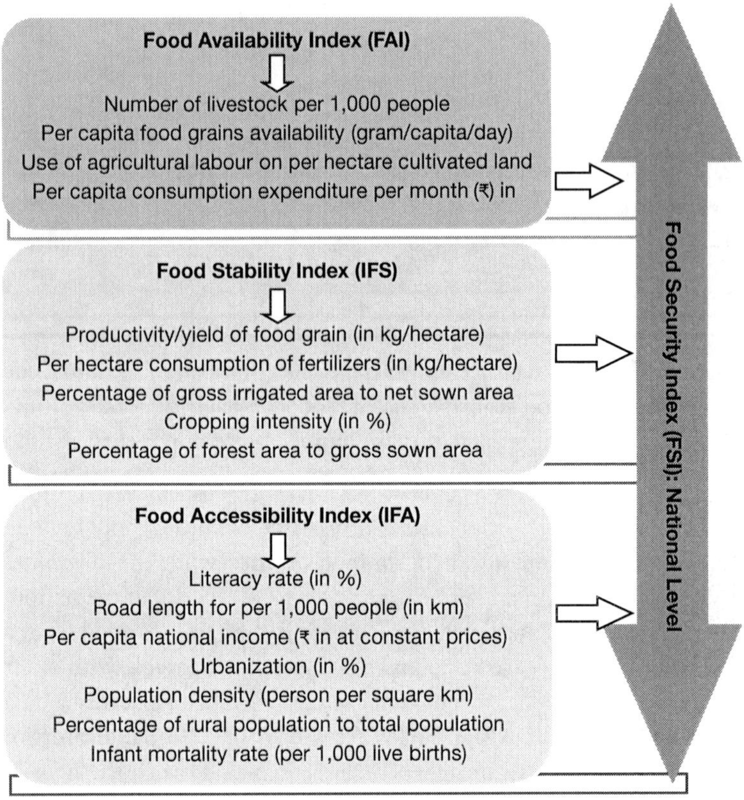

Figure 4.3 *Food Security and Its Components/Indicators at National Level*

Regression Models at National Level

Regarding Agriculture Productivity and Value of Output from Agriculture

Impact of Climatic Factors on Production and Productivity of Food Grains

The impact of climatic factors, namely, minimum temperature, maximum temperature and annual rainfall on food grain production (FGP) and productivity (YOF) during 1950–1951 to 2014–2015 (study period) as well as two sub-periods, namely, before economic reform

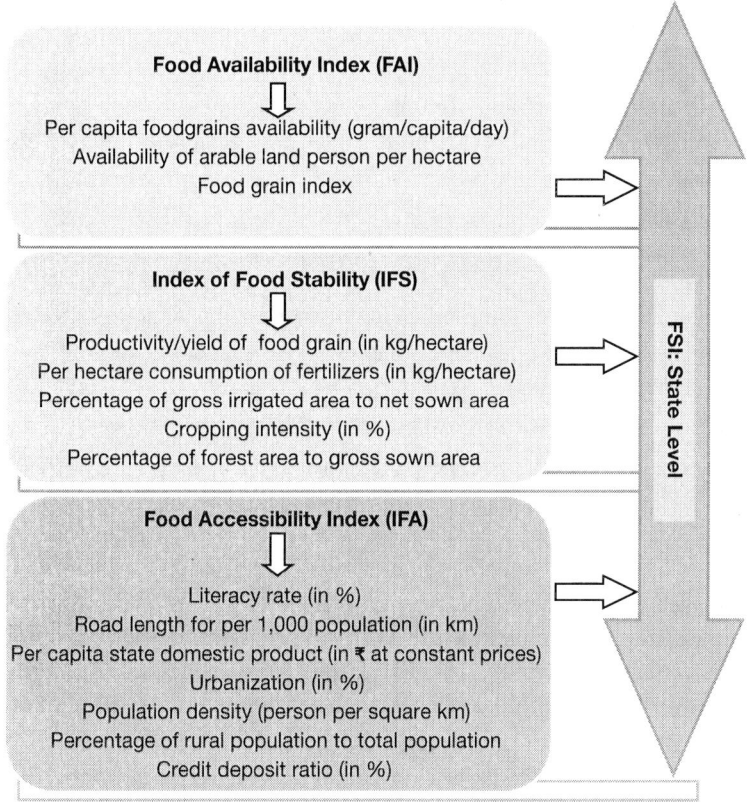

Figure 4.4 Food Security and Its Components/Indicators at State Level

period (1950–1951 to 1989–1990), and after economic reform period (1990–1991 to 2014–2015) at national level has been discussed by the following multiple regression models:

$$FGP = \beta_0 + \beta_1 RAIN + \beta_2 MINT + \beta_3 MAXT + Ui$$

$$YOF = \beta_0 + \beta_1 RAIN + \beta_2 MINT + \beta_3 MAXT + Ui,$$

where FGP and YOF are the food grain production and productivity of food grain; RAIN, MINT, MAXT are annual rainfall in millimetre, annual minimum temperature and maximum temperature respectively;

Ui is the stochastic error term; β_0 is constant coefficient; and β_1 to β_3 are coefficient of variables.

To avoid the problem of multicollinearity, annual growth rate has been taken of all dependent and independent variables.

Impact of Climatic and Non-climatic Factors on Productivity of Food Grain

The multiple regression models for the time series data was used to identify the impact of climate variables as well as socio-economic variables of crop productivity at the national level during 1980–1981 to 2014–2015. The regression equation is given as follows:

$$CSP = \beta_0 + \beta_1 RAIN + \beta_2 MINT + \beta_3 MAXT + \beta_4 GCFAG + \beta_5 LR + \beta_6 AL + \beta_7 NOTR + \beta_8 FERC + \beta_9 FANSA + \beta_{10} GIA + Ui,$$

where CSP is crop-specific productivity; RAIN, MINT and MAXT are average annual rainfall, average annual minimum and maximum temperature respectively; GCFAG is the gross capital formation of agriculture; LR, AL, NOTR, FERC and GIA are literacy rate, agricultural labour, number of tractors, consumption of fertilizers and gross irrigated area respectively; FANSA is the ratio of forest area to net sown area; βs are regression coefficient for respective variables; and Ui is stochastic error term.

To avoid the problems of multicollinearity, we have taken annual growth rate of all variables.

Impact of Climatic and Non-climatic Factors on Productivity of Non-food Grain

The following regression equation has been used to estimate the impact of climate and non-climate factors on the productivity of major non-food grain crops, namely, sugarcane, oilseeds, cotton and jute and mesta:

$$CSP_{NFC} = \beta_0 + \beta_1 RAIN + \beta_2 MINT + \beta_3 MAXT + \beta_4 GCFAG + \beta_5 LR + \beta_6 AL + \beta_7 NOTR + \beta_8 FERC + \beta_9 FANSA + \beta_{10} GIA + Ui,$$

where CSP_{NFC} is crop-specific productivity in case of non-food grain.

Impact of Climatic and Non-climatic Variables on Agricultural Value of Output

The impact of climatic and socio-economic factors on value of output of food grain crops and non-food-grain crops has been analysed by multiple regression model during 1980–1981 to 2014–2015. Per hectare value of output as dependent variables are regressed with non-climatic factors as well as climatic factors using time series date for the period of 1980–1981 to 2014–2015. All non-climatic variables (independent variables) have also been taken in term of per hectare value. The model can be written as following form:

$$PHVO = \beta_0 + \beta_1 RAIN + \beta_2 MINT + \beta_3 MAXT + \beta_4 PHGIA + \beta_5 PHFERC + \beta_6 PHNOTR + \beta_7 PHFA + \beta_8 PHGCFA + Ui,$$

where PHVO is per hectare value of output from agriculture and its components, namely, rice, wheat, cereals, coarse cereals, pulses, food grain, oilseeds, sugarcane, cotton and, jute and mesta. The value of output has taken at constant price of the agriculture sector as well as its components; RAIN, MINT and MAXT are average annual rainfall, average annual mean minimum and maximum temperature respectively; PHGIA is per hectare gross irrigated area as per cent to net sown area; PHFERC, PHNOTR, PHFA and PFGCFA are per hectare consumption of fertilizer, per thousand hectare availability of tractor, per hectare forest area and per hectare gross capital formation in agriculture respectively; β_0 is constant coefficient term and β_1 to β_8 are regression coefficient for respective variables; and Ui is stochastic error term.

Regarding Food Security and Its Components Regression Analysis

Impact of Climatic Variables on Food Security

FSI is considered as dependent variable and regressed with climatic variables such as rainfall, minimum temperature and maximum temperature as well as difference of maximum and minimum temperature by separate simple multiple regression models during 1980–1981 to 2014–2015 at the national level. The multiple regression models are as follows:

$$\text{FSI} = \beta_0 + \beta_1 \text{RAIN} + \beta_2 \text{MINT} + \beta_3 \text{MAXT} + Ui$$

$$\text{FSI} = \beta_{01} + \beta_1 \text{RAIN} + \beta_2 \text{ DIFF (MAXT–MINT)} + Ui,$$

where FSI is food security index; MINT is annual minimum temperature; MAXT is annual maximum temperature; and DIFF (MAXT–MINT) is the difference of annual maximum and minimum temperature; β_0 is constant coefficient term, β_1 to β_3 are regression coefficients for respective variables; and Ui is stochastic error term.

Impact of Climatic Variables on FAI

FAI is regressed with climatic variables such as rainfall, minimum temperature and maximum temperature as well as difference of maximum and minimum temperature by separate simple multiple regression models during 1980–1981 to 2014–2015 at national level. The regression models are as follows:

$$\text{FAI} = \beta_0 + \beta_1 \text{RAIN} + \beta_2 \text{MINT} + \beta_3 \text{MAXT} + Ui$$

$$\text{FAI} = \beta_0 + \beta_1 \text{RAIN} + \beta_2 \text{ DIFF (MAXT–MINT)} + Ui,$$

where FAI is food availability index. The rest of the variables are same as discussed earlier.

Impact of Climatic Variables on IFS

The impact of the climatic variables on the IFS during the study period, that is, 1980–1981 to 2014–2015 at national level are given by the following regression models:

$$\text{IFS} = \beta_0 + \beta_1 \text{RAIN} + \beta_2 \text{MINT} + \beta_3 \text{MAXT} + Ui$$

$$\text{IFS} = \beta_0 + \beta_1 \text{RAIN} + \beta_2 \text{ DIFF (MINT–MAXT)} + Ui,$$

where IFS is the food stability index and the rest of the variables are same as discussed earlier

Impact of Climatic Variables on IFA

The impact of climatic variables on IFA during 1980–1981 to 2014–2015 at national level are given by the following multiple regression models:

$$IFA = \beta_0 + \beta_1 RAIN + \beta_2 MINT + \beta_3 MAXT + Ui$$

$$IFA = \beta_0 + \beta_1 RAIN + \beta_2 \, DIFF \, (MINT-MAXT) + Ui,$$

where IFA is the food accessibility index and the rest of the variables are same as discussed earlier.

Impact of Climatic and Non-climatic Variables on FSI

The multiple regression models for the time period 1980–1981 to 2014–2015 have been used to estimate the impact of climatic and non-climatic variables on FSI at national level. The following is the multiple regression model:

$$FSI = \beta_0 + \beta_1 CI + \beta_2 (LIV/GSA) + \beta_3 (RL/GSA) + \beta_4 (TR/GSA) + \beta_5 (GIA/GSA) + \beta_6 (TFC/GSA) + \beta_7 (UR) + \beta_8 (POV) + \beta_9 (GCF/GSA) + \beta_{10} (RAIN) + \beta_{11} (MINT) + \beta_{12} (MAXT) + Ui,$$

where FSI is food security index; GSA is gross sown area at national level; CI is cropping intensity of the agriculture sector; (LIV/GSA),(RL/GSA),(TR/GSA),(GIA/GSA), (TFC/GSA) and (GCF/GSA) are ratio of gross sown area with gross livestock, road length, total number of tractor, gross irrigated area, consumption of total fertilizers and gross capital formation of agricultural and allied sector respectively; UR and POV are per cent of urbanization and poverty ratio; RAIN, MINT and MAXT are annual rainfall, annual minimum temperature and maximum temperature respectively; β_1 to β_{12} are regression coefficient for respective variables; β_0 is constant coefficient term; and Ui is stochastic error term.

To avoid the problems of multicollinearity, annual growth rate of all variables, that is, dependent as well as independent variables have been taken.

Regression Models At State Level

Impact of Climatic and Non-climatic Variables on Agricultural Productivity

The impact of the climatic and non-climatic variables on productivity of major food grain crops as well as non-food-grains crops in the selected states during the study period from 1980–1981 to 2014–2015 has been analysed by using the state-level panel data. To analyse the impact of the climatic and non-climatic variables, the productivity of various crops as well as crop sector has been taken as dependent variables. The state level panel data regression model is as follows:

$$CSP = \beta_0 + \beta_1 RAIN + \beta_2 MINT + \beta_3 MAXT + \beta_4 FERC + \beta_5 GIA/NSA + \beta_6 CI + \beta_7 FAGSA + \beta_8 RL + \beta_9 PD + \beta_{10} LR + Ui,$$

where CSP is crop specific/crop sector productivity; RAIN, MINT and MAXT are average annual rainfall, average annual minimum and annual maximum temperature; FERC, GIA/NSA, CI, FAGSA, RL, PD, LR are per hectare consumption of fertilizer, ratio of gross irrigated area to net sown area, cropping intensity, ratio of forest area to gross sown area, road length per 1,000 people, population density and literacy rate respectively; β_0 is constant coefficient term; β_1 to β_{10} are regression coefficients for respective independent variables and Ui is stochastic error term.

Impact of Climatic and Non-climatic Variables on Agricultural Value of Output

The impact of climatic and non-climatic variables on value of output of the agriculture sector and its crop sector during the study period from 1990–1991 to 2014–2015 has been analysed at state level by using panel data. To analyse the impact of the climatic and non-climatic variables on per hectare value of output from the agriculture sector and its crop sector are regressed with the climatic and non-climatic variables. The regression model is given the following form:

$$VAO = \beta_0 + \beta_1 CI + \beta_2 FERC + \beta_3 GIA/NSA + \beta_4 FAGSA + \beta_5 RL + \beta_6 LR + \beta_7 RAIN + \beta_8 MINT + \beta_9 MAXT + Ui,$$

where VAO is value of output from the agriculture sector and its crop sector; other independent variables are as same as discussed earlier. To avoid multicollinearity, we have changed the form of all variables, that is, dependent as well as independent variables.

Impact of Climatic and Non-climatic Variables on FSI

The impact of climatic factors and non-climatic factors/socio-eco-nomic variables on FSI and its components, that is, FAI, IFS and IFA has been estimated by panel data regression models for time period of 1980–1981 to 2014–2015 at state level. The details of the regression models have been discussed by the following regression equations:

$$\textbf{FSI} = \beta_0 + \beta_1 CI + \beta_2 RL + \beta_3 GIA/NSA + \beta_4 FAGSA + \beta_5 FERC + \beta_6 LR + \beta_7 UR + \beta_8 PD + \beta_9 RAIN + \beta_{10} MINT + \beta_{11} MAXT + Ui$$

$$\textbf{FAI} = \beta_0 + \beta_1 CI + \beta_2 RL + \beta_3 GIA/NSA + \beta_4 FAGSA + \beta_5 FERC + \beta_6 LR + \beta_7 UR + \beta_8 PD + \beta_9 RAIN + \beta_{10} MINT + \beta_{11} MAXT + Ui$$

$$\textbf{IFS} = \beta_0 + \beta_1 CI + \beta_2 RL + \beta_3 GIA/NSA + \beta_4 FAGSA + \beta_5 FERC + \beta_6 LR + \beta_7 UR + \beta_8 PD + \beta_9 RAIN + \beta_{10} MINT + \beta_{11} MAXT + Ui$$

$$\textbf{IFA} = \beta_0 + \beta_1 CI + \beta_2 RL + \beta_3 GIA/NSA + \beta_4 FAGSA + \beta_5 FERC + \beta_6 LR + \beta_7 UR + \beta_8 PD + \beta_9 RAIN + \beta_{10} MINT + \beta_{11} MAXT + Ui,$$

where FSI is food security index, FAI, IFS, IFA are food avail-ability index, index of food stability and index of food accessibility respectability; RAIN, MAXT and MINT are average annual rainfall, annual maximum temperature and annual minimum temperature respectively; CI, GIA/NSA and FERC are cropping intensity, gross irrigated area as per cent of net sown area and per hectare fertilizer consumption respectively; RL, LR, UR and PD are road length per thousand population, literacy rate, urbanization and population den-sity respectively; β_0 is constant coefficient; β_1 to β_{11} are the regression coefficients for respective independent variables and Ui is error term in the model.

The computation of the whole analysis has been done by using software packages, namely, SPSS, STATA and MS-Excel. The results for the analysis of the impact of climate change and non-climatic change/socio-economic variables on agricultural productivity and food security at national level as well as state level are being presented in succeeding chapters.

CHAPTER 5

Agro-Climatic Zones and Trends of Climatic Variables in India

We must face up to an inescapable reality: the challenges of sustainability simply overwhelm the adequacy of our responses. With some honorable exceptions, our responses are too few, too little, and too late.

—Kofi A. Annan

Introduction

Climate change has emerged as one of the major problems of the agriculture sector at both national and international levels. It is affecting the agriculture sector directly in terms of crop-specific productivity, soil fertility, biodiversity and national food security. Climatic variations such as occurrence of droughts and floods have a high impact on the agriculture sector of the economy as well as socio-economic conditions of the people of the nation. It is evident from the past studies that natural and human activities both are responsible for climate change. Natural activities consist of Earth's motion, sun's intensity, volcanic eruption, forest fires and the circulation of the ocean. On the other hand, human activities are also responsible for changing climatic variables due to rising population, rapid growth in urbanization, higher industrialization, use of advanced technology, innovation, higher economic development, transportation, building construction and decreasing forest area (Ahmad et al. 2011). All these activities are responsible for increasing GHGs in the atmosphere. Increasing quantity of GHGs in the atmosphere is a key factor for climatic variability.

The agro-climatic information system incorporates the physical properties of the atmosphere, land surface, soil and hydrology–vegetation interactions into a holistic tool which supports in planning and management of agricultural products (Unninayar 1989). Recently, farmers, commodity dealers, water managers and others have devised new strategies, which require agro-climatic information and use models to plan agricultural production. This agro-climatic information system intends to help National Agricultural Research System (NARS) by improving production efficiency and also targets their research efforts according to their specific agro-climatic situations. Further, it aims to modify the impact of new technology in each country. The end result of such a system is to obtain an optimum sustainable yield through better use of weather and climatic information, and to promote skilful crop production. This knowledge will also entail quantification in terms of analysing the degree of acceptable risk in sustained development of the agriculture sector including forestry, fisheries and aquaculture. At the country level, use of agro-climatic information system in the analysis of sustainability has already borne fruit and revealed a unique importance (Table 5.1). Box 5.1 represents a scheme indicating the functional units of an agro climatic-approach. It delineates procedures and interactions involved in implementing an agro-climatic system for short- or long-term economic benefits for a particular zone or country.

Box 5.1 Agro-Climatic Zones

ACZ refers to a land unit defined in terms of major climates, favourable for a certain range of crops and cultivars. The planning focusses on scientific management of regional resources in order to meet the food requirement, fibre, fodder and fuel wood without severely impacting the natural resources and environment (FAO 1983). Agro-climatic scenarios mainly refer to soil types, rainfall, temperature and water availability which influences the type of vegetation. AEZ is the land unit carved out of ACZ superimposed on landform which acts as modifier to climate and length of growing period.

ACZ of India

The geographical area of the country is 329 million hectares and consists of a large number of complex agro-climatic situations. A number of attempts have been made to delineate major AER with respect to soils, climate, physiographic and natural vegetation for macro-level planning on a more scientific basis. They are discussed in the following sections.

Agro-Climatic Regions by the Planning Commission

The salient characteristics of 15 ACZ in India are given in Table 5.1 and Figure 5.1.

The Planning Commission had categorized the country into 15 broad ACZ on the basis of physiography, soils, geological formation, climate, cropping patterns and development of irrigation and mineral resources for broad agricultural planning and developing future strategies. There were 14 regions in the mainland while 1 was in the islands of Bay of Bengal and the Arabian Sea. The primary reason was to enable policy development based on techno-agro-climatic considerations by holistically integrating plans of the agro-climatic regions with the state and national plans. In the agro-climatic regional planning, further sub-regionalization was done based on agro-ecological parameters.

ACZ under National Agricultural Research Project (NARP)

The National Agricultural Research Project (NARP) started by ICAR focused on initiating agricultural research in ACZ of the country with the objective of upgrading a zonal research station in each of the ACZ for generating location-specific, need-based research targeted for specific agro-ecological situations. The aim was analysing agro-ecological conditions and cropping patterns, and coming up with a targeted programme that would solve the major obstacles of agricultural performance in a zone based on natural resources, major crops, farming systems, production constraints and socio-economic conditions. Major focus was on technology generation. In NARP, 127 ACZ were identified across the country.

Table 5.1 Salient Characteristics of 15 ACZ in India

ACZ	No. of Sub-zones	Annual Rainfall (mm)	Area/States Represented	Nature of Climate	Major Crops
1. Western Himalayan Region	3	165–2000	Jammu and Kashmir, Himachal Pradesh and Uttarakhand	Cold arid to humid	Saffron, maize, barley, oats and wheat; peaches, apricot, pears, cherry, almond, litchis, walnut
2. Eastern Himalayan Region	5	1840–3528	Assam, West Bengal (Darjeeling) and North-east States	Per humid to humid	Rice, maize, potato and tea; orchards of pineapple, litchi, oranges and lime
3. Lower Gangetic Plain Region	4	1302–1607	West Bengal (except the hilly areas), eastern Bihar and the Brahmaputra valley	Moist sub-humid to dry sub-humid	Rice, jute, maize, potato, rapeseed and pulses
4. Middle Gangetic Plain Region	6	1211–1470	Parts of Uttar Pradesh and Bihar	Moist sub-humid to dry sub-humid	Rice, maize, millets, wheat, gram, barley, peas, mustard and potato
5. Upper Gangetic Plains Region	3	721–979	Central and western parts of Uttar Pradesh and plain area of Uttarakhand	Dry sub-humid to semi-arid	Wheat, rice, sugarcane, millets, maize, gram, barley, oilseeds, pulses and cotton
6. Trans-Ganga Plains Region	3	360–890	Punjab, Haryana, Delhi and Rajasthan (Ganganagar)	Extreme arid to dry sub-humid	Wheat, sugarcane, cotton, rice, gram, maize, millets, pulses and oilseeds
7. Eastern Plateau and Hills	5	1271–1436	Chhotanagpur Plateau, extending over Jharkhand, Orissa, Chhattisgarh and Dandakaranya	Moist sub-humid to dry sub-humid	Rice, millets, maize, oilseeds, ragi, gram, potato, tur, groundnut, soyabean, urad, castor and groundnut

8. Central Plateau and Hills	14	490–1570	Bundelkhand, Baghelkhand, Bhander Plateau, Malwa Plateau and Vindhyachal Hills	Semi-arid to dry sub-humid	Millets, wheat, rice, gram, oilseeds, cotton and sunflower
9. Western Plateau and Hills	4	602–1040	Southern part of Malwa plateau and Deccan plateau (Maharashtra)	Semi-arid	Wheat, cotton, pulses, groundnut, oilseeds, sugarcane, rice, oranges, grapes and bananas
10. Southern Plateau and Hills	6	677–1001	Southern Maharashtra, Karnataka, Andhra Pradesh, and Tamil Nadu uplands	Semi-arid	Millets, oilseeds, pulses, coffee, tea, cardamom and spices
11. Eastern Coastal Plains and Hills	6	780–1287	Circar coasts of Andhra Pradesh, Pondicherry and Orissa	Semi-arid to dry sub-humid	Rice, jute, tobacco, sugarcane, maize, millets, groundnut and oilseeds
12. Western Coastal Plains and Ghats	4	2226–3640	Malabar and Konkan coastal plains and the Sahyadris (Tamil Nadu, Kerala, Goa, Maharashtra, Karnataka)	Dry sub-humid per humid	Rice, coconut, oilseeds, sugarcane, millets, pulses and cotton
13. Gujarat Plains and Hills	7	340–1793	Hills and plains of Kathiawar and the fertile valleys of Mahi and Sabarmati rivers (Gujarat)	Arid to dry sub-humid	Groundnut, cotton, rice, millets, oilseeds, wheat and tobacco
14. Western Dry Region	–	395	West of Aravalli (Rajasthan)	Arid to extremely arid	Bajra, jowar, moth, wheat and gram
15. Island Region	2	1500–3086	Andaman and Nicobar Islands and Lakshadweep	Humid	Coconut, millets, pulses, arecanut, turmeric and cassava

Source: Author's classification based on Planning Commission of India.

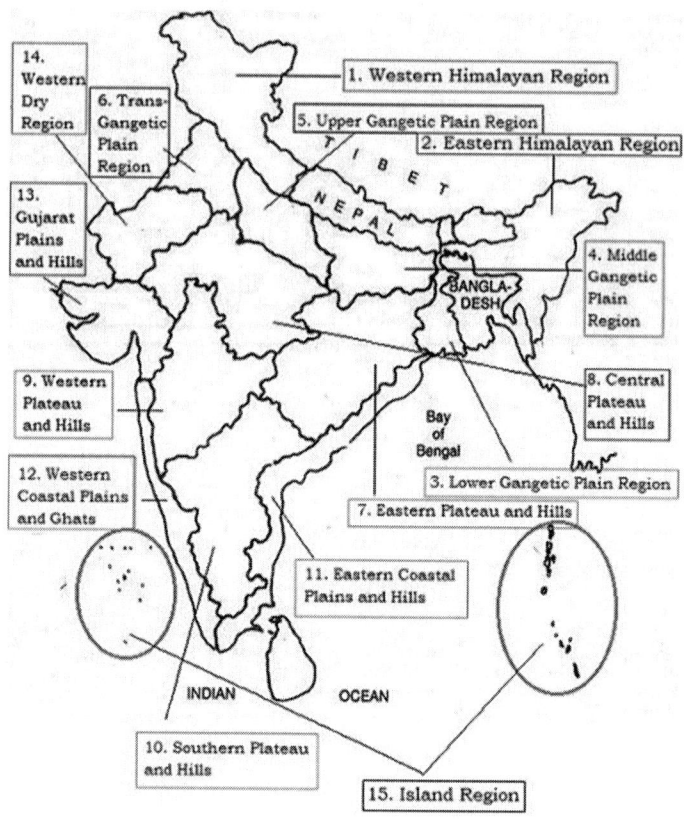

Figure 5.1 *ACZ by the Planning Commission*
Source: Planning Commission of India.

AEZ by the National Bureau of Soil Survey and Land Use Planning

The National Bureau of Soil Survey and Land Use Planning (NBSS & LUP) identified 20 AEZ based on the integrated criteria of effective rainfall, soil groups and delineated boundaries adjusted according to district boundaries with a negligible number of regions.

Eventually, these 20 AEZ were sub-divided into 60 sub-zones. The agro-ecological zone by NBSS and LUP are given in figure 5.2. The twenty agro-ecological zones are Western Himalayas; Western

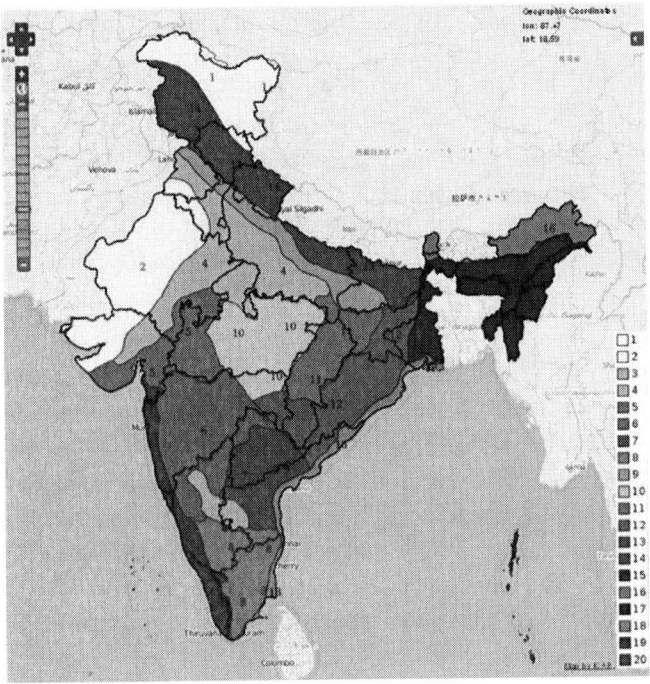

Figure 5.2 AEZ by NBSS & LUP

Source: https://www.nbsslup.in/
This figure has been redrawn by Sanjeev Kumar and is not to scale. It does not represent any authentic national or international boundaries and is used for illustrative purposes only.

Plain, Kachchh; and part of Kathiwara Peninsula, Deccan Plateau; Northern Plain and Central Highlands including Aravallis Central Malwa Highlands; Gujarat Plains, and Kathiawar Peninsula; Deccan Plateau, hot semi-arid ecoregion; Deccan (Telengana) Plateau and Eastern Ghats; Eastern Ghats, Tamil Nadu Plateau and Deccan (Karnataka); Northern Plain, hot sub-humid (dry) eco-region; Central Highlands (Malwas, Budelkhand, and Eastern Satpura); Eastern Plateau (Chattisgarh), hot sub-humid eco-region; Eastern (Chotanagpur) Plateau and Eastern Ghats; Eastern Plain; Western Himalayas; Bengal and Assam plains; Eastern Himalayas; North Eastern Hills (Purvanchal); Eastern Coastal Plain; Western Ghats and Coastal Plain and Island of Andaman Nicobar and Lakshadweep.

ACZ division will aid in achieving optimum utilization in a suitable manner within the framework of resource constraints and potential of each region. This classification of ACZ will support the development of the agriculture sector in terms of efficient farming systems and crop improvement research programmes besides establishing principles for improved resource management.

Trends of Climate Variables in India

The rising world population, degradation in environment, limited natural resources and changes in climatic factors pose a great challenge to agricultural productivity and food security. As per the estimation of FAO, WFP and IFAD (2012), about 870 million people are under-nourished and 98 per cent of these reside in developing countries like India. Moreover, a billion people lack adequate nutrition. Hunger and malnutrition alone are killing almost six million children each year worldwide. The situation in India is far more pathetic, about 17.5 per cent of the population is undernourished and the country stands at 63rd rank out of 69 nations in GHI (IFPRI 2013).

Food security is actually an outcome of the food production process. Climate change will affect food security by influencing the availability of food, access to food, stability of food supplies and volatility in food prices. Climate and its variability have been influencing food security and its components, that is, availability of food, accessibility of food and stability of food at national and global levels. Climate change adversely affects food security through agriculture production. It affects to food security in four dimensions, that is, food availability, food accessibility, food utilization and food system stability in India.

Rainfall

India has a tropical monsoon climate and rainfall is an important element for the economic development of India. Most of the India's population is dependent on agriculture and 40 per cent of the cropped area does not have any kind of irrigation facility other than the rain. Majority of the population waits for the rains for sowing major seeds and depends on monsoon for agricultural activities. It is also said that

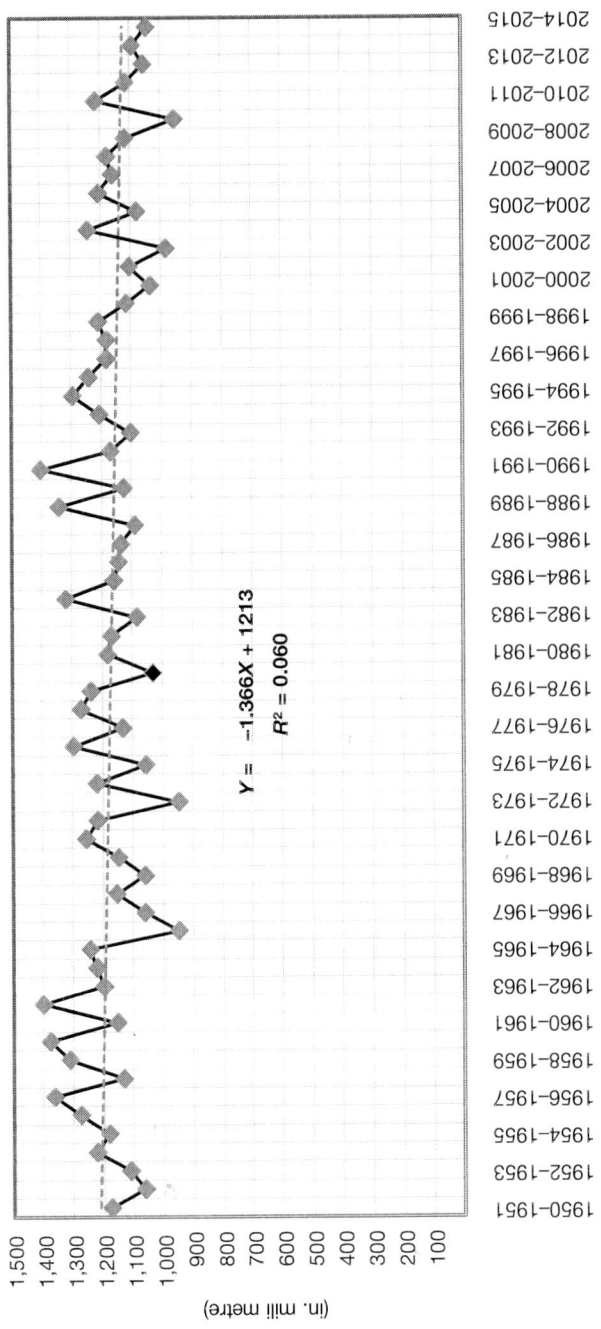

Figure 5.3 *Trends of Annual Rainfall in India*

Source: India Meteorological Department, GoI.

Indian agriculture has been gamble of monsoon. There is a strong positive and negative linkage between growth of agriculture and rainfall in India. Figure 5.3 shows the annual rainfall (in millimetre) during 1950–1951 to 2014–2015 in India.

Figure 5.3 reveals that the annual rainfall was 1174.20mm in 1950–1951 and became 1045.20mm in 2014–2015 in India. Similarly, the mean of the annual rainfall was 1168mm whereas the standard deviation of the annual rainfall was 105.37mm during 1950–1951 to 2014–2015. It is observed that annual rainfall shows fluctuating trends during the same periods. It is observed that the annual rainfall decreased during 1950–1951 to 2014–2015 in India. The trend value of annual rainfall shows declining trends at magnitude of –1.366 during the study period.

Minimum Temperature

Temperature is one of the most important climatic factors for the agricultural development in India. However, the temperature is fluctuating between minimum and maximum temperatures. Figure 5.4 shows the annual minimum temperature during 1950–1951 to 2014–2015 in India. The figure highlights that the annual minimum temperature was 18.95 °C in 1950–1951 and increased to 19.77 °C in 2014–2015 in India. The mean of the annual minimum temperature was 19.38 °C and the standard deviation was 0.34 °C during the same period in India. It is observed that about 1 °C minimum temperature increased during 1950–1951 to 2014–2015 in India.

Maximum Temperature

Figure 5.5 reveals the annual maximum temperature in India during 1950–1951 to 2014–2015. It is found that the annual maximum temperature was 28.47 °C in 1950–1951 and increased to 29.72 °C in 2014–2015 in India. On the other hand, the mean of the annual maximum temperature was 29.40 °C and the standard deviation was 0.40 °C in India during 1950–1951 to 2014–2015.

It is observed that the annual maximum temperature has been increased during 1950–1951 to 2014–2015 in India at the rate of 0.016

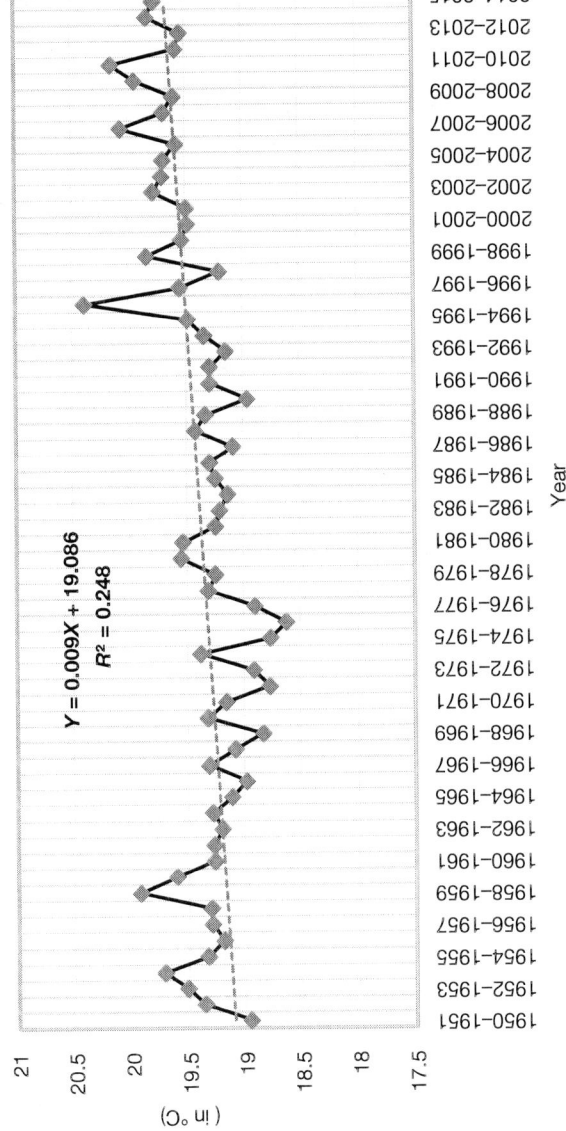

Figure 5.4 *Trends of Annual Minimum Temperature in India*

Source: Author's own creation based on India Meteorological Department Database.

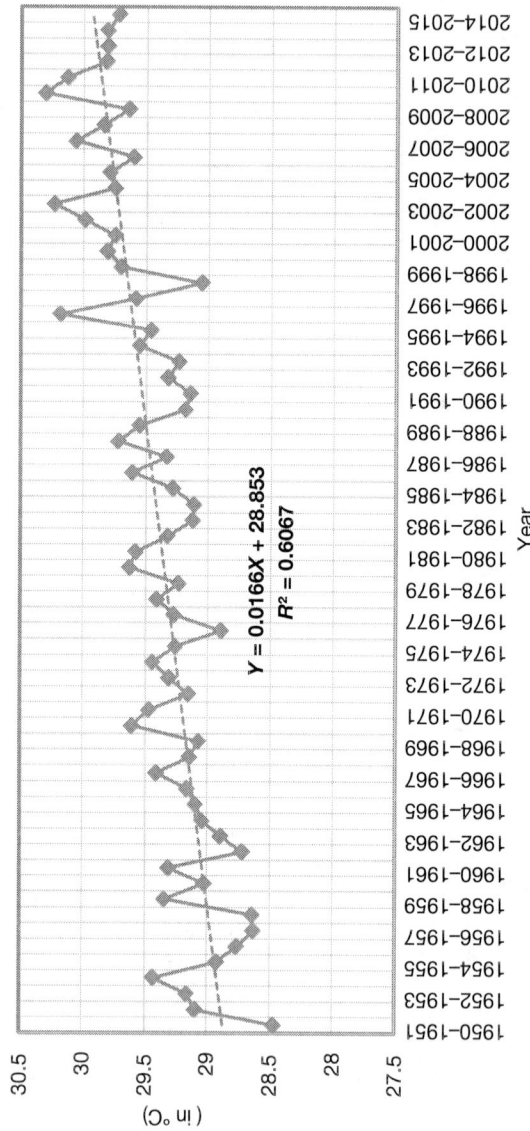

Figure 5.5 *Trends of Annual Maximum Temperature in India*
Source: Author's own creation based on India Meteorological Department Database.

per cent annual during the study period. Temperature has affected the productivity of various crops in India. It was estimated by Ranuzzi and Richa (2012) that if the temperature goes up to 20 °C, then the rice production will be decreased by almost one tonne/hectare. Similarly, 10 °C rise in mean temperature, would decrease wheat yield by 7.0 million tonnes or around $1.5 billion at current prices per year in India.

Comparison of Climatic Variables at National Level

It is a fact that Indian agriculture is highly dependent on monsoon. Majority of the agriculture area is left uncultivated due to deficient rainfall which decreases the productivity of agriculture and increases food prices and problem of food security of the nation. The trends of annual rainfall (in millimetre), annual minimum temperature (in °C) and annual maximum temperature (in °C) during 1980–1981 to 2014–2015 at national level are presented in Figure 5.6. It is found that the annual rainfall was 1182.30mm in 1980–1981 and decreased to 1045.20mm in 2014–2015 at national level. On the other hand, it grew at a rate of −0.307 per cent during the study period. Regarding annual minimum temperature, it was 19.53°C in 1980–1981 and increased to 19.77°C in 2014–2015 at national level. Similarly, the growth rate of annual minimum temperature went up with the rate of 0.102 per cent during the overall period at national level. In case of the annual maximum temperature, it was 29.58°C in 1980–1981 and increased to 29.72°C in 2014–2015 in the country. Considering the growth rate, it grew at the rate of 0.072 per cent during the study period. Overall it is found that climatic variability is affecting the socio-economic conditions of the people. Rising temperature has been influencing agricultural productivity and food security of the nation.

Trends of Climatic Variables at State Level

India is endowed with a vast and rich diversity of natural resources particularly soil, water, climate and agro-biodiversity at both national and state levels. In order to tap the potential of the agricultural production system on a sustainable basis, there is a need to focus our attention to

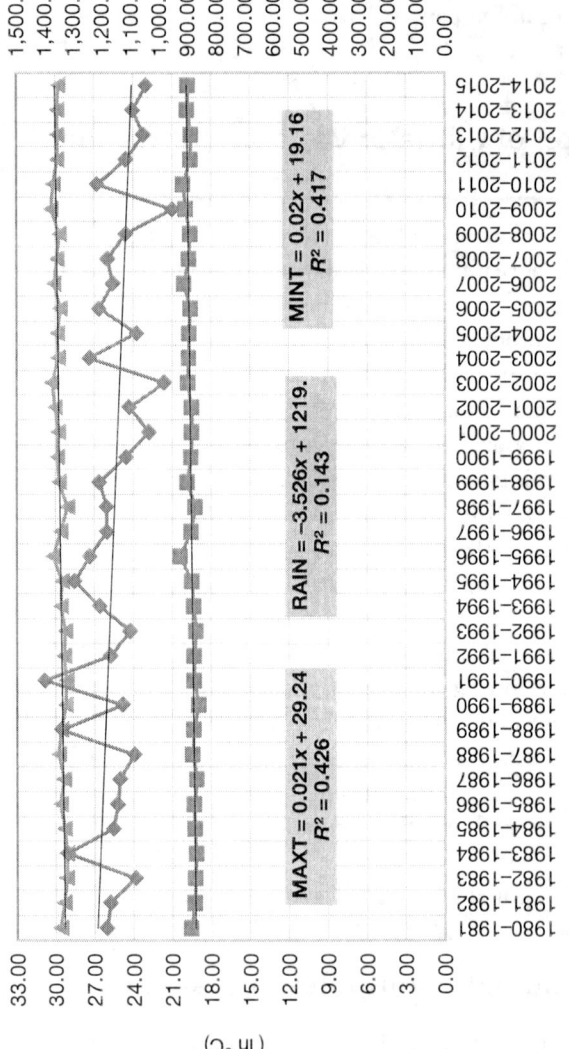

Figure 5.6 Trends of Rainfall, Minimum and Maximum Temperature in India

Source: Author's own creation based on India Meteorological Department Database.

the arena of efficient management of natural resources. Rainfall and temperature tend to be significant variables in this regard.

Rainfall

The agriculture sector is highly dependent on weather in India. Weather is the most important input for agricultural development, raising multiple cropping and increasing crop productivity. However, there is widespread variation in climate variability among all the states. Majority area of agriculture is uncultivated due to deficient rainfall, which is a major cause of decreasing agricultural productivity, and further it increases food prices as well as food security problems across the states. Figure 5.7 presents the trends of annual average rainfall (in millimetre) in major states during 1980–1981 to 2014–2015. It has

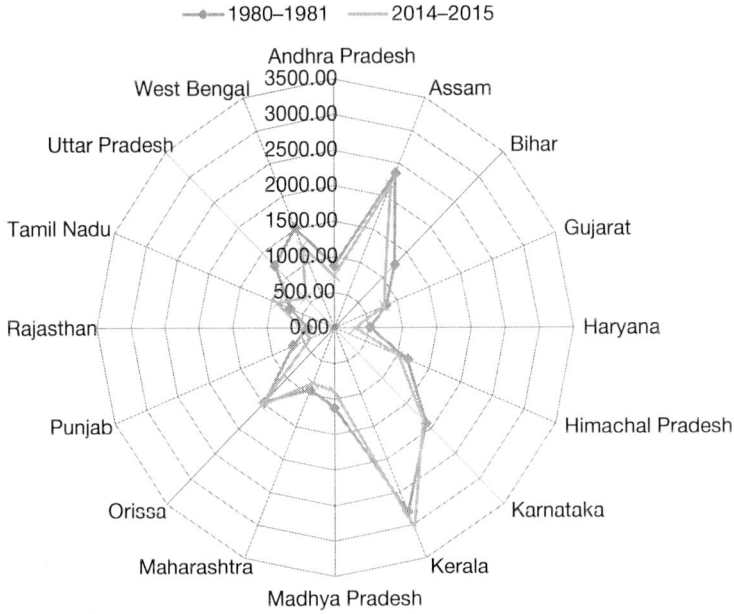

Figure 5.7 *State-Level Trends of Annual Average Rainfall (in mm) in India*

Source: Author's own creation based on India Meteorological Department Database.

been observed that there are large variations in terms of rainfall at state level. The annual average rainfall in Assam, Karnataka, Kerala and West Bengal was very high as compared to other states of the study during the study period, while the states namely Haryana, Punjab and Rajasthan showed the lowest rainfall during the study period in the country. The CAGR of annual rainfall is presented in Table 5.2. The trend shows that there is a declining growth rate of annual rainfall during the study period in all selected states except Karnataka, Kerala, Madhya Pradesh, Maharashtra, Odisha and Rajasthan. This is a serious indicator for Indian agriculture.

Figure 5.8 highlights the levels of state-wise growth rate of annual rainfall during the study period. The state level growth trends of annual rainfall during the study period can be divided into two

Table 5.2 *Growth Trends of Climatic Variables during 1980–1981 to 2014–2015*

States	Rainfall	Minimum Temperature	Maximum Temperature
Andhra Pradesh	−0.320	0.127	0.052
Assam	−1.123	0.307	0.208
Bihar	−0.581	0.108	0.086
Gujarat	−0.715	0.125	0.095
Haryana	−0.703	0.058	0.044
Himachal Pradesh	−0.808	0.433	−0.158
Karnataka	0.581	0.002	0.154
Kerala	0.189	0.029	0.025
Madhya Pradesh	0.024	−0.100	0.025
Maharashtra	0.176	0.045	−0.122
Orissa	0.123	0.253	0.137
Punjab	−1.086	−0.314	−0.140
Rajasthan	0.193	0.248	0.135
Tamil Nadu	−0.095	0.097	0.118
Uttar Pradesh	−0.959	0.191	0.025
West Bengal	−0.398	0.322	0.139

Source: Author's calculations.

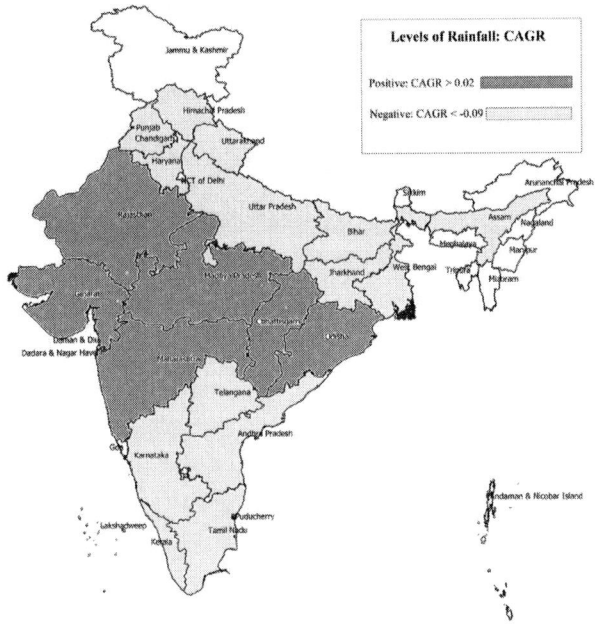

Figure 5.8 *State-Wise Growth Rate Levels of Annual Rainfall from 1980–1981 to 2014–2015*

Source: Author's own creation.

This figure has been redrawn by Sanjeev Kumar and is not to scale. It does not represent any authentic national or international boundaries and is used for illustrative purposes only.

categories: positive rainfall states (CAGR>0.02) and negative rainfall states (CAGR<−0.09). Figure 5.8 shows that the growth rate of annual rainfall showed fluctuating trends across the selected states during the study period. It is seen that variations highly fluctuated in terms of rainfall across the states during the study period.

Minimum Temperature

Figure 5.9 shows the state-wise annual average minimum temperature of selected Indian states during 1980–1981 to 2014–2015. The annual average minimum temperature in Andhra Pradesh, Assam, Bihar, Gujarat, Haryana, Himachal Pradesh, Karnataka, Kerala, Madhya Pradesh,

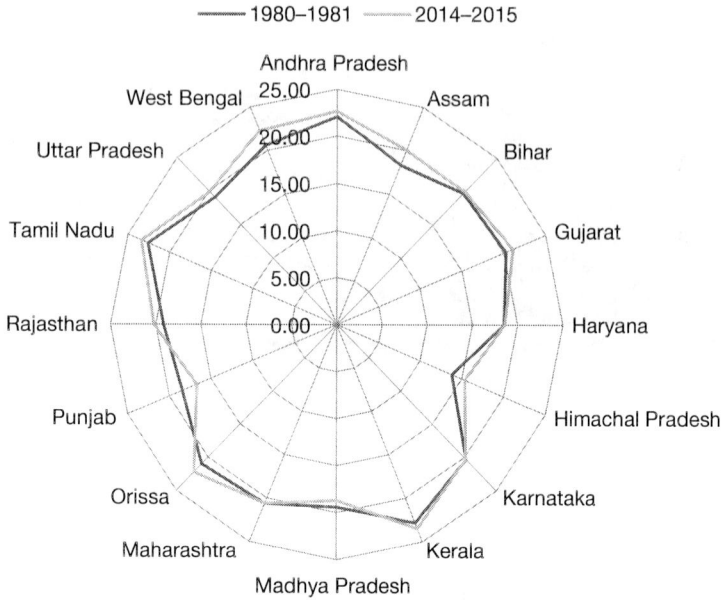

Figure 5.9 *State-Level Trends of Annual Average Minimum Temperature in India*

Source: Author's own creation based on India Meteorological Department Database.

Maharashtra, Odisha, Punjab, Rajasthan, Tamil Nadu, Uttar Pradesh and West Bengal was in the range of 15 to 20 °C during the study period. Overall it can be seen that almost all the states had fluctuating trends in annual average minimum temperature during the study period and its sub-period. Therefore, there are wide disparities at state level in terms of average annual minimum temperature. The CAGR of annual minimum temperature is presented in Table 5.2. The trend shows that there are increasing growth rate of annual rainfall during the study period in all selected states except Punjab and Madhya Pradesh.

Maximum Temperature

The state-wise annual average maximum temperatures during 1980–1981 to 2014–2015 are presented in Figure 5.10 and Table 5.2.

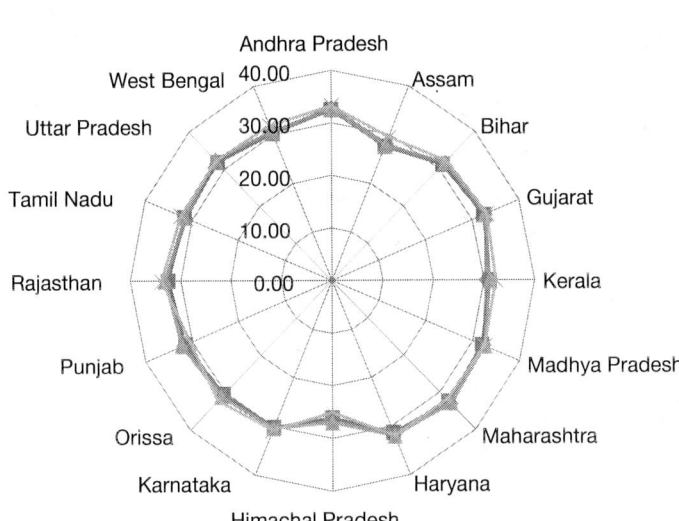

Figure 5.10 *State-Level Trends of Annual Average Maximum Temperature in India*

Source: *Author's own creation based on India Meteorological Department Database.*

It is found that Andhra Pradesh, Assam, Bihar, Gujarat, Haryana, Himachal Pradesh, Karnataka, Kerala, Madhya Pradesh, Maharashtra, Odisha, Punjab, Rajasthan, Tamil Nadu, Uttar Pradesh and West Bengal had small fluctuating trends during the study period. The ranges of maximum temperature during the study period are from 30 °C to 35 °C. The CAGR trend shows that there are increasing growth rate of annual maximum temperature during the entire study period in all selected states except Punjab, Maharashtra and Himachal Pradesh.

The state-wise growth rate of temperature difference during the study period has been presented in Figure 5.11. The state level growth rate of temperature difference during the study period can be divided into three categories, namely high growth rate in temperature difference states (CAGR>0.12), moderate growth rate in temperature difference states (CAGR between −0.11 and 0.11) and low growth rate in temperature difference states (CAGR<−0.11). Figure 5.11 reveals

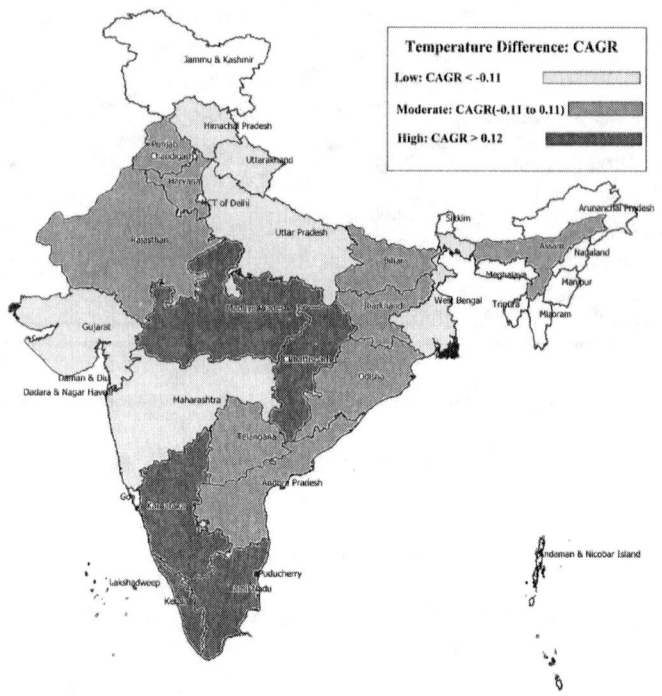

Figure 5.11 *State-Wise Growth Rate of Annual Temperature Difference Levels*

Source: Author's own creation.

This figure has been redrawn by Sanjeev Kumar and is not to scale. It does not represent any authentic national or international boundaries and is used for illustrative purposes only.

that the growth rate of temperature difference states has widespread fluctuations across the selected states during the study period. It is observed that the variations are highly fluctuated across the states during the study period.

Conclusion of the Chapter

Undertaking sustainable measures particularly in the domain of rainfall and temperature in managing natural resources can help in addressing the impact of climate change on agricultural productivity and food security. Moreover, the following points can also be taken into account for achieving the same:

1. Increasing productivity with the help of integrated land resources.
2. Allocating land for different uses based upon land capability, land productivity and national production goals.
3. Promoting for optimum use of land by promoting mixed farming systems wherein production program include fodder and tree crops on marginal and sub-marginal land of farmers.
4. Coordinating the formulation and implementation of water resource management policies, forest management policies and urban planning within the overall resource allocation by way of comprehensive national land use policy.

CHAPTER 6

Indian Agriculture and Climate Change
A National Level Analysis

Tackling climate change is closely linked to poverty alleviation and economic development;

I would call them different sides of the same coin.

—Paul Polman

Introduction

It is well known that there is a direct relationship between agriculture and climate. Changes in climatic variables have emerged as a major problem of the Indian agriculture sector. The agriculture sector is affected directly by climate change in terms of crop level productivity, soil fertility, biodiversity and national food security. Changes in climatic variables, namely, occurrence of drought and flood have a high impact on productivity of the agriculture sector of the economy as well as socio-economic conditions of the people of the nation. It is obvious from most of the past studies that natural and human activities both are accountable for climate change. These two broad activities are responsible for increasing GHGs in the atmosphere. This is the key factor of climatic variability.

Moreover, the demand of food is increasing in a country like India. It is observed that food demand will be doubled by 2050 due to growth of population and it will also increase the use of land, water and other important natural resources. Therefore, food security becomes a major concern in many ways such as increasing demand of food with growing population, poverty and declining agricultural productivity due to climate change in India.

There are several studies on impact of climate change on the agriculture sector at global as well as national level. Most of the studies have focused on the various issues of climate change and agriculture. Asha lata, Gopinath and Bhat (2012) have found that climate variations such as occurrence of droughts have a high level of impact on the yield of rainfed crops and cause reduction in net revenue in India. Joshi and Chaturvedi (2013) in their study have noticed that global temperature is rising and climate conditions have become a more erratic threat to the vegetation, biodiversity progression and have an enduring effect on food security as well as human health in the country. Javeed and Manuhaar (2013) have shown that climate change is responsible for the decrease in the agricultural productivity. Cereal crops such as rice and wheat are the most vulnerable to the impact of climate change. Small and marginal farmers are the most vulnerable groups because these people have small farm sizes, low capital and technological development.

The main focus of this chapter is to provide the performance of the agriculture sector at national level and to establish the relationship between the agriculture sector and climate change at national level through regression analysis. It also attempts to analyse the impact of climate as well as non-climate variables on agricultural productivity and value of agricultural output with respect to food grain and non-food grain crops at the national level.

Performance of Food Grain and Non-food Grain Crops

Food Grain Crops

Agriculture is the backbone of the Indian economy and majority of the population is directly or indirectly dependent on the agriculture sector for their livelihood. The share of agriculture in the GDP was 52 per cent in 1951–1952 and became 17.60 per cent in 2014–2015, but the dependency of population remained the same. It was found that the area under rice was 30.81million hectares in 1950–1951 and increased to 43.86million hectares in 2014–2015. Similarly, the area of wheat was 9.75million hectares in 1950–1951 and became 30.97million hectares in 2014–2015. The area under coarse cereals was 37.67million hectares in 1950–1951 and decreased to 24.17million hectares in 2014–2015. In the same way, the area under pulses was 19.09million hectares in 1950–1951 and increased to 23.10million hectares in the year 2014–2015. However, the area under food grains was 97.32million hectares in 1950–1951 and became 122.07million hectares in 2014–2015 in India (GoI 2016). The performance of production of coarse cereals and pulses was not as good when compared to that of rice and wheat. It is noticed that the growth of area under rice was higher during pre-GR period as compared to GR period.

CAGR of area, production and productivity (yield) of food grain as well as its components, that is, rice, wheat, coarse cereals and pulses from 1950–1951 to 2014–2015 and its sub-periods, that is, pre-GR period, GR period, GR Phase I, GR Phase II and GR Phase II are given in Table 6.1. The overall growth rate of area under food grains was positive at the magnitude of 0.20 per cent but not significant as compared to pre-GR period. The mean and standard deviation of area under food grains was 120.68 and 7.14 during the study period in India.

The growth of wheat production has shown an impressive trend during the GR Phase I. The overall growth rate of wheat production was 4.47 per cent whereas the mean and standard deviation of wheat production was 42.66 and 27.92 during 1950–1951 to 2014–2015 in India. The overall growth of yield of wheat was 2.71 per cent while mean and standard deviation was 2.03 and 821.56 quintal per hectare during 1950–1951 to 2014–2015 in India.

It is clear that the growth rate of yield of coarse cereals was 1.34 per cent in pre-GR period, 1.85 per cent in GR Phase I, 1.73 per

Table 6.1 Growth Trends of Area, Production and Productivity of Food Grain and Its Components in India

Crops	APY	PGRP	GRP	GRP- Phase I	GRP- Phase II	GRP- Phase III	Study Period (1950–1951 to 2014–2015)		
							Growth Rate	Average APY	Standard Deviation
Rice	A	1.37	0.40	0.82	0.47	0.08	0.58	39.25	4.39
	P	3.69	2.36	2.71	4.13	1.46	2.48	59.67	26.10
	Y	2.29	1.96	1.87	3.65	1.37	1.90	1.52	516.21
Wheat	A	2.32	1.25	3.43	0.26	0.95	1.72	20.99	6.30
	P	3.80	3.58	6.58	3.19	2.03	4.47	42.66	27.92
	Y	1.45	2.31	3.04	2.93	1.10	2.71	2.03	821.56
Coarse cereal	A	0.71	-1.37	-0.88	-1.42	-1.25	-0.93	37.64	7.02
	P	2.26	0.87	0.94	0.28	1.55	1.06	29.17	6.47
	Y	1.34	2.27	1.85	1.73	2.79	2.01	0.77	345.43
Pulses	A	1.47	0.08	0.40	-0.36	0.28	0.08	22.81	1.37
	P	1.61	0.99	0.25	0.94	1.31	0.74	12.42	2.34
	Y	0.14	0.90	-0.14	1.30	1.09	0.66	0.054	86.21
Food grains	A	1.23	-0.02	0.51	-0.32	-0.01	0.20	120.68	7.14
	P	2.96	2.26	2.82	2.76	1.66	2.43	143.93	61.58
	Y	1.72	2.28	2.30	3.09	1.67	2.22	1.19	481.38

Source: Author's calculation based on Ministry of Agriculture and Farmers Welfare Database.

Note: PGRP, Pre-GR Period (1950–1951 to 1965–1966); GRP, GR period (1966–1967 to 2014–2015); GRP Phase I, GR Phase I (1966–1967 to 1980–1981); GRP Phase II, GR Phase II (1981–1982 to 1989–1990); GRP Phase III, GR Phase III (1990–1991 to 2014–2015); Study period, 1950–1951 to 2014–2015. Further, average area (A) in million hectares, production (P) in MT, productivity (Y) in tonnes per hectare.

cent in GR Phase II and 2.79 per cent in GR Phase III in India. The overall growth of yield of coarse cereals was 2.01 per cent while mean and standard deviation was 830.15 and 345.43 quintal per hectare during 1950–1951 to 2014–2015 in India. It was observed that the productivity of coarse cereals was significant during GR Phase III compared to other phases.

With regard to pulses, the yield grew at a compound rate of 0.14 per cent in pre-GR period. The growth rate of yield of pulses was negative (–0.14%) in GR Phase I, 1.30 per cent in GR Phase II and 1.09 per cent in GR Phase III at national level. The overall growth rate of yield of pulses was 0.66 per cent during 1950–1951 to 2014–2015. The mean and standard deviation of productivity of pulses was 542.66 and 86.21quintal per hectare during 1950–1951 to 2014–2015 in India.

The growth rate of food grain was 1.72 per cent in pre-GR period, 2.30 per cent in GR Phase I, 3.09 per cent in GR Phase II and grew to 1.67 per cent during GR Phase III in India. The overall growth rate of productivity of food grain was 2.22 during 1950–1951 to 2014–2015 at the national level. The average productivity and standard deviation of food grains was 1178.48 and 481.38quintal per hectare during 1950–1951 to 2014–2015 in India. In short, it can be said that performance of cereals was much better than coarse cereals and pulses during the last 65 years.

Non-food Grain Crops

CAGR of area, production and productivity (yield) of non-food-grain as well as its components, that is, oilseeds, sugarcane, jute and mesta, cotton and tobacco during the period from 1960–1961 to 2014–2015 and its sub-periods, that is, pre-GR period, GR period, GR Phase I, GR Phase II and GR Phase III are given in Table 6.2.

Non-food grain crops show a change from subsistence cropping to commercial cropping during the study period. Thus the share of non-food grain crops in total agricultural production substantially increased in India. Table 6.2 reveals that growth rate of area of oilseeds grew at 2.55 per cent during GR Phase II which was the highest compared to all other phases. On the other hand, the growth rate of production

Table 6.2 Growth Trends of Area, Production and Productivity of Non-food Grain Crops in India

Crops	APY	PGRP	GRP	GRP Phase I	GRP Phase II	GRP Phase III	Study Period	(1960–1961 to 2014–2015) Average APY	Standard Deviation
Oilseeds	A	1.65	1.39	1.15	2.55	0.30	1.37	21.02	4.76
	P	0.05	3.33	2.14	5.08	2.05	3.18	16.31	8.20
	Y	-1.61	1.91	0.98	2.47	1.71	1.78	0.78	221.81
Sugarcane	A	2.81	1.64	1.72	0.71	1.38	1.54	3.47	0.89
	P	3.49	2.59	3.10	2.2	1.54	2.54	212.53	83.86
	Y	0.63	0.96	1.67	1.49	0.14	1.00	61.25	9774.52
Cotton	A	1.23	0.79	0.02	-1.35	1.91	0.61	8.40	1.37
	P	-0.11	3.77	2.59	2.91	6.03	3.39	12.00	8.76
	Y	-1.24	2.97	2.59	4.28	4.07	2.77	1.43	120.05
Jute and Mesta	A	2.21	-0.47	1.17	-2.44	-0.76	-0.48	1.04	0.15
	P	1.02	1.47	2.15	0.13	0.95	1.29	8.77	2.06
	Y	-1.14	1.97	0.97	2.68	1.75	1.79	8.43	459.71
Tobacco	A	-0.73	-0.16	0.01	-3.06	0.38	-0.11	0.42	0.05
	P	-0.30	1.29	2.13	-1.50	1.01	1.35	0.50	0.14
	Y	0.80	1.45	2.14	1.70	0.65	1.45	1.19	284.53

Source: Author's calculation based on Ministry of Agriculture and Farmers Welfare Database.

Note: PGRP, Pre-GR Period (1950–1951 to 1965–1966); GRP, GR period (1966–1967 to 2014–2015); GRP Phase I, GR Phase I (1966–1967 to 1980–1981); GRP Phase II, GR Phase II (1981–1982 to 1989–1990); GRP Phase III, GR Phase III (1990–1991 to 2014–2015); Study period, 1950–1951 to 2014–2015. Further, average area (A) in million hectares, production (P) in MT, productivity (Y) in tonnes per hectare.

of oilseeds was 0.05 per cent in pre-GR period, 3.33 per cent in GR period, 2.14 per cent in GR Phase I, 5.08 per cent in GR Phase II—which was the highest, 2.05 per cent in GR Phase III and 3.18 per cent during the overall period in India. In case of oilseeds productivity, the growth rate was maximum with 2.47 per cent in the GR Phase II and was negative with −1.61 per cent in pre-GR period in India.

Growth rate of production of sugarcane was 3.49 per cent during pre-GR period and became 2.59 per cent in GR period, 3.10 per cent in GR Phase I, continuously decreased during GR Phases II and III and became 2.54 per cent during overall period. On the other hand, the growth rate of sugarcane productivity was 0.63 per cent in pre-GR period and continuously increased to 1.67 per cent during GR Phase I and further decreased during GR Phase II and GR Phase III and became 1.00 per cent during overall period in India. The growth rate of productivity of sugarcane was impressive during GR Phase I. But overall it is found that the growth rate of area, production, and productivity of sugarcane was positive and impressive during all phases in India. The mean and standard deviation of sugarcane production was 212.00 and 84.0MT during 1960–1861 to 2014–2015.

With regards to cotton, the growth rate of area was 1.23 per cent during pre-GR period and thereafter continuously decreased for two phases, that is, GR period and GR Phase I. It further became negative in GR Phase II and 1.91 per cent for GR Phase III, 0.61 per cent for overall period in India. The CAGR of production and productivity of cotton was negative during pre-GR period and further became positive in all phases in India. The growth rate of production was impressive with 6.03 per cent in GR Phase III, 3.39 per cent in overall study period at national level. On the other hand, the growth rate of productivity of cotton was highest with 4.28 per cent in GR Phase II and became 2.77 per cent during overall study period in India. The mean and standard deviation of production was 12.00 and 8.76MT during 1960–1961 to 2014–2015.

The growth rate of production of jute and mesta was 1.02 per cent during pre-GR period, 1.47 per cent in GR period, 2.15 per cent in GR Phase I, 0.13 per cent in GR Phase II, 0.95 per cent in GR Phase III, and 1.29 per cent during overall period. On the other hand, the growth rate of productivity of jute and mesta was −1.14 per cent during pre-GR period, 1.97 per cent in GR period, 0.97 per cent in GR Phase I, 2.68 per cent in GR Phase II, 1.75 per cent in GR Phase III and 1.79 per cent during overall period. The growth rate of area of jute and mesta was positive during pre-GR period and in GR Phase I at national level.

In the case of tobacco, the growth rate of production was positive during GR period, GR Phase I, GR Phase III and during overall period, and showed negative growth rate in other phases. On the other hand, the growth rate of productivity of tobacco was positive during all phases in India. From the above analysis, it is observed that the growth rate of commercial crops such as oilseeds, sugarcane, cotton, jute and mesta, and tobacco grew at positive growth rate during the overall study period at the national level. The national performance of the Indian agriculture sector in terms of the CAGR of area, production and productivity food grain crops (1950–1951 to 2014–2015) and major non-food grain crops (1960–1961 to 2014–2015) is also depicted in Figure 6.1.

Impact of Climatic and Non-climatic Variables on Agriculture

The global warming effects have not even kept India untouched. The earlier part of this chapter has highlighted the change in temperature and rainfall over the past few decades. Maximum and minimum temperature variations have surged and the number of rainy days has reduced. Agriculture is the only sector which is majorly influenced by the changing climatic conditions. The impact of climate change on crop productivity is difficult to predict in India due to the variety of cropping systems and levels of technology used. However, the use of regression model is one way, and probably representing the best method, in which these effects can be studied along with socio-economic factors. This section is divided into four sub-sections: The

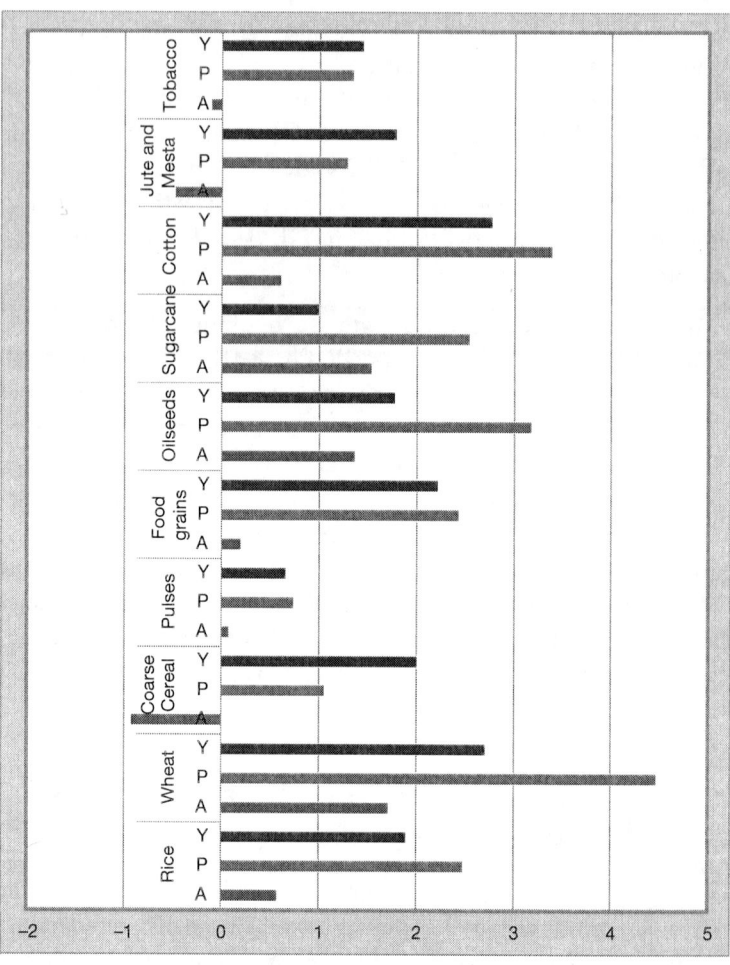

Figure 6.1 *Growth Trends of Area, Production and Productivity of Agricultural Crops in India*

Source: Author's calculation based on Ministry of Agriculture and Farmers Welfare Database.

first sub-section explains the impact of climatic factors on production and productivity of food grains; the second sub-section explores the impact of climate as well as non-climate factors on productivity of food grain crops and the third sub-section explains the relationship of these factors with non-food-grain crops and the fourth sub-section shows the impact of climate and non-climate factors on value of output by agriculture sector.

Impact of Climatic Factors on Production and Productivity of Food Grains

The growth and performance of the agriculture sector are influenced by several factors such as use of agricultural inputs, capital formation, irrigation facilities, climate changes and government policies. It is very difficult to analyse the effect of all the factors in a simple framework. However, this sub-section of the chapter elaborates the impact of climatic factors, namely, minimum temperature, maximum temperature and annual rainfall (IV) on food grain production and productivity during 1950–1951 to 2014–2015 (study period) as well as two sub-periods, namely, before economic reform period (1950–1951 to 1989–1990) and after economic reform period (1990–1991 to 2014–2015) at national level. The regression models are as follows:

$$FGP = \beta_0 + \beta_1 RAIN + \beta_2 MINT + \beta_3 MAXT + Ui$$

$$YOF = \beta_0 + \beta_1 RAIN + \beta_2 MINT + \beta_3 MAXT + Ui,$$

where, FGP and YOF are the food grain production and productivity of food grain; RAIN, MINT, MAXT are annual rainfall in millimetre, annual minimum temperature and maximum temperature respectively; and Ui is the stochastic error term; β_0 is constant coefficient, β_1 to β_3 are coefficients of variables. To avoid the problem of multicollinearity, annual growth rate has been taken of all dependent and independent variables. The regression results of food grain production and food grain productivity are presented in Tables 6.3 and 6.4, respectively.

Food Grain Production

The results (Table 6.3) indicate that the value of R-square is high during all periods of study. The magnitude of F-value also indicates that the given model is a good fit for production of food grains. The effect of maximum temperature and rainfall had positive and significant impact, whereas minimum temperature had negative and significant impact on food grain production during 1950–1951 to

Table 6.3 Regression Results between Food Grain Production and Climatic Variables

Independent Variables	Dependent Variable: Food Grain Production								
	Period for Study (1950–1951 to 2014–2015)		Before Economic Reform (1950–1951 to 1989–1990)			After Economic Reform (1990–1991 to 2014–2015)		
	Coefficient	t-value	p-value	Coefficient	t-value	p-value	Coefficient	t-value	p-value
Rainfall	0.720	10.020	0.000	0.747	7.850	0.000	0.0004	2.800	0.011
Minimum temperature	−3.950	−4.440	0.000	−3.779	−2.840	0.007	−1.203	−0.870	0.395
Maximum temperature	4.975	3.730	0.000	5.294	2.890	0.007	−0.590	−0.270	0.793
Constant	0.024	3.340	0.001	0.027	2.620	0.013	−0.481	−2.680	0.014
R-squared	0.642			0.653			0.405		
F-value	35.980			21.970			4.780		
No of observations	64			39			25		

Source: Author's own calculations.

2014–2015. Similarly, the effect of maximum temperature and rainfall had positive and significant impact on food grain production whereas minimum temperature had negative but significant impact on food grain production during pre-reform period. On the other hand, annual maximum and minimum temperature have negative and insignificant effect on food grain production during the post-reform period of study while rainfall had positive and significant impact on food grain production during this period. In indicates that temperature has affected food grain production during recent years. It has serious implications for food security of the nation.

Productivity of Food Grains

Table 6.4 indicates that during the study period and its sub-period, the value of R-square is high. The model explains more than 50 per cent of variation in study period as well as sub-periods at the national level. The effect of maximum temperature and rainfall had positive and significant impact on productivity of food grains, whereas minimum temperature had negative but significant impact on productivity of food grains during the study period. Similarly, maximum temperature and rainfall had positive and significant impact on productivity of food grains, whereas minimum temperature had negative but significant impact on productivity of food grain during the pre-reform period. During the post-reform period, maximum temperature had a negative and insignificant impact on productivity of food grains and minimum temperature had negative but significant impact on productivity of food grains. The effect of rainfall had positive and significant impact on productivity of food grains at the national level.

Impact of Climatic and Non-climatic Factors on Productivity of Food Grain

Agricultural productivity of food grain plays a very vital role for agriculture development and improving food security of the nation. However, productivity of food grain and its components has been influenced by many climatic and non-climatic variables. The impact of climatic and non-climatic variables on productivity of food grain and its components, that is, rice, wheat, cereals, coarse cereals and

Table 6.4 Regression Results between Food Grain Productivity and Climatic Variables

Independent Variables	Dependent Variable: Food Grain Productivity								
	Period for Study (1950–1951 to 2014–2015)			Before Economic Reform (1950–1951 to 1989–1990)			After Economic Reform (1990–1991 to 2014–2015)		
	Coefficient	t-value	p-value	Coefficient	t-value	p-value	Coefficient	t-value	p-value
Rainfall	0.500	8.47	0.000	0.529	6.46	0.000	0.00034	3.42	0.003
Minimum temperature	–3.428	–4.68	0.000	–3.202	–2.79	0.008	–1.984	–2.23	0.037
Maximum temperature	4.358	3.97	0.000	4.391	2.78	0.009	–1.277	–0.89	0.381
Constant	0.020	3.38	0.001	0.021	2.29	0.028	–0.374	–3.24	0.004
R-squared	0.5537			0.5516			0.4668		
F-value	24.82			14.35			6.13		
No. of observations	64			39			25		

Source: Author's own calculations.

pulses has been analysed in this section. The regression model for the time series data was used to identify the impact of climate variables as well as socio-economic variables of crop productivity at national level during 1980–1981 to 2014–2015. The details of the regression model have been discussed in chapter 4. The regression equation is as follows:

$$CSP = \beta_0 + \beta_1 RAIN + \beta_2 MINT + \beta_3 MAXT + \beta_4 GCFAG + \beta_5 LR + \beta_6 AL + \beta_7 NOTR + \beta_8 FERC + \beta_9 FANSA + \beta_{10} GIA + Ui,$$

where, CSP is crop-specific productivity; RAIN, MINT and MAXT are average annual rainfall, average annual minimum and maximum temperature respectively; GCFAG is gross capital formation of agriculture; LR, AL, NOTR, FERC, GIA are literacy rate, agricultural labour, number of tractors, consumption of fertilizers and gross irrigated area respectively; FANSA is the ratio of forest area to net sown area; β's are regression coefficients for respective variables; and Ui is stochastic error term. To avoid the problems of multicollinearity, we have taken annual growth rate of all variables. The results of regression model are presented in Table 6.5.

The values of R-square have been found highest at the magnitude of 0.8072 in case of food grain followed by rice, cereals, pulses, coarse cereals and wheat, in that order, which implies that the regression model explain a significant level of variation to the total variations in case of food grain and its component crops during the study period. The magnitude of F-value indicates that the given model is a good fit in all crops except wheat. The value of variance inflation factor (VIF) between independent variables is 2.82, which implies that there is absence of multicollinearity in the regression model.

The regression result revealed that rainfall had positive and statistically significant impact on the productivity of food grain and its components except coarse cereals during the study period. On the other hand, annual average minimum temperature had negative and significant impact on the productivity of most of the crops except pulses and coarse cereals, and it had positive and significant impact on rice, cereals and food grain. The results attest that average annual maximum temperature has a statistically significant and negative impact on crop productivity of food grain, rice and cereals except wheat throughout

Table 6.5 Regression Results of Food Grain Productivity and Its Determinants during 1980–1981 to 2014–2015

DV: Productivity	Regression Values	RAIN	MINT	MAXT	GCF in Agriculture (GCFAG)	Literacy Rate (LR)	Agricultural Labour (AL)	No. of Tractors (NOTR)	Fertilizer Consumption (FERC)	Forest Area as % of NSA	Gross Irrigated Area	Constant
Rice	Coefficient	0.4115	3.8940	-5.2625	-0.0207	-0.9238	0.6493	0.0422	-0.0658	-1.1025	0.2828	0.0127
	t-value	4.990	4.330	-3.910	-0.510	-0.480	0.380	0.620	-0.500	-2.350	0.840	0.280
	p-value	0.000	0.000	0.001	0.618	0.634	0.707	0.541	0.623	0.028	0.411	0.781
	R-squared=0.8052	Adj. R-squared =0.7234				$F_{(10,23)}$=9.51			Prob.>F=0.0000		No. of Obs.=34	Mean VIF=2.82
Wheat	Coefficient	0.1687	-2.1658	3.7530	0.0238	1.4036	0.1912	0.0497	0.0339	-0.0240	0.4132	-0.0291
	t-value	1.630	-1.920	2.230	0.460	0.590	0.090	0.580	0.210	-0.040	0.980	-0.510
	p-value	0.116	0.067	0.036	0.648	0.564	0.929	0.566	0.839	0.968	0.338	0.612
	R-squared=0.3963	Adj. R-squared =0.1339				$F_{(10,23)}$=1.51			Prob.>F= 0.1987		No. of Obs.=34	Mean VIF=2.82
Cereals	Coefficient	0.2829	2.3775	-3.1248	0.0401	0.4090	0.1682	0.0598	-0.1172	-0.4943	0.6521	-0.0076
	t-value	4.120	3.180	-2.790	1.180	0.260	0.120	1.060	-1.070	-1.270	2.320	-0.200
	p-value	0.000	0.004	0.010	0.252	0.799	0.907	0.302	0.297	0.218	0.029	0.842
	R-squared=0.7811	Adj. R-squared =0.6859				$F_{(10,23)}$=8.20			Prob.>F= 0.0000		No. of Obs.=34	Mean VIF=2.82

Coarse cereals	Coefficient	0.2798	−0.1975	−1.8392	0.1651	1.8765	−2.0113	0.0804	−0.7600	−1.1914	1.4058	0.0438
	t-value	1.160	−0.080	−0.470	1.380	0.340	−0.410	0.410	−1.980	−0.870	1.430	0.330
	p-value	0.256	0.941	0.643	0.180	0.739	0.689	0.689	0.060	0.393	0.166	0.742
	R-squared=0.4855	Adj. R-squared =0.2618	F (10,23)=2.17	Prob.>F= 0.0603	No. of Obs.=34	Mean VIF=2.82						
Total pulses	Coefficient	0.3596	−2.2442	3.1103	0.1726	−2.3762	2.9086	0.0684	−0.4052	−1.0178	1.2955	−0.0726
	t-value	2.200	−1.260	1.160	2.120	−0.630	0.860	0.510	−1.540	−1.090	1.930	−0.810
	p-value	0.039	0.222	0.256	0.045	0.538	0.399	0.618	0.136	0.286	0.066	0.427
	R-squared=0.5466	Adj. R-squared =0.3495	F (10,23)=2.77	Prob.>F= 0.0209	No. of Obs.=34	Mean VIF=2.82						
Food grain	Coefficient	0.2472	2.2905	−2.9365	0.0559	0.3657	0.1108	0.0162	−0.1090	−0.5488	0.7778	−0.0070
	t-value	3.91	3.320	−2.850	1.780	0.250	0.080	0.310	−1.080	−1.520	3.010	−0.200
	p-value	0.001	0.003	0.009	0.089	0.805	0.933	0.759	0.292	0.141	0.006	0.842
	R-squared=0.8072	Adj. R-squared =0.7234	F (10,23)=9.63	Prob.>F= 0.0000	No. of Obs.=34	Mean VIF=2.82						

Source: Author's own calculations.

the study period, while on the other hand it had a negative impact on coarse cereals. This result of regression indicates that climatic factors are affecting food grain productivity in both ways—some had positive impact and some had negative impact on crop-specific productivity in food grain crops during the study period.

In case of non-climatic variables of regression, the result indicates that capital formation in agriculture and gross irrigated area had a positive and significant impact on productivity of food-grain throughout the study period. The other socio-economic variables such as fertilizer consumption, number of tractors, agricultural labour, forest area as per cent of total sown area and literacy rate had an insignificant impact on food grain productivity in India. In case of rice crop, all socio-economic variables except forest area as per cent of total sown area had an insignificant impact on productivity of rice crops.

The variables, namely, gross capital formation in agriculture, literacy rate, agricultural labour, number of tractors, consumption of fertilizers and gross irrigated area had positive and insignificant impact, whereas forest area had negative impact on the wheat productivity during the study period. In case of cereal productivity, gross irrigated area and capital formation in agriculture had positive and significant impact, whereas other socio-economic factors had insignificant impact on cereal productivity during 1980–1981 to 2014–2015. Gross capital formation in agriculture, literacy rate, number of tractors and gross irrigated area had positive but statistically insignificant impact, whereas agricultural labour and forest area had negative and insignificant impact on the coarse cereals productivity during the study period. In the case of pulses, it was found that the factors such as gross capital formation in agriculture and gross irrigated area had positive and statistically significant impact on pulses productivity during the study period. On the other hand, other five socio-economic variables had an insignificant impact on productivity of pulses at the national level. From the above analysis, it was concluded that the climatic and non-climatic variables had mixed impact on productivity of food grain as well as its components during 1980–1981 to 2014–2015 at the national level.

Impact of Climatic and Non-climatic Factors on Productivity of Non-food Grain

Productivity of non-food grain crops is also important in the point of view of agricultural development as well as food security of the nation. The aforementioned regression equation has been used to estimate the impact of climate and non-climate factors on the productivity of major non-food grain crops, namely, sugarcane, oilseeds, cotton and jute and mesta. The estimated regression results are presented in Table 6.6.

The values of R-square have been found highest at the magnitude of 0.7268 in case of oilseeds followed by jute and mesta, sugarcane and cotton in that order, which implies that the regression model explains a significant level of variation to the total variations in case of non-food grain crops during the study period. The magnitude of F-value indicates that the given model is a good fit in sugarcane, and jute and mesta. The value of VIF between independent variables is 2.82, which implies that there is absence of multicollinearity in the regression model.

The regression result highlighted that rainfall had positive and significant impact, whereas consumption of fertilizers and forest area had negative and statistically significant impact on oilseeds productivity during the study period. On the other hand, maximum temperature, agricultural labour, number of tractors and gross irrigated area had positive and insignificant impact, whereas minimum temperature, gross capital formation in agriculture, literacy rate had negative and insignificant impact on oilseeds productivity during the study period. In case of sugarcane, the variables such as consumption of fertilizer had positive and significant impact during the period 1980–1981 to 2014–2015. The variables such as rainfall, maximum temperature, tractors, forest area and gross irrigated area had positive and insignificant impact whereas minimum temperature, government expenditure, literacy rate and agricultural labour had negative and insignificant impact on the sugarcane productivity.

Maximum temperature had positive impact, whereas minimum temperature had negative and statistically significant impact on the jute and mesta productivity. Similarly, rainfall, agricultural labour and

Table 6.6 Regression Results of Non-food Grain Productivity and Its Determinants during 1980–1981 to 2014–2015

DV: Productivity	Regression Values	RAIN	MINT	MAXT	GCF in Agriculture	Literacy Rate	Agricultural labour	No. of Tractors	Fertilizer Consumption	Forest Area as % of NSA	Gross Irrigated Area	Constant
Oilseeds	Coefficient	0.8771	-2.1604	2.5425	-0.0619	-1.1431	3.5324	0.2063	-0.6642	-2.8344	0.7702	-0.0512
	t-value	3.9800	-0.9000	0.7100	-0.5700	-0.2200	0.7800	1.1400	-1.8800	-2.2600	0.8600	-0.420
	p-value	0.001	0.378	0.486	0.577	0.825	0.446	0.268	0.072	0.034	0.401	0.675
	R-squared=0.7268	Adj. R-squared =0.6079		F (10,23)=6.12		Prob.>F= 0.0002			No. of obs. = 34		Mean VIF = 2.82	
Sugarcane	Coefficient	0.0701	-1.1801	1.6975	-0.0560	-0.6488	-0.1335	0.1190	0.2465	0.3549	0.1109	0.0103
	t-value	0.810	-1.250	1.200	-1.300	-0.320	-0.070	1.660	1.780	0.720	0.310	0.220
	p-value	0.427	0.225	0.242	0.207	0.75	0.941	0.11	0.089	0.479	0.757	0.83
	R-squared=0.3824	Adj. R-squared =0.2138		F (10,23)=1.50		Prob.>F= 0.1957			No. of obs. = 34		Mean VIF = 2.82	

Jute and Mesta	Coefficient	0.1129	−3.6648	5.1666	−0.1143	−0.7707	0.9095	−0.0121	0.2052	−1.0968	−0.4873	0.0884
	t-value	0.760	−2.250	2.120	−1.540	−0.220	0.290	−0.100	0.860	−1.290	−0.800	1.080
	p-value	0.457	0.034	0.045	0.137	0.826	0.771	0.923	0.399	0.210	0.433	0.291
	R-squared=0.4280	Adj. R-squared =0.1793		$F_{(10,23)}=1.72$		Prob.>F= 0.1359		No. of obs.=34		Mean VIF=2.82		
Cotton	Coefficient	0.0656	1.1153	−2.0355	−0.0719	−12.0503	8.4303	0.2930	−0.5649	−1.8885	1.7728	−0.0409
	t-value	0.180	0.280	−0.340	−0.390	−1.420	1.110	0.970	−0.960	−0.910	1.180	−0.200
	p-value	0.860	0.783	0.736	0.697	0.170	0.277	0.343	0.346	0.375	0.249	0.841
	R-squared=0.3005	Adj. R-squared =0.1036		$F_{(10,23)}=1.00$		Prob.>F =0.4800		No. of obs.=34		Mean VIF=2.82		

Source: Author's own calculations.

consumption of fertilizer had positive and insignificant impact whereas gross capital formation, literacy rate, number of tractors, forest area and gross irrigated area had negative and insignificant impact on jute and mesta productivity. Productivity of cotton was affected positively and statistically significant by rainfall, minimum temperature, agricultural labour, number of tractors and gross irrigated area, whereas average maximum temperature, government expenditure on agriculture, literacy rate, consumption of fertilizers and forest area had negative and insignificant impact on cotton productivity. It was concluded from the above analysis that climatic and non-climatic factors are influencing directly or indirectly the productivity of non-food grain crops in India during the period of study.

Impact of Climatic and Non-climatic Variables on Value of Output by the Agriculture Sector

The impact of climatic and socio-economic factors on value of output of food grain crops and non-food grain crops has been analysed by multiple regression model for the study period, that is, during 1980–1981 to 2014–2015. Per unit (per hectare) value of output as dependent variable is regressed with non-climatic factors as well as climatic factors, using time series date for the period from1980–1981 to 2014–2015. All non-climatic variables (independent variables) have also been taken in term of per hectare value. The model can be written as follows:

$$PHVO = \beta_0 + \beta_1 RAIN + \beta_2 MINT + \beta_3 MAXT + \beta_4 PHGIA + \beta_5 PHFERC + \beta_6 PHNOTR + \beta_7 PHFA + \beta_8 PHGCFA + Ui,$$

where, PHVO is per hectare value of output from agriculture and its components, namely, rice, wheat, cereals, coarse cereals, pulses, food-grain, oilseeds, sugarcane, cotton, and jute and mesta; the value of output has been taken at constant price of the agriculture sector as well as its components; RAIN, MINT and MAXT are average annual rainfall, average annual mean minimum and maximum temperature respectively; PHGIA is per hectare gross irrigated area as per cent to net sown area; PHFERC, PHNOTR, PHFA and PFGCFA are per hectare consumption of fertilizer, per thousand-hectare availability of tractors, per hectare forest area and per hectare gross capital formation in agriculture respectively; β_0 is constant coefficient term, β_1 to β_8 are regression coefficients for respective variables; and Ui is stochastic error term. The regression results are presented in Table 6.7.

The value of R-square has been found very high (>90%) in case value of output of the agriculture sector as well as its components crops, which implies that the regression model explains a high significant level of variation to the total variations during the study period. The magnitude of F-value indicates that the given model is a good fit in case of all crop sectors. The value of VIF between independent variables is 8.72 (<10), which implies that there is absence of multicollinearity in the regression model.

The regression result indicates that rainfall had a positive and statistically significant impact on value of output by the agriculture sector and its major components, namely, rice, cereals, food grain, pulses, oilseeds and cotton during the study period. In case of wheat and coarse cereals, it had positive but not statistically insignificant impact. On the other hand, annual rainfall had a negative and insignificant impact on value of output of sugarcane, and jute and mesta during study period.

Average minimum temperature had negative and significant impact on value of output by the agriculture sector and its crop sectors except rice, cotton, jute and mesta, and coarse cereals. In case of value of output by coarse cereals, and jute and mesta, it had a negative and insignificant impact.

The results attest that average annual maximum temperature has a statistically significant and positive impact on value of output of the agriculture sector and its components except rice and cotton. These results of regression indicate that climatic factors are affecting the value of output by the agriculture sector in both ways; most of the factors have positive impact and some have negative impact on value of output in food grain crops, non-food grain crops and the agriculture sector during the study period.

In case of non-climatic factors, it was found that gross irrigated area and gross capital formation in agriculture had positive and statistically significant impact on value of agriculture during the study

Table 6.7 Regression Results of Value of Output by Agriculture and Its Determinants

DV: PHVO	Regression Values	Independent Variables								
		RAIN	MINT	MAXT	PHGIA	PHFERC	PHNOTR	PHFA	PHGCFA	Constant
Agriculture sector	Coefficient	5.897	−2802.51	2786.521	50123.3	19.06	−5733.06	585.655	0.399	−32492.2
	t-value	2.98	−2.75	2.75	8.62	1.51	−1.40	0.03	8.27	−1.88
	p-value	0.006	0.011	0.011	0.00	0.144	0.174	0.978	0.00	0.071
	R-squared=0.9932				**Adj. R²=0.9911**		**F (8,26)=474.47**		**Prob.>F= 0.000**	**No. of obs.=35**
	Mean VIF=8.72									
Cereals	Coefficient	4.32	−2442.471	2171.299	29350.42	8.839	102.731	−47637.4	−0.008	4854.768
	t-value	3.23	−3.54	3.17	7.47	1.03	0.04	−3.42	−0.25	0.42
	p-value	0.003	0.002	0.004	0.00	0.311	0.971	0.002	0.806	0.681
	R-squared=0.9749				**Adj. R²=0.9672**		**F (8,26)=126.39**		**Prob.>F= 0.000**	**No. of obs.=35**
Wheat	Coefficient	1.755	−1645.99	2104.322	29216.72	12.472	3673.816	−34474.8	−0.113	−16094.86
	t-value	0.93	−1.69	2.18	5.27	1.03	0.94	−1.75	−2.45	−0.98
	p-value	0.361	0.103	0.039	0.00	0.311	0.357	0.091	0.021	0.338
	R-squared=0.9518				**Adj. R²=0.937**		**F (8,26)=64.18**		**Prob.>F=0.0000**	**No. of obs.=35**
Rice	Coefficient	4.166	2563.449	−2385.081	30386.67	3.752	346.561	−52995.2	−0.004	424.362
	t-value	3.56	4.24	−3.97	8.83	0.5	0.14	−4.34	−0.15	0.04
	p-value	0.001	0.00	0.001	0.00	0.621	0.888	0.00	0.879	0.967
	R-squared=0.9788				**Adj. R²=0.9722**		**F (8,26)=149.85**		**Prob.>F=0.0000**	**No. of obs.=35**

Coarse cereal	Coefficient	1.468	-576.584	71.931	12796.81	0.703	-2394.915	-11581.8	0.08	13276.44
	t-value	1.26	-0.96	0.12	3.73	0.09	-0.99	-0.95	2.81	1.30
	p-value	0.22	0.347	0.905	0.001	0.926	0.332	0.35	0.009	0.204
	R^2=0.9368	Adj. R^2=0.9173	$F_{(8,26)}$=48.16	Prob.>F=0.0000	No. of obs.=35					
Pulses	Coefficient	2.938	-1440.862	1293.586	15192.17	-18.145	1621.596	-23602.7	0.12	-237.203
	t-value	2.72	-2.59	2.34	4.79	-2.63	0.72	-2.10	4.54	-0.03
	p-value	0.011	0.016	0.027	0.00	0.014	0.475	0.046	0.00	0.98
	R^2=0.9051	Adj. R^2=0.8758	$F_{(8,26)}$=30.98	Prob.>F=0.0000	No. of obs.=35					
Food grain	Coefficient	2.3679	-1714.564	1558.802	27602.5	-0.97	-54.916	-32689.5	0.012	-1108.934
	t-value	2.40	-3.38	3.09	9.53	-0.15	-0.03	-3.18	0.50	-0.13
	p-value	0.024	0.002	0.005	0.00	0.879	0.979	0.004	0.624	0.898
	R^2=0.9802	Adj. R^2=0.9741	$F_{(8,26)}$=160.97	Prob.>F=0.0000	No. of obs.=35					
Oilseeds	Coefficient	8.8119	-1155.72	1634.229	25576.5	10.273	-849.694	-47880.2	0.088	-10599.55
	t-value	3.39	-0.86	1.23	3.35	0.62	-0.16	-1.77	1.38	-0.47
	p-value	0.002	0.397	0.231	0.003	0.542	0.876	0.089	0.179	0.645
	R^2=0.9244	Adj. R^2=0.9012	$F_{(8,26)}$=39.76	Prob.>F=0.0000	No. of obs.=35					
Sugarcane	Coefficient	-10.034	-15549.9	16281.2	104000.9	80.975	-52892.06	9211.109	-0.642	-140104.4
	t-value	-0.76	-2.29	2.41	2.68	0.96	-1.93	0.07	-1.99	-1.22
	p-value	0.453	0.031	0.023	0.012	0.346	0.064	0.947	0.057	0.235
	R^2=0.8677	Adj. R^2=0.827	$F_{(8,26)}$=21.32	Prob.>F=0.0000	No. of obs.=35					

(Contiuned)

Table 6.7 Continued

DV: PHVO	Regression Values	RAIN	MINT	MAXT	PHGIA	PHFERC	PHNOTR	PHFA	PHGCFA	Constant
Cotton	Coefficient	4.939	2586.905	−3052.559	24364.66	22.231	−1125.116	−64404.6	0.548	64929.04
	t-value	0.72	0.74	−0.87	1.22	0.51	−0.08	−0.91	3.29	1.09
	p-value	0.475	0.468	0.39	0.235	0.614	0.937	0.373	0.003	0.285
	R-squared=0.8722			Adj. R^2=0.8329		F $(8,26)$=22.18		Prob.>F=0.0000		No. of obs.=35	
Jute and Mesta	Coefficient	−0.013	−1318.95	1484.909	33342.83	−14.175	3040.943	−26182.3	0.138	−7415.822
	t-value	−0.01	−1.06	1.20	4.69	−0.92	0.61	−1.04	2.34	−0.35
	p-value	0.996	0.30	0.242	0.00	0.368	0.549	0.308	0.027	0.728
	R-squared=0.9452			Adj. R^2=0.9284		F $(8,26)$=56.1		Prob.>F=0.0000		No. of obs.=35	

Source: Author's own calculations based on MoSPI data set.

period. On the other hand, consumption of fertilizer and area under forest had positive but not significant impact on value of output from the agriculture sector; whereas number of tractors had negative but statistically insignificant impact on the value of output of agriculture. In case of value of output of cereals, gross irrigated area had positive and significant impact on this crop. On the other hand, forest area had negative and statistically significant impact on the output value of cereals. Other variables have an insignificant impact.

Gross irrigated area had positive and significant impact whereas forest area and gross capital formation in agriculture had negative and statistically significant impact on value of wheat. On the other hand, other non-climatic factors had a significant impact on value of output in case of wheat crop. The value of output of rice crop was affected positively and significantly by gross irrigated area, whereas negatively and statistically significantly by forest area. In the case of coarse cereals, gross irrigated area and gross capital formation had positive and statistically significant impact during the period of study. On the other hand, fertilizer consumption had positive but statistically insignificant impact, whereas number of tractor and forest area had negative and statistically insignificant impact on value of coarse cereals. In case of pulses, the variables such as gross irrigated area and gross capital formation in agriculture had positive and statistically significant impact whereas the variables such as consumption of fertilizer and forest area had negative and significant impact on value of output of pulses during the period 1980–1981 to 2014–2015.

Gross irrigated area and gross capital formation in the agriculture sector had positive impact on value of output in food grain during the study period, whereas forest area had negative and significant impact on value of food grain. In case of value of output by oilseeds, gross irrigated area had positive and statistically significant impact, whereas forest area had negative and statistically significant impact on value of oilseeds. Consumption of fertilizer and gross capital formation in the agriculture sector had positive and insignificant impact, whereas number of tractors per hectare had negative and insignificant impact on value of output by oilseeds. On the other hand, gross irrigated area had positive and statistically significant impact on sugarcane value of output during the period of study, whereas per hectare number of tractor and gross capital formation in agriculture had negative and statistically significant impact on sugarcane value of output.

Gross capital formation in agriculture had positive and statistically significant impact on value of output by cotton. While gross irrigated area and consumption of fertilizer had positive and insignificant impact on cotton value of output during the study period, number of tractor and per cent area of forest had negative and insignificant impact on cotton value of output. In case of jute and mesta crops, gross irrigated area and gross capital formation in agriculture had positive and significant impact on value of output during the study period. The variable such as number of tractor had positive and insignificant impact, whereas consumption of fertilizer and area under forest had negative and insignificant impact on value of output by jute and mesta.

Conclusion of the Chapter

Climatic as well as non-climatic factors had been influencing the agriculture sector in India in terms of crop-specific agricultural productivity and value of output during the study period. They had been affecting the food grain production, productivity and farm income. Further, they had serious implication for national food security system. It was observed that the compound growth rate of food grain production is not significant during 1950–1951 to 2014–2015. The regression result shows that climatic variables are influencing the productivity of food grain, non-food grain and value of output from the agriculture sector. The effect of annual rainfall has positive impact on crop-specific productivity, while in the case of value of output, it was found positive in all crops except sugarcane, and jute and mesta during the study period at national level. Maximum temperature has negative impact on productivity of all crop except wheat, pulses, sugarcane and oilseeds, whereas the impact of minimum temperature has been also found negative on productivity of all crops except rice, cereals, food grain and cotton during the study period at national level.

The non-climatic factors such as gross capital formation in agriculture and gross irrigated area had positive and statistically significant impact on agricultural productivity of most of the crops as well as value of output by the crop sector. On the other hand, area under forest had negative and significant impact on productivity and value of output of various crops. It is concluded that the climatic and non-climatic factors had mixed impact on productivity and value of output of various crop sector during study period at national level.

There is need for intervention, which can help the farmers to adopt climate changes and reduce the loss of agricultural production and value of output. Farmers should change the cropping pattern with the changing in rainfall and temperature. Similarly, huge financial support for efficient land management, balanced fertilizers use and enhanced irrigated area as well as capital formation in agriculture is equally important. Overall development of the agriculture sector, pro-grammes and policies must be focused on reducing GHGs emission through raising the forest coverage areas, improving conservation and efficient management, developing scientific instruments and increasing expenditure on agricultural research and development. The govern-ment should focus towards the changing the type of crops which are grown to better match changed pattern of temperature and rainfall. Effective adaptation strategies involving technological innovation and intuitional development are the key factors which would help to improve agricultural productivity as well as food security of the nation.

CHAPTER 7

Trends of Food Security and Its Components at National Level

FAO's vision of a world without hunger is one in which most people are able, by themselves, to obtain the food they need for an active and healthy life, and where social safety nets ensure that those who lack resources still get enough to eat.

—**FAO**

Introduction

Food is very vital for life and is one of the pivotal basic needs of people (Rukhsana 2011). Food security has emerged as the main problem in India where about one-third of the population is poor and one-half of all children are malnourished (Dev and Sharma 2010). The problem of food security arises mainly due to the fluctuation in food production and insufficient availability of food. In recent years, food security has undergone considerable changes and food problems are the major problems in the country. However, the government is trying for achieving self-sufficiency by increasing food production as well as improving capacity to cope-with year-to-year fluctuations in food production at national level. But as Indian agriculture is continuing its dependence upon weather conditions, the production of food grains is fluctuating with the variation of climate conditions.

Food security has been defined at the household, national, regional and global level as a situation in which all people at all times have physical and economic accessibility to sufficient, safe and nutritious food in order to meet their dietary needs and food preferences for an active and healthy life. The definition is 'Food security exists when all people, at all times, have physical and economic access to sufficient, safe and nutritious food that meets their dietary needs and food preferences for an active and healthy life' (FAO 1996). The definition introduced three basic and distinctive characters of food security that are:

1. **Food availability**: It refers to the availability of sufficient quantities of food, along with appropriate quality, generally supplied through domestic production or imports (including food aid).
2. **Accessibility to food**: Access to adequate resources by individuals in order to obtain appropriate food for a nutritious diet. Entitlements refer to a set of all commodity bundles over which a person can establish command given the legal, political and socio-economic arrangements of the community in which they live (including traditional rights such as access to common resources).
3. **Stability of food**: Food security entails a population, household or individual that must have access to adequate food at all times without any risk of losing access to food as a consequence of sudden shocks (e.g., an economic or climatic crisis) or cyclical events (e.g., seasonal food insecurity). The concept of stability can therefore refer to both the availability and access dimensions of food security.

To achieve food security at national level, National Food Security Act (NFSA), 2013 has been implemented in India. The basic features of the bill are given in Box 7.1.

Box 7.1   President of India Promulgates National Food Security Ordinance 2013

- Inclusion of two-thirds population to get highly subsidized foodgrains
- Poorest of the poor continue to get 35 kg per household
- Eligible households to be identified by the states
- Special focus on nutritional support to women and children
- To provide food security allowances in case of non-supply of foodgrains
- States to get assistance for intra-state transportation
- Women empowerment: Eldest women will be the head of the household
- Aadhaar for unique identification of beneficiaries
- Grievance redressal mechanism at district level
- Social audits and vigilance committees to ensure transparency
- Penalty for non-compliance

This chapter analyses the trends of various dimensions of food security and its components at national level. The present chapter is divided in three sections except introduction. The first section analyses the performance of food security and its indicators. The second section describes trends of FSI and its components, that is, FAI, IFS and IFA. Lastly, the third section describes conclusion of the present chapter. The methodological framework and data sources of the present chapter have already been discussed in Chapter 4.

Performance of Food Security and Its Indicators

Trends of Food Grain Production and Population

Food availability means availability of sufficient stocks of food to meet domestic demand of people in India. An important concern for food security is whether the food production would remain higher than the population growth rate. Table 7.1 and Figure 7.1 show the trends of population and food grain production in India during 1950–1951 to 2014–2015. It is observed that during 1950–1951 the population was 363 million while food grain production was 50.83MT. During

Table 7.1 *Trend of Population and Food Grain in India*

Year	Population (Million)	Food Grain Production (MT)
1950–1951	363.20	50.83
1960–1961	442.40	82.02
1970–1971	551.30	108.42
1980–1981	688.50	129.59
1990–1991	851.70	176.39
2000–2001	1033.20	196.81
2010–2011	1201.90	244.49
2014–2015	1283.00	252.02

Source: Author's estimation based on Ministry of Agriculture and Farmers Welfare database (https://eands.dacnet.nic.in/)

the last 65 years, population has increased from 363 million to 1,283 million and food grain production has increased from 50.83MT to 252MT at national level. The data indicates that population and food grain both have positive trends during the last 65 years. But the slope of trend value of population has been found to be higher than the slope of trend value of food grain production during the last 65 years.

It is also observed that at the time of independence the country had shortage of food grain but GR initiated in the late 1960s increased the agricultural production and improved food security of the nation. It increased food grain production over the next three or four decades and reduced both the levels of food insecurity and poverty by 50 per cent. In spite of the increasing population, the nation has achieved self-sufficiency in food grain production. But in present scenario hungriness exists in the country due to non-availability of food grain production and its unequal distribution.

The per Capita Net Availability of Food Grain and Non-food Grain Crops

Food grain crops: Trends of the per capita net availability of food grain, cereals and pulses during 1950–1951 to 2014–2015 at national

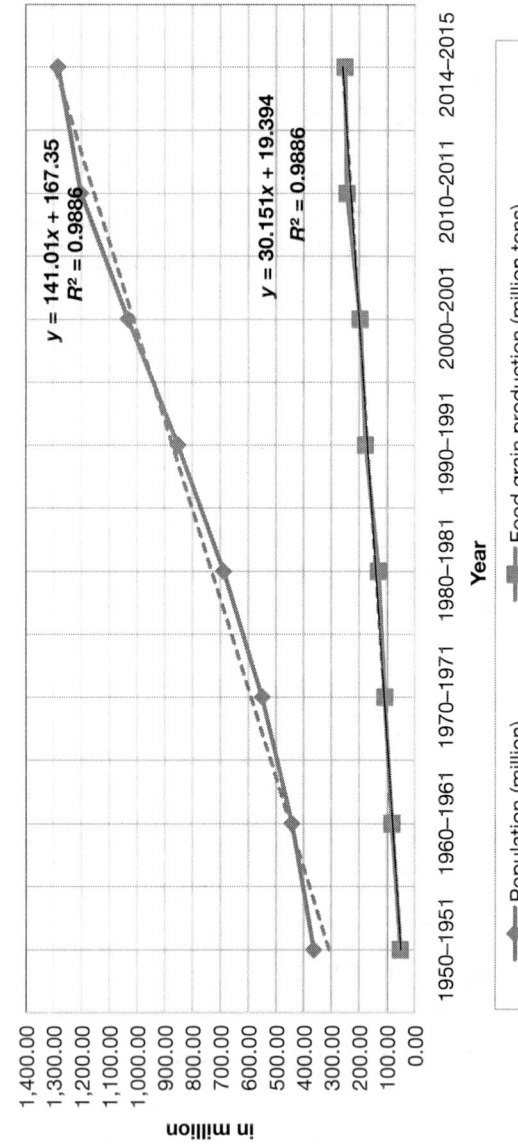

Figure 7.1 *Trend of Population and Food Grain Production in India*

Source: Author's estimation based on Ministry of Agriculture and Farmers Welfare database (https://eands.dacnet.nic.in/).

Table 7.2 *The per Capita Net Availability of Food Grain and Non-food Grain in India*

Year	Per Capita Net Availability per Fay (Grams)			Non-food Grain Crops		
	Cereals	Pulses	Food Grain	Edible oil (kg)	Vanaspati (kg)	Sugar (Nov–Oct) (kg)
1950–1951	334.20	60.70	394.90	2.50	0.70	5.00
1960–1961	399.70	69.00	468.70	3.20	0.80	4.80
1970–1971	417.60	51.20	468.80	3.50	1.00	7.40
1980–1981	417.30	37.50	454.80	3.80	1.20	7.30
1990–1991	468.50	41.60	510.10	5.50	1.00	12.70
2000–2001	386.20	30.00	416.20	8.20	1.30	15.80
2010–2011	410.60	43.00	453.60	13.00	1.00	17.00
2014–2015	444.10	47.20	491.20	16.80	0.80	19.50

Source: Author's calculation based on RBI database (https://www.rbi.org.in/).

level are given in Table 7.2. It shows that the per capita availability of food grain and cereals increased from 1950–1951 to 1990–1991, and then showed a declining trend. However, the per capita availability of pulses was not good during the study period. These trends indicate the serious implications for food security at national level.

Non-food grain crops: Table 7.2 also indicates the trends of the per capita net availability of non-food grain during 1950–1951 to 2014–2015 at national level. It shows that the per capita net availability of edible oil was 2.50 kg in 1950–1951 and increased to 16.80 kg in 2014–2015. However, the per capita availability of *vanaspati* was 0.70 kg in 1950–1951 and became 0.80 kg in 2014–2015. In case of sugar (November–October), the per capita availability was 5 kg in 1950–1951 and it increased to 19.5 kg in 2014–2015 in India.

The per Capita Availability of Quality Food in India

The per capita availability of quality food items, namely, milk, fish, eggs, fruits and vegetables, from 1950–1951 to 2014–2015 at national

Table 7.3 *The per Capita Availability of Quality Food Items from 1950–1951 to 2014–2015*

Year	Milk (Gram/ Day)	Fish (Gram/ Day)	Eggs (Gram/ Day)	Fruits (Gram/ Day)	Vegetable (Gram/ Day)
1950–1951	–	–	–	–	–
1960–1961	124	0.7	0.02	–	–
1970–1971	112	0.9	0.03	–	–
1980–1981	128	1.0	0.04	–	–
1990–1991	176	1.2	0.07	87	160
2000–2001	217	1.5	0.09	133	263
2009–2010	263	1.7	0.13	145	302
2014–2015	322	2.1	0.16	189	357

Source: Author's calculation based on RBI database (https://www.rbi.org.in/).

level are given in Table 7.3. It reveals that the per capita net availability of nutritious food such as milk, fish, eggs, fruits and vegetables increased substantially during the study period. Even though the per capita availability of quality food items increased during the last 60 years, the rate of enhancement of quality food items is less when compared to developed countries as well as many developing countries. So farmers should emphasize to produce these quality food items in the present scenario. These crops will be more profitable for farmers.

Buffer Stock of Food Grain Crops

Buffer stock of food grain crops (mainly rice and wheat) is very important to provide food to the country. It is favoured when either due to weather conditions or due to man-made factors the food demand shoots up. It is used to fulfil the food requirements of people during adverse climatic conditions such as droughts, floods and plant diseases. Table 7.4 shows the actual level of buffer stocks of food grain as on 1 July during the period 2002–2003 to 2014–2015 at national level. It is found that due to continuous rise in procurement prices, the buffer stocks of rice and wheat were accumulated to the extent of 63MT by

Table 7.4 Buffer Stock of Rice and Wheat Food Grain Crops (in MT)

Year	Actual Buffer Stock (1 July)	Norm of Buffer Stock (1 July)
2002–2003	63.00	24.30
2003–2004	35.20	24.30
2004–2005	29.90	24.30
2005–2006	24.50	26.90
2006–2007	19.40	26.90
2007–2008	23.90	26.90
2008–2009	36.20	29.90
2009–2010	52.50	31.90
2010–2011	57.80	31.90
2011–2012	64.00	31.90
2012–2013	80.50	31.90
2013–2014	73.90	31.90
2014–2015	61.00	31.90

Source: Author's estimation based on Department of Food and Public Distribution System database.

July 2002–2003 which was much above the optimal minimum buffer norms (MBN) of 24.3MT.

It is clear that this stock of 63MT was much above the optimal stocks of 15 to 25MT recommended by various committees. Further, the actual buffer stock started to decline and became 23.90MT in 2007–2008, which was below the prescribed norm of 26.9MT in 2007–2008. It is found that drought was the reason that food stocks reduced in 2003–2004 and actual buffer stocks were below the set norms during 2005–2006, 2006–2007 and 2007–2008 at national level. It was the time when the government had to import wheat in the country. However, further buffer stocks accumulated and become maximum 80.50MT in 2012–2013 compared to the norm of 31.90MT. Thereafter, the buffer stocks started to decline and the actual buffer stocks were 61MT in 2014–2015 as compared to the norm of 31.90MT in the same year in India. It is observed that there were several up and down trends in actual buffer stocks as compared to the norms of buffer stocks of rice and wheat during 2002–2003 to 2014–2015 in the country. Therefore, the government should ensure food security of the people by building adequate buffer stocks from the surpluses of food production in the country. It is seen that during the last 15 years there are no remarkable changes in the buffer stocks to fulfil the need of growing population at national level.

Trends of Food Security and Its Components Index

This section is devoted to analyse the trend of FSI and its components, that is, FAI, IFS and IFA, during 1980–1981 to 2014–2015 at national level. To calculate the FSI and its components index, the technique of Z-score has been used. If the parameters/indicators are the favourable for food security and its components, then the following formula has been used to estimate the Z-score for various indicators of food security and its components:

$$CI_i = \{(x_i - \text{Min}(x))/(\text{Max}(x) - \text{Min}(x)\},$$

where CI means composite index of Z score (Z-index) {http://www.foodsecurityindex.eiu.com/}; Min (x) and Max (x) are lowest and highest value in each indicator/parameter during the study period for food security or its components. If the parameters are the unfavourable for food security and its components, then the following formula has been used to estimates the Z-score:

$$CI_i = \{(x_i - \text{Max}(x))/(\text{Max}(x) - \text{Min}(x)\}$$

With the help of composite Z-score (CI), we have calculated FAI, IFS and IFA with their respective indicators/parameters in the following manners:

$$\text{FAI or IFS or IFA} = \Sigma CI_i/n$$

Final FSI is based on the simple average of food availability, food stability and food accessibility Z-score and it is calculated by the following:

$$\text{FSI} = \Sigma \text{CI}_c / n,$$

where FSI is food security index, CI_c is the composite Z-value of the components of food security, that is, food availability, food stability and food accessibility and n is the number of components of food security.

It is clear that the high values of variables indicate a more favourable conditions of environment for food security, while low values indicate an unfavourable environment for food security of the nation. Further, the normalized value of Z-score is then transformed from a 0–1 value to a 0–100 score to make it directly comparable with other indicators. This in effect means that the country with the highest raw data value will score 100, while the lowest will score 0. The details of construct index of food security and its components have been discussed in Chapter 4.

Food Availability Index

The pattern of food availability is influenced by many socio-economic variables in India. Therefore, FAI has been calculated by including variables/indicators such as number of livestock per 1,000 population (NLPTP), per capita food grain availability in gram/capita/day (PCFA), use of agricultural labour on per hectare-cultivated land (PHAL) and monthly per capita consumption expenditure (MPCCE).

Table 7.5 analyses the trends of FAI and its sub-components in India during 1980–1981 to 2014–2015. It was found that the trend of composite index of livestock per thousand population had been declining throughout the study period. The mean value of NLPTP was 0.527 and coefficient of variation (CV) around 55 per cent during the study period. The contribution of this parameter towards food availability had been declining with respect to time. On the other hand, the value of Z-score in case of per capita availability of food grain increased with high fluctuations during the study period. The mean and coefficient of variations of PCAF are 0.506 and 48.63 per cent respectively during the study period at national level. The trend of Z-score was positive and highly significant with mean value of 0.434 and high variations in case of agricultural labour on per hectare cultivated land. The value of

Table 7.5 Trends of FAI and Its Components Index in India

			Value of Composite Indices: Z-score			
Year	Number of Livestock on per 1,000 Population (NLPTP)	Per Capita Food Grain Availability (Gram/Capita/Day) (PCFA)	Use of Agricultural Labour on per Hectare-Cultivated Land (PHAL)	Per Capita Consumption Expenditure per Month (MPCCE)	Food Availability Index (FAI)	FAI Score/100
1980–1981	**1.000**	**0.000**	**0.000**	**0.000**	**0.250**	**25.0**
1981–1982	0.963	0.445	0.017	0.005	0.358	35.8
1982–1983	0.929	0.448	0.035	0.009	0.355	35.5
1983–1984	0.907	0.267	0.050	0.014	0.309	30.9
1984–1985	0.884	0.693	0.069	0.020	0.417	41.7
1985–1986	0.862	0.431	0.090	0.028	0.353	35.3
1986–1987	0.840	0.673	0.108	0.045	0.416	41.6
1987–1988	0.818	0.610	0.130	0.053	0.403	40.3
1988–1989	0.797	0.373	0.143	0.062	0.344	34.4
1989–1990	0.776	0.832	0.162	0.070	0.460	46.0
1990–1991	**0.748**	**0.624**	**0.177**	**0.075**	**0.406**	**40.6**
1991–1992	0.731	1.000	0.210	0.083	0.506	50.6
1992–1993	0.699	0.586	0.238	0.091	0.404	40.4
1993–1994	0.669	0.539	0.269	0.111	0.397	39.7
1994–1995	0.623	0.610	0.303	0.121	0.414	41.4
1995–1996	0.586	0.854	0.335	0.148	0.481	48.1
1996–1997	0.553	0.650	0.365	0.154	0.431	43.1

1997–1998	0.508	0.930	0.396	0.187	0.505	50.5
1998–1999	0.463	0.367	0.426	0.210	0.367	36.7
1999–2000	0.420	0.555	0.459	0.241	0.419	41.9
2000–2001	**0.379**	**0.441**	**0.490**	**0.248**	**0.390**	**39.0**
2001–2002	0.341	0.058	0.526	0.264	0.297	29.7
2002–2003	0.304	0.840	0.574	0.289	0.502	50.2
2003–2004	0.319	0.273	0.604	0.291	0.372	37.2
2004–2005	0.333	0.525	0.639	0.353	0.462	46.2
2005–2006	0.348	0.120	0.676	0.385	0.382	38.2
2006–2007	0.362	0.350	0.712	0.397	0.455	45.5
2007–2008	0.315	0.325	0.746	0.425	0.453	45.3
2008–2009	0.270	0.257	0.778	0.566	0.468	46.8
2009–2010	0.226	0.337	0.822	0.680	0.516	51.6
2010–2011	**0.184**	**0.268**	**0.852**	**0.735**	**0.510**	**51.0**
2011–2012	0.150	0.433	0.892	0.811	0.572	57.2
2012–2013	0.111	0.400	0.930	0.846	0.572	57.2
2013–2014	0.037	0.817	0.963	0.964	0.696	69.6
2014–2015	**0.000**	**0.791**	**1.000**	**1.000**	**0.698**	**69.8**
Mean Value and Coefficient of Variation (CV)						
Mean	0.527	0.506	0.434	0.285	0.438	
CV	54.848	48.630	72.095	103.037	22.188	

Source: Author's calculation.

Z-score in case of per capita consumption expenditure per month had an increasing trend at a higher rate during the study period.

Regarding FAI, the value (Z-score) has been increased continuously during the study period at national level with some fluctuations. The performance of all parameters of food availability has been found quite well except NLPTP during the study period.

The value of FAI score out of 100 increased from 25 in the year 1980–1981 to 69.8 in the year 2014–2015 with some fluctuations. It was impressive growth in case of availability of food grain at national level. It was also noticed that the score of FAI rapidly increased in the recent five years. Yet FAI score is lesser than 75. Therefore, there are scopes to enhance the value of FAI through reallocation of resources. As we know that availability of food grain is the major components of food security, it means that the FAI has been influenced by food security of the nation at a positive rate during the study period. The result of FAI also indicates that there are high fluctuations in food availability and its sub-components during the study period. To avoid these fluctuations, the government should emphasize on managing the food availability aspects.

Food Stability Index

Food stability is also a very important component of food security. Food stability depends on several other sub-components, that is, productivity (kg/hectare), cropping intensity, the ratio of forest area to sown area, consumption of fertilizers on per hectare cultivated land (kg/hectare) and ratio of gross irrigated area to net sown area. These sub-components/indicators except the ratio of forest area to net sown area have a positive impact on IFS. IFS as well as its sub-components/indicators have been estimated through Z-score at national level during 1980–1981 to 2014–2015. The value of Z-score in case of IFS is also transformed from a 0–1 value to a 0–100 score. The value of IFS and its components index at national level during the study period are presented in Table 7.6.

IFS was found negative during the first seven years of study due to negative Z-value of forest area. The mean value of all indicators except

Table 7.6 Trends of FSI and its Components Index in India

Year	Productivity (kg/Hectare)	Cropping Intensity	Forest Area as % to Net Sown Area	Fertilizer Consumption on Per Hectare of Cultivated Land	Gross Irrigated Area as % to Net Sown Area	Food Stability Index (IFS)	IFS Score/100
			Value of Composite Indices: Z-score				
1980–1981	0.000	0.019	−0.736	0.000	0.000	−0.143	−14.34
1981–1982	0.008	0.085	−0.858	0.024	0.020	−0.144	−14.43
1982–1983	0.011	0.000	−0.764	0.038	0.042	−0.135	−13.48
1983–1984	0.126	0.136	−1.000	0.095	0.063	−0.116	−11.62
1984–1985	0.114	0.124	−0.916	0.117	0.093	−0.094	−9.35
1985–1986	0.137	0.200	−0.835	0.130	0.088	−0.056	−5.59
1986–1987	0.095	0.187	−0.782	0.137	0.129	−0.047	−4.67
1987–1988	0.136	0.234	−0.436	0.146	0.184	0.053	5.26
1988–1989	0.278	0.291	−0.892	0.242	0.222	0.028	2.84
1989–1990	0.295	0.271	−0.850	0.266	0.233	0.043	4.29
1990–1991	0.323	0.369	−0.878	0.307	0.255	0.075	7.51
1991–1992	0.325	0.302	−0.781	0.317	0.319	0.096	9.61
1992–1993	0.392	0.375	−0.829	0.289	0.331	0.112	11.16
1993–1994	0.432	0.420	−0.773	0.299	0.365	0.149	14.87
1994–1995	0.473	0.446	−0.769	0.354	0.408	0.182	18.25
1995–1996	0.423	0.461	−0.700	0.368	0.431	0.197	19.67
1996–1997	0.534	0.499	−0.708	0.387	0.520	0.246	24.62
1997–1998	0.478	0.562	−0.635	0.470	0.523	0.280	27.97
1998–1999	0.546	0.583	−0.685	0.496	0.576	0.303	30.31

(Continued)

Table 7.6 Continued

			Value of Composite Indices: Z-score				
Year	Productivity (kg/Hectare)	Cropping Intensity	Forest Area as % to Net Sown Area	Fertilizer Consumption on Per Hectare of Cultivated Land	Gross Irrigated Area as % to Net Sown Area	Food Stability Index (IFS)	IFS Score/100
1999–2000	0.616	0.548	−0.592	0.553	0.607	0.346	34.63
2000–2001	0.545	0.426	−0.569	0.493	0.540	0.287	28.71
2001–2002	0.643	0.550	−0.567	0.522	0.585	0.346	34.65
2002–2003	0.463	0.459	0.000	0.474	0.575	0.394	39.40
2003–2004	0.637	0.610	−0.490	0.502	0.584	0.368	36.82
2004–2005	0.569	0.665	−0.501	0.572	0.645	0.390	38.97
2005–2006	0.626	0.698	−0.542	0.658	0.702	0.428	42.84
2006–2007	0.663	0.751	−0.495	0.717	0.763	0.480	47.97
2007–2008	0.757	0.794	−0.422	0.755	0.808	0.538	53.84
2008–2009	0.801	0.754	−0.492	0.856	0.810	0.546	54.57
2009–2010	0.703	0.661	−0.543	0.933	0.719	0.495	49.46
2010–2011	0.820	0.850	−0.374	1.000	0.835	0.626	62.62
2011–2012	0.954	0.810	−0.517	0.988	0.863	0.620	61.95
2012–2013	1.000	0.818	−0.486	0.890	0.880	0.621	62.05
2013–2014	0.975	0.973	−0.294	0.841	0.948	0.688	68.83
2014–2015	0.947	1.000	−0.327	0.842	1.000	0.692	69.24
Mean Value and Coefficient of Variation (CV)							
Mean	0.481	0.484	−0.630	0.459	0.476	0.254	
CV	60.69	55.95	−33.78	64.67	62.25	102.56	

Source: Author's calculation.

ratio of forest area to net sown area of IFS is near about 0.50 during the study period with some fluctuations. The value of Z-score in case of IFS was −0.143 in 1980–1981 and increased to 0.692 in 2014–2015. There was a rapid improvement in the situation of food stability at national level in India during the study period. The value of IFS score out of 100 has increased from very low (−14.3) in the year 1980–1981 to very high (69.2) in the year 2014–2015 with some fluctuations at national level. Overall from the above analysis it is reflected that IFS and its complements had positive trends during the study period except the first seven years in the country.

However, the government needs to maintain these trends as well as strengthen agricultural inputs, that is, land and capital, efficiency of irrigation inputs, organic fertilizers, and agricultural research and development to remove the instability of food stability in India. In this recent era, food security not only requires conventional agricultural policies oriented towards the stability of food but also policies focused towards procuring healthy and environmentally sustainable food. Now it is high time to formulate an index that pursues both 'food security' in the conventional sense as well as current concerns such as sustainability and conservation of food. In the 21st century, food security must be attained in the context of both, that is, food stability and food safety. Mostly, there is an inverse relationship between stability and safety, but promotion of coexistence of both should be set as a food policy goal.

Food Accessibility Index

Accessibility of food to all people at the right time is very important. Food security not only depends on food availability indicators/components and food stability components but also on accessibility indicators of food security such as literacy rate, road length, urbanization, per capita net national income, population density and infant mortality rate. These variables are directly related to food accessibility. IFA as well as its sub-components/indicators have been estimated through Z-score at national level during 1980–1981 to 2014–2015. The value of Z-score in case of IFA is also transformed from a 0–1 value to a 0–100 score. The Z-value of IFA and its components index at national level during the study period are presented in Table 7.7.

Table 7.7 Trends of Food Accessibility Index and Its Components Index in India

				Value of Composite Indices: Z-score					
Year	Literacy Rate (%)	Road Length for Per 1,000 Population	Urbanization (%)	Rural Population As % of Total Population	Per Capita Net National Income On Market Prices	Population Density (Pd)	Infant Mortality Rate	Food Accessibility Index (FAI)	FAI Score/ 100
1980–1981	0.000	0.000	0.425	1.000	0.000	0.000	1.000	0.346	34.6
1981–1982	0.026	0.245	0.464	0.980	0.007	0.027	0.935	0.384	38.4
1982–1983	0.053	0.216	0.503	0.964	0.009	0.054	0.935	0.390	39.0
1983–1984	0.079	0.187	0.538	0.942	0.019	0.081	0.922	0.395	39.5
1984–1985	0.105	0.159	0.570	0.917	0.021	0.108	0.830	0.387	38.7
1985–1986	0.132	0.050	0.600	0.891	0.027	0.135	0.817	0.379	37.9
1986–1987	0.158	0.106	0.629	0.865	0.033	0.162	0.804	0.394	39.4
1987–1988	0.184	0.080	0.655	0.836	0.035	0.189	0.791	0.396	39.6
1988–1989	0.211	0.056	0.680	0.808	0.052	0.216	0.752	0.396	39.6
1989–1990	0.237	0.032	0.703	0.778	0.061	0.243	0.608	0.380	38.0
1990–1991	0.263	0.303	0.717	0.726	0.069	0.270	0.608	0.422	42.2
1991–1992	0.302	0.358	0.758	0.719	0.065	0.301	0.595	0.442	44.2
1992–1993	0.340	0.459	0.797	0.712	0.074	0.332	0.530	0.463	46.3
1993–1994	0.379	0.593	0.836	0.707	0.080	0.362	0.530	0.498	49.8
1994–1995	0.417	0.611	0.851	0.643	0.093	0.393	0.530	0.505	50.5
1995–1996	0.456	0.690	0.875	0.605	0.108	0.424	0.504	0.523	52.3
1996–1997	0.494	0.673	0.902	0.581	0.125	0.454	0.491	0.532	53.2

1997–1998	0.533	0.601	0.928	0.558	0.131	0.485	0.504	0.534	53.4
1998–1999	0.572	0.605	0.953	0.535	0.144	0.516	0.478	0.543	54.3
1999–2000	0.610	0.589	0.977	0.512	0.168	0.547	0.452	0.551	55.1
2000–2001	**0.649**	**0.583**	**1.000**	**0.490**	**0.173**	**0.577**	**0.426**	**0.557**	**55.7**
2001–2002	0.674	0.581	0.914	0.451	0.182	0.608	0.386	0.542	54.2
2002–2003	0.699	0.603	0.831	0.412	0.190	0.638	0.347	0.531	53.1
2003–2004	0.724	0.620	0.750	0.375	0.215	0.668	0.321	0.525	52,5
2004–2005	0.749	0.682	0.673	0.341	0.239	0.698	0.321	0.529	52.9
2005–2006	0.774	0.688	0.599	0.310	0.271	0.728	0.308	0.525	52.5
2006–2007	0.799	0.724	0.527	0.281	0.306	0.758	0.282	0.525	52.5
2007–2008	0.824	0.740	0.458	0.255	0.348	0.789	0.256	0.524	52,4
2008–2009	0.849	0.876	0.392	0.231	0.357	0.819	0.217	0.534	53.4
2009–2010	0.875	0.898	0.327	0.208	0.393	0.849	0.178	0.532	53.2
2010–2011	**0.900**	**0.918**	**0.264**	**0.187**	**0.441**	**0.879**	**0.138**	**0.532**	**53.2**
2011–2012	0.925	0.974	0.213	0.198	0.473	0.909	0.112	0.544	54.4
2012–2013	0.950	0.984	0.155	0.182	0.874	0.940	0.070	0.594	59.4
2013–2014	0.975	0.976	0.055	0.017	0.932	0.970	0.034	0.565	56.5
2014–2015	**1.000**	**1.000**	**0.000**	**0.000**	**1.000**	**1.000**	**0.000**	**0.571**	**57.1**
Mean Value and Coefficient of Variation(CV)									
Mean	0.512	0.527	0.615	0.549	0.220	0.489	0.486	0.486	48.6
CV	62.01	59.40	43.35	53.26	116.87	62.25	57.48	14.90	14.90

Source: Author's calculation.

During the study periods, the trends of Z-score of food accessibility indicators had increased at a significant rate except rural population and infant mortality rate. High growth in value of Z-score has been found in the case of literacy rate, urbanization, per capita net national product and population density during the study period at national level. The mean value of all indicators of IFA is near about 50 during the study period with high fluctuations.

With regards to IFA, the value (Z-score) increased at a low rate during the study period at national level with some fluctuations. The performance of all parameters of food availability has been found quite well except rural population and infant mortality rate during the study period.

The value of the IFA score out of 100 increased from 34.6 in the year 1980–1881 to 57.1 in the year 2014–2015 with some fluctuations. The growth in case of accessibility of food at national level was not so impressive. It was also noticed that the score of IFA had not rapidly increased during the recent years. Therefore, there are scopes to enhance the value of IFA through reallocation of resources.

A food accessibility system must originate by expanding the number of items certified as safe as well as by certifying producers and facilities. This will call for implementation of the existing five management systems in the context of food, that is, Good Agricultural Practices (GAP), farm-to-table traceability, Hazard Analysis and Critical Control Points, food products identification and food safety investigations. The task of upgrading food safety lies between the two axes of 'enhancement of environmental friendliness and sustainability' and 'improvement of food safety and accessibility of food'.

Food Security Index

Food is the basic necessity of life and food security means to provide sufficient, safe and nutritious food items to meet the dietary needs and food preferences of people for an active and healthy lifestyle. Food security ensures enough food for more than one-third of the population including children and malnourished in the country. The trends of food security and its components/dimensions, that is, FAI, IFA and FSI are presented in Table 7.8 and Figure 7.2. The trend of food security score in India revealed that it increased from 15 in 1980–1981 to 65 in 2014–2015. Food stability as well as food availability indices are the major contributors towards enhanced food security during the study period. It is found that FSI was 0.218 in 1980–1981 and increased to 0.721 in 2014–2015. The CAGR of FSI was 4.8 per cent per annum during the pre-reform period, that is, 1980–1981 to 1990–1991. But, during the reform period, that is, 1990–1991 to 2014–2015, it was only 2.37 per cent per annum and increased at the rate of 56 per cent per annum at national level.

The value of the FAI was 0.250 in 1980–1981 and increased to 0.698 in 2014–2015 at national level. The CAGR of FAI was found to be 4.0 per cent per annum from 1980–1981 to 1990–1991, which further decreased to 1.55 per cent during the sub-period, that is, 1990–1991 to 2014–2015, and become 1.49 per cent during the study period at national level. In case of IFS, the index was -0.143 in 1980–1981 and increased to 0.688 in 2014–2015. For 1980–1981 to 1990–1991, the data is not available while during the sub-period of 1990–1991 to 2014–2015 it was 8.481 per cent during the period, at national level. With regards to the IFA, the trend of Z-score was 0.346 in 1980–1981 and increased to 0.571 in 2014–2015 and it grew at the rate of 0.67 per cent during 1980–1981 to 1990–1991, which further increased to 0.74 per cent after new economic reform period, that is, 1990–1991 to 2014–2015 and become 1.38 per cent during the study period at national level. The trends lines indicate that the composite Z-score of FSI and its components had positive and significant at national level during study period. But it is a matter of concern that the growth rate of FSI declined during the reform period of the study.

Despite substantial progress having been made in reducing food insecurity during the last four decades, maintaining food security at the national and household levels still continues to be a major obstacle in attaining complete food security in India. Various government initiatives in order to improve food security include concerted efforts

Table 7.8 Trends of Food Security Index and Its Components in India

Year	Food Availability Index (FAI)		Food Stability Index (IFS)		Food Accessibility Index (IFA)		Food Security Index (FSI)	
	Value	Score/100	Value	Score/100	Value	Score/100	Value	Score/100
1980–1981	0.25	25.0	−0.143	−14.3	0.346	34.6	0.151	15.1
1990–1991	0.406	40.6	0.075	7.5	0.422	42.2	0.301	30.1
2000–2001	0.390	39.0	0.287	28.7	0.557	55.7	0.411	41.1
2010–2011	0.510	51.0	0.626	62.6	0.532	53.2	0.556	55.6
2014–2015	0.698	69.8	0.688	68.8	0.565	56.5	0.650	65.0
Compound Annual Growth Rate (CAGR)								
CAGR (1980–1981/ 1990–1991)	4.055			NA	0.671			6.352
CAGR (1990–1991/2014–2015)	1.552		8.481		0.746			2.736
CAGR (1980–1981/ 2014–2015)	1.492			NA	1.382			3.585

Source: Author's calculation.

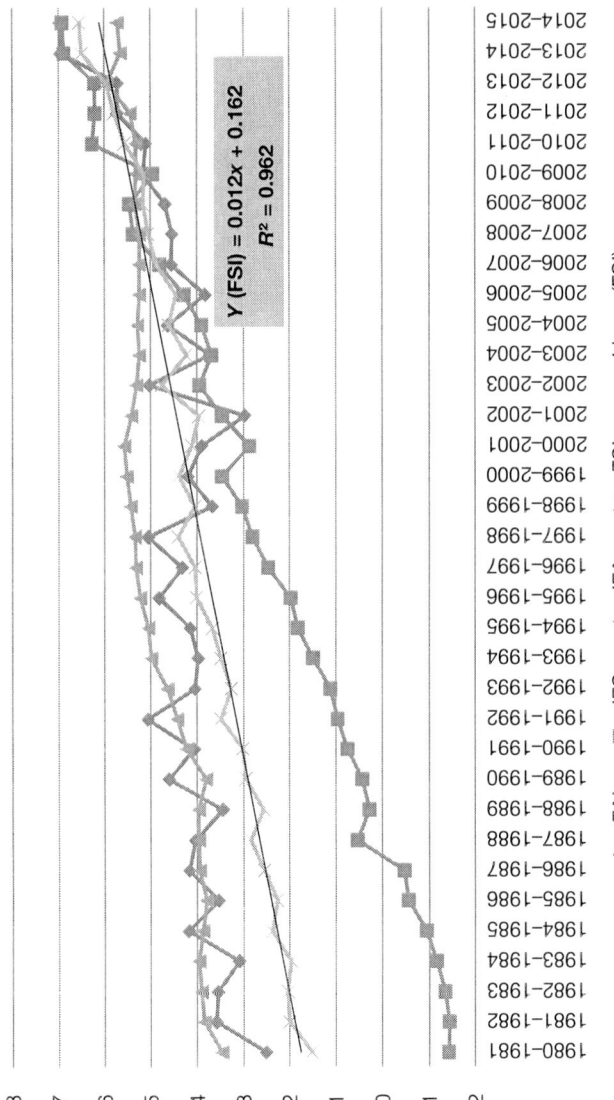

Figure 7.2 Trends of Food Security Index and Its Components Index in India

Source: Author's own calculation.

to increase food grain production, intervention in the grain markets, setting up of public distribution system and maintenance of stocks for major food grain. The rolling out of the NFSA is in the offing to ensure socio-economic accessibility to adequate food and a living with dignity for all persons in the country. However, in spite of several initiatives and strategies taken by government at national as well as state level, the problems of food and nutritional security continue to persist in the country. Nearly one-third of the world's undernourished children live in India out of which almost half of the children are stunted and 40 per cent are underweight. Moreover, one-third of the Indian women are also underweight (Joshi et al. 2011).

Matrix Correlation between Food Security and Its Indicators

The performance of food security depends on its dimensions such as food availability, food stability and food accessibility. For the identification of relationship among them, matrix correlation has been used. The matrix correlation among food security index and its components, that is, FAI, IFA and IFA at national level during 1980–1981 to 2014–2015 are presented in Table 7.9. Karl Pearson's correlation coefficient technique has been used to find out the relationship. It was found that FSI is positively correlated with FAI (r=0.81), IFS (r=0.98) and IFA (r=0.90). FAI had positively correlated with FSI

Table 7.9 *Matrix Correlation of Food Security Index and Its Dimensions*

Variables	Food Security Index	Food Availability Index	Food Stability Index	Food Accessibility Index
Food security index	1.000			
Food availability index	0.811	1.000		
Food stability index	0.985	0.716	1.000	
Food accessibility index	0.909	0.572	0.896	1.000

Source: Author's calculation.

(r=0.71) and IFA (r=0.57). Similarly, IFS was positively correlated with IFA (r=0.89).

It is observed that all components of FSI are highly correlated to each other. The value of correlation coefficient among food security and its dimension was found to be positive and significant at 1 per cent level of significance.

Conclusion of the Chapter

India is basically an agrarian economy where majority of the population depends on the agriculture sector for their livelihood. From the above analysis it is clear that the population increased at a very high rate as compared to the production of food grain at national level. The trends of population and food grain both had positive trends but the trends of population were more progressive, which was the major cause of the slow growth rate of the per capita net availability of food grain production. On the other hand, the per capita net availability of nutritious food items such as milk, fish, eggs, fruits and vegetables went up substantially during the study period at national level. The trends of the buffer stocks of food grain crops fluctuated highly during the study period at national level. It is a fact that increasing agriculture production not only achieved food security but also improved the overall income of farmers as a part of the Honourable prime minister's vision for doubling the income of Indian farmers at national level. Agricultural growth will not only improve the level of production of agriculture as well as food security but its linkages with other sectors will enhance the overall economic growth. Also, it will reduce poverty and increase the level of farmer's income and purchasing power.

CHAPTER 8

Food Security and Climate Change

A National Level Analysis

> Our early 21st century civilization is in trouble. We need not go beyond the world food economy to see this. Over the last few decades we have created a food production bubble—one based on environmental trends that cannot be sustained, including over pumping aquifers, over plowing land, and overloading the atmosphere with carbon dioxide.
>
> **—Lester R. Brown**

Introduction

Ending hunger, attaining food security and improving nutrition are the main targets and heart of the SDGs. Food security continues to be one of the main development priorities of India because the country's relatively high rates of economic growth have not led to a reduction in hunger and undernutrition. In the current era, food security is one of the leading concerns associated with climate change at both national and global levels. Climate change affects food security directly in complex ways. Climate change impacts productivity of crops, livestock, forestry, fisheries and aquaculture, and can have grave social and economic consequences in the form of reduced incomes of farmers,

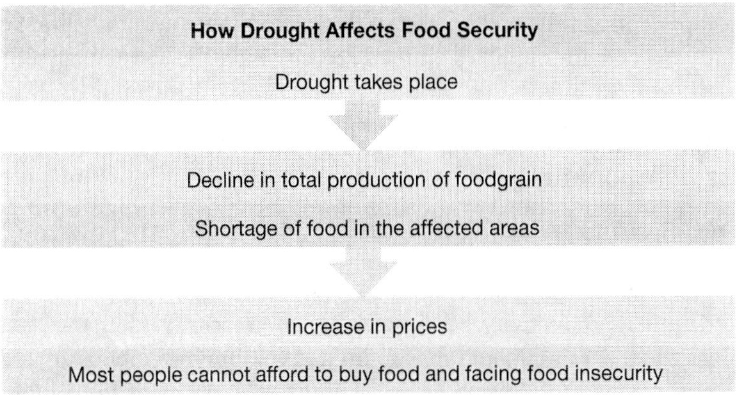

How Drought Affects Food Security
Drought takes place

Decline in total production of foodgrain
Shortage of food in the affected areas

Increase in prices
Most people cannot afford to buy food and facing food insecurity

Figure 8.1 *Impact of Drought on Food Security*
Source: Author's own creation.

eroded livelihoods, trade disruption and health issues. Moreover, it is important to note that the net impact of climate change depends not only on the extent of the climatic upset but also on the underlying vulnerabilities. As per the Food and Agriculture Organization (2016), both biophysical and social vulnerabilities determine the net impact of climate change on food security and its dimensions.

There is a very close relationship between climate change and food security. Food security can be directly affected by the changes in climate variables. In India, drought was the main reason for food insecurity in the past years. The impact of drought on food security can be shown by Figure 8.1.

This chapter analyses the impact of climatic variables as well as non-climatic variables on FSI and its components through regression analysis.

Impact of Climatic and Non-climatic Variables on FSI

This section is divided into two parts. The first part analyses the relationship between climatic variables and food security as well as its components. In the second part of the section, the impact of climatic and non-climatic variables on food security index has been analysed.

Impact of Climatic Variables on Food Security and Its Components

Food Security Index

The impact of climatic variables is worldwide in terms of influencing agricultural productivity, biodiversity and food security. Climatic variables, that is, rainfall, and maximum and minimum temperature are directly related to agriculture sector and food security of the nation. Here, FSI is considered as dependent variable and regressed with climatic variables such as rainfall, minimum temperature and maximum temperature as well as difference of maximum and minimum temperature by separate simple multiple regression models during 1980–1981 to 2014–2015 national level. The multiple regression models are as follows:

$$\text{FSI} = \beta_0 + \beta_1 \text{RAIN} + \beta_2 \text{MINT} + \beta_3 \text{MAXT} + Ui \qquad (1)$$

$$\text{FSI} = \beta_0 + \beta_1 \text{RAIN} + \beta_2 \text{DIFF (MAXT–MINT)} + Ui, \qquad (2)$$

where, FSI is food security index; MINT is annual minimum temperature; MAXT is annual maximum temperature and DIFF (MAXT–MINT) is the difference of annual maximum and minimum temperature; β_0 is constant coefficient term, β_1 to β_3 are regression coefficients for respective variables; and Ui is stochastic error term.

To remove the problems of multicollinearity, we have taken both sides in annual growth rate of all variables, that is, dependent as well as independent variables. The regression results of equation (1) are presented in Table 8.1. The results indicate that the value of R-square was 0.257; it means that only 26 per cent variation in FSI is explained by the variation in climatic variables during the study period at national level. Further, rainfall had negative and significant impact on FSI, whereas maximum temperature had negative but insignificant impact on FSI during the study period at national level. In the case of annual minimum temperature, it had positive but insignificant impact on FSI

Table 8.1 Results of Regression Equation (1) of FSI and Climatic Variables

Dependent Variable: Food Security Index (FSI)			
	Period for Study: 1980–1981 to 2014–2015		
Independent Variables	Coefficient	t-value	p-value
Annual rainfall	−0.365	−3.220	0.003
Annual minimum temperature	2.222	1.600	0.120
Annual maximum temperature	−3.452	−1.590	0.122
Constant	0.0392	3.390	0.002
R-squared	0.257		
F-value	0.028		
No. of observations	34		

Source: Author's calculation.

during the same period at national level. Overall it is found from the regression results that variability in climatic variables, that is, rainfall and temperature is the major cause of lack of sustainability in food security at national level.

The results of regression equation (2) are represented in Table 8.2. In this regression model, we have regressed FSI with annual rainfall and difference of the maximum and minimum temperature during 1980–1981 to 2014–2015 at national level. The result shows that the data had positive intercept and a negative slope coefficient during the study period at national level. On the other hand, the annual rainfall had negative and statistically significant impact on FSI whereas the difference of annual maximum and minimum temperature had negative but insignificant impact on FSI during the study period at national level. The result highlights that the value of R-square is 0.256; it means that 25 per cent of variation in FSI is explained by climate variables. The F-value indicates that the given model is good fit for FSI at national level. Overall the regression results show that high variability in climatic factors had negative impact on food security at national level.

Table 8.2 Results of Regression Equation (2) of FSI and Climatic Variables

Dependent Variable: Food Security Index (FSI)			
	Period for Study: 1980–1981 to 2014–2015		
Independent Variables	Coefficient	t-value	p-value
Annual rainfall	−0.362	−3.260	0.003
Diff. (MAXT–MINT)	−1.134	−1.650	0.108
Constant	0.0395	3.470	0.002
R-squared		0.256	
F-value		0.010	
No. of observations		34	

Source: Author's calculation.

Food Availability Index

The performance of FAI is directly influenced by climatic variables. It is a very crucial factor to determine the growth of the food security at national level. Here, FAI is regressed with climatic variables such as rainfall, minimum temperature and maximum temperature as well as difference of maximum and minimum temperature by separate simple multiple regression models during 1980–1981 to 2014–2015 at national level. The regression models are as follows:

$$FAI = \beta_0 + \beta_1 RAIN + \beta_2 MINT + \beta_3 MAXT + Ui \qquad (3)$$

$$FAI = \beta_0 + \beta_1 RAIN + \beta_2 DIFF (MAXT–MINT) + Ui, \qquad (4)$$

where, FAI is food availability index; the rest of the variables are same as discussed earlier.

The regression results of equation (3) are given by Table 8.3. It shows the regression results of FAI and climatic variables during 1980–1981 to 2014–2015 at national level. The regression results reveal that climatic variables such as annual rainfall and annual maximum temperature had negative and statistically significant impact on FAI at national level. On the other hand, annual minimum temperature had positive and significant impact on FAI. The value of R-square

Table 8.3 Results of Regression Equation (3) of FAI and Climatic Factors

Dependent Variable: Food Availability Index (FAI)

Independent Variables	Period for Study: 1980–1981 to 2014–2015		
	Coefficient	t-value	p-value
Annual rainfall	−1.302	−4.440	0.000
Minimum temperature	7.511	2.090	0.045
Maximum temperature	−11.840	−2.110	0.043
Constant	0.0535	1.790	0.083
R-squared	0.398		
F-value	0.0015		
No. of observations	34		

Source: Author's calculation.

was around 0.398; which implies that at least 40 per cent variation in FAI is explained by the variation in climatic factors at national level. The magnitude of F-value shows that that the given model is a good fit between the FAI and climatic variables at national level.

The results of regression equation (4) are presented in Table 8.4. It shows the relationship between FAI and climatic variables such as annual rainfall and difference of maximum and minimum temperature during 1980–1981 to 2014–2015 at national level. The regression result shows that annual rainfall had negative and statistically significant impact on FAI during the study period at national level. Difference of maximum and minimum temperatures had negative and statistically significant impact on FAI at national level. The regression results reveal that fluctuation in the rainfall and temperatures leads to low productivity of land and influences the FAI and its dimensions at national level.

Food Stability Index

Food stability is a very important component of FSI. It is considered that if any disturbances arise in the components of IFS, they would

Table 8.4 Results of Regression Equation (4) of FAI and Climatic Factors

Dependent Variable: Food Availability Index (FAI)

Independent Variables	Period for Study: 1980–1981 to 2014–2015		
	Coefficient	t-value	p-value
Annual rainfall	–1.291	–4.500	0.000
Diff (MAXT–MINT)	–3.873	–2.190	0.036
Constant	0.0545	1.850	0.073
R-squared	0.396		
F-value	0.0004		
No. of observations	34		

Source: Author's calculation.

affect the overall components of FSI. Hence, this sub-section discusses the impact of the climatic variables on IFS during the study period, that is, from 1980–1981 to 2014–2015 at national level. The multiple time series regression models are as follows:

$$IFS = \beta_0 + \beta_1 RAIN + \beta_2 MINT + \beta_3 MAXT + Ui \qquad (5)$$

$$IFS = \beta_0 + \beta_1 RAIN + \beta_2 DIFF (MINT-MAXT) + Ui, \qquad (6)$$

where, IFS is the food stability index; the rest of the variables are same as discussed earlier.

The results of multiple regression model (5) are presented in Table 8.5. The results show the relationship between IFS and climate variables during 1980–1981 to 2014–2015 at national level. They indicate that annual rainfall and maximum temperature had positive but insignificant impact on IFS during the study period at national level.

On the other hand, the impact of annual minimum temperature had negative but insignificant impact on IFS. The value of R-square is very low (0.1269) which implies that only 12.7 per cent variation in IFS is explained by the variation in climatic factors during the study period at national level.

Table 8.5 Results of Regression Equation (5) of IFS and Climatic Factors

Dependent Variable: Food Stability Index (IFS)			
	Period for Study: 1980–1981 to 2014–2015		
Independent Variables	Coefficient	t-value	p-value
Annual rainfall	0.172	0.73	0.473
Minimum temperature	–1.574	–0.54	0.591
Maximum temperature	5.139	1.13	0.266
Constant	0.0907	3.76	0.001
R-squared		0.1269	
F-value		0.5496	
No. of observations		34	

Source: Author's calculation.

Table 8.6 Results of Regression Equation (6) of IFS and Climatic Factors

Dependent Variable: Food Stability Index (IFS)			
	Period for Study: 1980–1981 to 2014–2015		
Independent Variables	Coefficient	t-value	p-value
Annual rainfall	0.147	0.620	0.538
Diff (MINT–MAXT)	1.158	0.790	0.435
Constant	0.091	3.750	0.001
R-squared		0.091	
F-value		0.714	
No. of observations		34	

Source: Author's calculation.

The results of multiple regression model (6) are given by Table 8.6. It analyses the impact of IFS on climate factors, that is, annual rainfall, and difference of maximum and minimum temperature during study period (1980–1981 to 2014–2015) at national level. The regression results show that coefficient of intercept and slope both had positive impact during the study period at national level. On the other hand, the results highlight that the climatic factors such as annual rainfall and difference of minimum and maximum temperature had positive but insignificant impact on the IFS at national level. The value of R-square (0.091) and F-value are very low which implies that only 9 per cent variation in food stability is explained by the variation in climatic factors during the same period at national level.

Food Accessibility Index

Climate variability, that is, rainfall, and maximum and minimum temperature are influencing IFA as well as food security of the nation. Food accessibility refers to access by individuals to adequate resources for acquiring appropriate foods for a nutritious diet. Hence, this sub-section describes the impact of climatic variables on IFA during 1980–1981 to 2014–2015 at national level. The regression models are as follows:

$$IFA = \beta_0 + \beta_1 RAIN + \beta_2 MINT + \beta_3 MAXT + Ui \qquad (7)$$

$$IFA = \beta_0 + \beta_1 RAIN + \beta_2 DIFF\ (MINT-MAXT) + Ui, \qquad (8)$$

where, IFA is the food accessibility index; and the rest of the variables are same as discussed earlier.

The results of multiple regression model (7) are presented in Table 8.7. It shows the relationship between IFA and climate variables during the study period at national level. The regression result shows that annual rainfall and annual maximum temperature had positive and statistically insignificant impact on IFA at national level. On the other hand, it is found that annual minimum temperature had negative and insignificant impact on IFA at national level. The results indicate that the value of R-square was very low, that is, 0.100 which implies that only 10 per cent variation in IFA is explained by climatic factors.

The results of regression equation (8) are presented in Table 8.8. It shows that the impact of climatic variables such as annual rainfall and difference of minimum and maximum temperature during 1980–1981 to 2014–2015 at national level.

Table 8.7 Results of Regression Equation (7) of IFA and Climatic Factors

Dependent Variable: Food Accessibility Index (IFA)			
	Period for Study (1980–1981 to 2014–2015)		
Independent Variables	Coefficient	t-value	p-value
Annual rainfall	0.0293	0.450	0.658
Minimum temperature	−0.0250	−0.030	0.975
Maximum temperature	0.0280	0.020	0.982
Constant	0.0150	2.310	0.028
R-squared	0.100		
F-value	0.665		
No. of observations	34		

Source: Author's calculation.

Table 8.8 Results of Regression Equation (7) of IFS and Climatic Factors

Dependent Variable: Food Accessibility Index (IFA)			
	Period for Study (1980–1981 to 2014–2015)		
Independent Variables	Coefficient	t-value	p-value
Annual rainfall	0.0302	0.47	0.640
Diff (MINT–MAXT)	0.0210	0.05	0.958
Constant	0.0154	2.35	0.025
R-squared	0.099		
F-value	0.670		
No. of observations	34		

Source: Author's calculation.

The regression results also show that annual rainfall and difference of annual minimum and maximum temperature had positive and insignificant impact on IFA at national level. A very low value of R-square, 0.099, indicates that only 10 per cent variation in IFA is explained by climatic factors. The F-value is also very low.

Impact of Climatic and Non-climatic Variables on FSI

Food security is considered a necessity for a healthy life and achievement of the goal of development at national level. In the previous section of the present chapter, we have discussed the impact of climatic variables on FSI as well as its components. Non-climatic variables or socio-economic variables are also important for food security. Hence, the present sub-section is devoted to analyse the impact of climatic and socio-economic variables on FSI at national level during 1980–1981 to 2014–2015. The multiple regression models for the time period 1980–1981 to 2014–2015 have been used to estimate the impact of climatic and non-climatic variables FSI at national level. The following is the multiple regression model:

$$FSI = \beta_0 + \beta_1(CI) + \beta_2(LIV/GSA) + \beta_3(RL/GSA) \\ + \beta_4(TR/GSA) + \beta_5(GIA/GSA)$$

$$+ \beta_6(TFC/GSA) + \beta_7(UR) + \beta_8(POV) + \beta_9(GCF/GSA) \\ + \beta_{10}(RAIN) + \beta_{11}(MINT)$$

$$+ \beta_{12}(MAXT) + Ui \qquad (I)$$

where, FSI is food security index; GSA is gross sown area at national level; CI is cropping intensity of agriculture sector; (LIV/GSA), (RL/GSA), (TR/GSA), (GIA/GSA), (TFC/GSA) and (GCF/GSA) are ratio of gross sown area with gross livestock, road length, total number of tractors, gross irrigated area, consumption of total fertilizers and gross capital formation of agricultural and allied sector respectively; UR and POV are urbanization and poverty ratio respectively; RAIN, MINT, and MAXT are annual rainfall, annual minimum temperature and maximum temperature respectively, β_1 to β_{12} are regression coefficient for respective variables and; β_0 is constant coefficient term and Ui is stochastic error term.

To avoid the problems of multicollinearity, annual growth rate of all variables, that is, dependent as well as independent variables have been taken. The results of the multiple regression model (9) are presented in Table 8.9.

Table 8.9 Results of Regression Equation (9) of FSI and Non-climatic Factors

Independent Variables	Dependent Variable: Food Security Index (FSI)		
	Coefficient	t-value	p-value
RAIN	−0.384	−2.70	0.013
MINT	0.761	0.59	0.559
MAXT	−2.650	−1.40	0.177
CI	4.682	3.13	0.005
LIV/GSA	1.529	2.42	0.025
RL/GSA	0.509	3.29	0.004
TR/GSA	0.064	0.68	0.502
GIA/GSA	0.037	0.07	0.945
TFC/GSA	0.248	1.34	0.194
UR	−0.024	−0.03	0.975
POV	0.307	0.44	0.663
GCF/GSA	0.143	2.53	0.019
Constant	0.007	0.34	0.736
R-squared = 0.6976		Adj. R-squared = 0.5248	
Prob. > =0.0026		Mean VIF = 2.94	
No. of observations = 34			

Source: Author's calculation.

In case of non-climatic variables, the regression results show that cropping intensity, livestock as ratio of gross sown area, road length network as ratio of gross sown area and gross capital formation in agriculture sector as ratio of gross sown area had positive and statistically significant impact on the FSI during study period at national level. On the other hand, number of tractors as ratio of gross sown area, fertilizer consumption as ratio of gross sown area, gross irrigated area as ratio of gross sown area and poverty ratio had positive and insignificant impact on FSI, while urbanization had negative impact on FSI at national level.

In case of climatic variables, the results indicate that annual rainfall and maximum temperature had a negative and significant impact on FSI during 1980–1981 to 2014–2015 at national level, whereas the impact of minimum temperature on food security index was found negative during the study period. The model shows that value of R-square is 0.6976; which means that about 70 per cent variation in FSI is explained by the climatic and non-climatic variables. The magnitude of F-value also indicates that the given model is a good fit for analysing the impact of climatic and non-climatic variables on FSI at national level. On the other hand, the value of VIF between independent variables is 2.94, which implies that there is absence of multicollinearity in the regression model. Overall from above results it can be concluded that there is a need to improve the condition of non-climatic variables and mitigate the effects of climatic changes by implementing effective government programmes, policies and technology to achieve the sustainability in food and nutrition security.

Conclusion of the Chapter

Climatic and non-climatic factors are influencing the agriculture sector in terms of production, productivity and food security of the nation. From the above regression results it is found that climatic variability in terms of rainfall, and minimum and maximum temperature has affected FSI and its components, that is FAI, IFS and IFA during the study period at national level. The non-climatic variables, that is, cropping intensity, number of livestock, gross capital formation in agriculture and road length network had positive and statistically significant impact on the food security. On the other hand, annual rainfall and maximum temperature had negative and significant impact on FSI during the study period.

Impact of climate variability in terms of rainfall and temperature has become one of the emerging issues of the agriculture sector and food security in the nation. It is obvious that majority of India's population depends on climate-sensitive sectors such as agriculture, forestry and fishery for their livelihood. Due to the adverse impact of climatic variability, rainfall is declining and temperatures have been increasing. Thus, droughts and floods are increasing and affecting food security and livelihoods of the people in the country. There is a need to change national level policy planning and public–private partnerships, and lay out a global vision for modifying long time trends for sustainable development and reducing the food security problems in India.

CHAPTER 9

Performance of Indian Agriculture at State Level

An ever-green revolution implies the enhancement of productivity in perpetuity without associated ecological harm."

—M. S. Swaminathan

Introduction

India is a country with myriad agro-climatic zones. More than 60 per cent of the agricultural land is dependent on monsoon. It is witnessed that climate change affects agriculture globally. But the effects are more visible in countries like India which are dominated by high agriculture dependence coupled with excessive pressure on natural resources. For instance, it has been found that the warming trend in India from 1901 to 2007 was 0.5 °C with warming rate accelerating at 0.2 °C per every 10 years since 1970 (Kumar 2009).

It is observed that fluctuations in agricultural development arise due to vast regional diversities in agro-climatic environment, resource endowment and growth of population among various regions of the country. The regional disparities in agricultural productivity arise due to differential resource endowments in the country in terms of soil fertility, land patterns, average annual rainfall, irrigation, varying levels of investment in rural infrastructure, technological innovations and climatic variability in different regions/states of the country. These regional disparities have widened over the years and significantly across the economy at state level. Therefore, it is very important to deeply look into these disparities pertaining to agricultural productivity across different states.

The main objective of the present chapter is to examine the productivity performance of food grain as well as non-food grain crops during 1980–1981 to 2014–2015 at state level and explain the state level trends of value of output from agriculture and its components.

Productivity Trends of Food Grain and Non-food Grain Crops

The agricultural productivity performance in India depends on its constituent states. But several features such as land holdings, irrigation inputs, soil nutrients, financial services, climatic variability and access to modern technology are diverse in different states of India. Consequently, a variety of crops are grown in the states of the country. In the present study, we have selected 16 major states of India, which contribute more than 90 per cent in terms of gross cropped area as well as agricultural production. This section is divided into two sub-sections. The first sub-section describes about the food grain crops and non-food grain crops are analysed in the second sub-section.

Food Grain Crops

During the study period the production of food grain increased from 198.40MT in 2004–2005 to 265.04MT in 2014–2015. The enhancement of food grain production during 2014–2015 was due to a good monsoon year, while the pre-monsoon rains were 99 per cent of the long period average and both monsoon and post-monsoon rains were deficient, and deficient rainfall affected the food grain production of both crop seasons. Increase in agricultural production during the last decade was largely a result of growth in productivity. At state level, food grain production share reveals a different scenario. Also, rising levels of food grain production is a quintessential aspect of national food security. Figure 9.1 shows the top 10 food grain producing states in India during 2014–2015. Because of the states falling in different climatic regions, there tend to be wide fluctuations in food grain production among the states during 2014–2015.

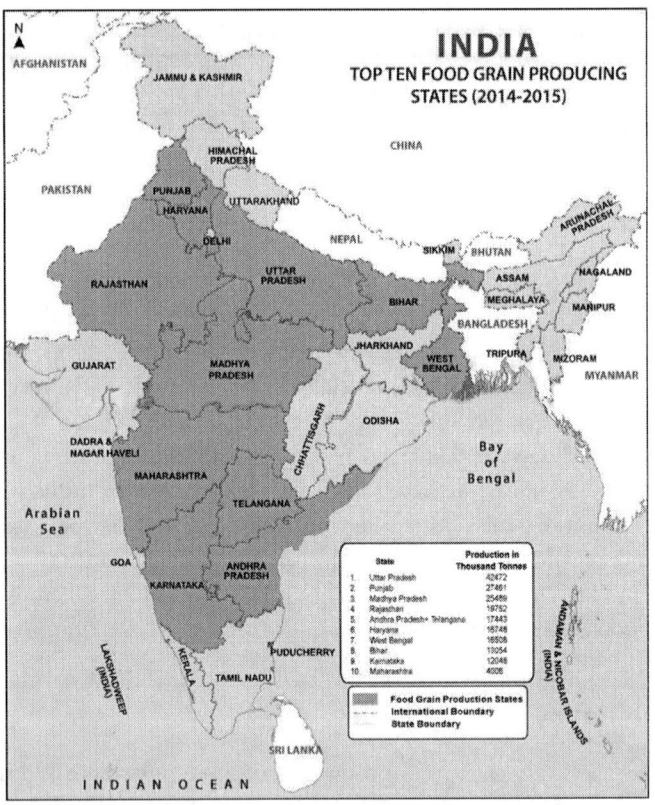

Figure 9.1 *Top 10 Food Grain Producing States in India in 2014–2015*

Source: https://www.mapsofindia.com/top-ten/india-crops/foodgrain.html
This figure has been redrawn by Sanjeev Kumar and is not to scale. It does not represent any authentic national or international boundaries and is used for illustrative purposes only.

Productivity supplements food grain production, while natural resources are limited. At the state level, there are widespread regional variations in food grain productivity. Thus, this sub-section primarily spells out trends of food grain productivity at state level in India by identifying productivity gaps at crop level among the states. Tables 9.1 shows the state level CAGR of food grain productivity/yield along with its components for rice (paddy), wheat, cereals, coarse cereals and pulses during 1980–1981 to 2014–2015 and its sub-periods. Further analysis is done by dividing the study period into three sub-phases: first phase from 1980–1981 to 1989–1990 (mature GR), second phase from 1990–1991 to 1999–2000 (early economic reforms) and third phase from 2000–2001 to 2014–2015 (economic reforms). The results indicate that the CAGR of food grain productivity during the study period was found highest in Rajasthan followed by Andhra Pradesh, Gujarat, Haryana, Karnataka, West Bengal, Madhya Pradesh and Bihar in that order. On the other hand, food grain productivity growth rate of other states such as Kerala, Assam, Maharashtra, Uttar Pradesh, Himachal Pradesh, Odisha, Tamil Nadu and Punjab was lower than the national average, that is, 2.06 per cent per annum during the study period. In case of wheat crop, it was highest in Andhra Pradesh and lowest in Odisha.

In rice crop, it was highest in Kerala and lowest in Maharashtra. The CAGR of pulses productivity during the study period was found to be more than 2.0 per cent per annum in the case of Himachal Pradesh, Andhra Pradesh and Maharashtra. The CAGR of pulses productivity during the study period was found negative in the case of Uttar Pradesh and Odisha. In the case of cereals productivity, it grew at the highest rate of 3.04 per cent in Rajasthan and lowest at the rate of 1.19 per cent in Himachal Pradesh during the study period. On the other hand, the growth rate of total cereals productivity was 2.17 per cent at national level during the study period. Considering productivity of coarse cereals, it grew at the highest rate of 5.17 per cent in Andhra Pradesh and lowest 1.81 per cent in Assam, but the growth rate of productivity of the coarse cereals grew at rate of 2.63 per cent at national level during the study period. Concerning productivity of wheat, it grew at positive rate in the all states except Assam, Gujarat, Karnataka, Odisha and West Bengal during the mature GR period.

Table 9.1 State Level Trends of Productivity (Yield) of Food Grain and Its Components Crops

State	Year	Wheat	Rice	Cereals	Coarse Cereals	Pulses	Food Grain
Andhra Pradesh	1980–1981 to 1989–1990	2.62	1.96	3.28	0.96	5.55	1.73
	1990–1991 to 1999–2000	-4.13	1.13	2.42	5.51	0.41	3.73
	2000–2001 to 2014–2015	6.1	0.4	2.07	3.14	3.65	2.29
	1980–1981 to 2014–2015	2.39	1.45	2.93	5.17	2.6	2.7
Assam	1980–1981 to 1989–1990	-1.59	0.57	0.49	0.37	0.69	0.49
	1990–1991 to 1999–2000	-0.78	0.96	0.91	0.84	2.93	1.11
	2000–2001 to 2014–2015	0.69	2.71	2.74	4.99	1.44	2.65
	1980–1981 to 2014–2015	0.13	1.83	1.81	1.51	1.33	1.81
Bihar	1980–1981 to 1989–1990	2.5	3.87	3.82	5.76	1.12	3.06
	1990–1991 to 1999–2000	2.56	2.94	2.98	3.39	1.63	3.56
	2000–2001 to 2014–2015	1.08	2.85	2.23	-0.93	1.68	2.29
	1980–1981 to 2014–2015	1.13	1.85	2.03	2.98	1.18	2.14
Gujarat	1980–1981 to 1989–1990	-0.51	-0.64	-0.47	-3.11	-3.01	-1.87
	1990–1991 to 1999–2000	1.08	1.73	4.01	5.5	2.9	4.37
	2000–2001 to 2014–2015	4.8	4.56	4.46	13.52	5.78	4.73
	1980–1981 to 2014–2015	1.81	1.86	2.9	4.57	1.66	2.69

State	Period						
Haryana	1980–1981 to 1989–1990	3.93	–0.14	4.13	0.47	5.37	4.84
	1990–1991 to 1999–2000	1.51	–1.64	1.24	3.03	–0.22	2.09
	2000–2001 to 2014–2015	–4.4	1.28	1.54	8.67	0.94	1.6
	1980–1981 to 2014–2015	0.65	0.69	2.18	4.58	0.98	2.63
Himachal Pradesh	1980–1981 to 1989–1990	1.75	–0.37	0.93	0.6	–6.36	0.63
	1990–1991 to 1999–2000	0.86	1.86	0.98	1.04	4.5	1.36
	2000–2001 to 2014–2015	1.07	1.31	1.09	7.06	9.73	1.22
	1980–1981 to 2014–2015	0.92	1.46	1.19	2.56	6.12	1.34
Karnataka	1980–1981 to 1989–1990	–2.76	–0.14	1.33	0.69	–0.88	0.34
	1990–1991 to 1999–2000	0.73	1.89	3.1	3.57	0.36	3.69
	2000–2001 to 2014–2015	3.62	0.76	3.15	11.95	3.76	2.76
	1980–1981 to 2014–2015	1.88	1.21	2.7	4.35	1.44	2.4
Kerala	1980–1981 to 1989–1990	–	1.23	1.18	1.76	1.64	0.85
	1990–1991 to 1999–2000	–	10.17	–1.64	–0.12	–0.81	–1.52
	2000–2001 to 2014–2015	–	–5.59	2	8.35	1.71	2.09
	1980–1981 to 2014–2015	–	2.51	1.57	1.91	0.91	1.64
Madhya Pradesh	1980–1981 to 1989–1990	3.39	1.67	2.7	2.75	0.3	1.67
	1990–1991 to 1999–2000	2.47	–0.85	1.8	1.72	3.79	2.74
	2000–2001 to 2014–2015	4.05	6.16	4.61	5.07	2.01	3.9
	1980–1981 to 2014–2015	2.32	0.92	2.57	3	1.91	2.28

(Continued)

Table 9.1 Continued

State	Year	Wheat	Rice	Cereals	Coarse Cereals	Pulses	Food Grain
Maharashtra	1980–1981 to 1989–1990	2.2	-0.58	1.19	1.61	3.87	0.61
	1990–1991 to 1999–2000	1.73	2.15	1.37	0.85	4.16	2.29
	2000–2001 to 2014–2015	1.19	2.14	2.86	10.85	2.7	2.64
	1980–1981 to 2014–2015	1.97	0.77	1.62	3.21	2.13	1.58
Orissa	1980–1981 to 1989–1990	-1.52	3.56	3.4	1.97	-0.4	1.14
	1990–1991 to 1999–2000	-2.73	-1.44	-1.24	-0.59	-4.24	0.93
	2000–2001 to 2014–2015	1.46	3.62	3.72	7.4	3.02	3.42
	1980–1981 to 2014–2015	-0.56	1.69	1.73	1.83	-0.56	1.98
Punjab	1980–1981 to 1989–1990	3.0	1.28	2.69	0.3	3.33	2.9
	1990–1991 to 1999–2000	1.98	5.6	1.26	2.52	-1.23	1.48
	2000–2001 to 2014–2015	0.65	0.72	0.72	5.45	1.17	0.73
	1980–1981 to 2014–2015	1.4	0.9	1.31	3.21	0.85	1.44
Rajasthan	1980–1981 to 1989–1990	3.77	1.33	2.47	1.17	-3.63	0.99
	1990–1991 to 1999–2000	1.47	-5.44	3.44	0.78	4.89	4.7
	2000–2001 to 2014–2015	1.29	5.44	3.37	10.17	4.22	3.13
	1980–1981 to 2014–2015	1.96	2.5	3.04	4.45	1	2.86

State	Period						
Tamil Nadu	1980–1981 to 1989–1990	8.89	6	5.08	2.68	5.06	2.64
	1990–1991 to 1999–2000	-1.95	-1.19	0.25	1.02	0.29	1.86
	2000–2001 to 2014–2015	1.64	0.86	2.72	15.73	3.55	2.53
	1980–1981 to 2014–2015	0.95	1	1.82	4.53	0.96	1.81
Uttar Pradesh	1980–1981 to 1989–1990	2.87	5.65	4	3.75	-0.61	3.19
	1990–1991 to 1999–2000	2.24	2.22	2.31	1.45	0.33	2.76
	2000–2001 to 2014–2015	0.57	1.32	1.03	9.09	-0.59	1.08
	1980–1981 to 2014–2015	1.61	1.95	1.92	3.39	-0.18	1.9
West Bengal	1980–1981 to 1989–1990	-0.66	5.65	5.28	7.57	2.95	5.01
	1990–1991 to 1999–2000	0.98	1.93	1.9	1.96	1.3	2.38
	2000–2001 to 2014–2015	2	1	1.16	5.45	1.36	1.17
	1980–1981 to 2014–2015	0.96	2.31	2.25	3.45	1.43	2.37
All India	1980–1981 to 1989–1990	3.1	3.19	3.11	1.71	0.58	2.97
	1990–1991 to 1999–2000	1.82	1.34	2.15	2.14	2.15	2.18
	2000–2001 to 2014–2015	1.17	1.88	2.2	3.94	2.3	2.11
	1980–1981 to 2014–2015	1.68	1.73	2.17	2.63	1.14	2.06

Source: Author's calculation based on Directorate of Economics and Statistics, Department of Agriculture, Cooperation and Farmer's Welfare, Ministry of Agriculture and Farmer's Welfare, Government of India.

Rice grew at a positive rate in all the states rather than Gujarat, Haryana, Himachal Pradesh, Karnataka and Maharashtra remained at a negative growth rate during the mature GR period. On the other hand, growth rate of cereals showed positive trends in Andhra Pradesh, Assam, Bihar, Haryana, Himachal Pradesh, Karnataka Kerala, Madhya Pradesh, Maharashtra, Odisha, Punjab, Rajasthan, Tamil Nadu, Uttar Pradesh and West Bengal, while Gujarat showed negative growth rate during mature GR period. In case of coarse cereals, all states grew at positive rate except Gujarat during mature GR period. The growth rate of food grain was positive in all the states except Gujarat during the mature GR period. The growth rate of food grain crops, that is, wheat, rice, cereals, coarse cereals, pulses and total food grain was found fluctuating and showed mixed growth rate during the early economic reforms and economic reforms periods in the different states of the country. Overall, from the above analysis, the results reveal that productivity of food grain crops grew at positive rate but there were fluctuating trends across the states and study periods.

Furthermore, we have tried to show the state-wise food grain productivity levels during the study period with the help of Figure 9.2.

The state level growth trends of food grain productivity during the study period can be divided into three categories, namely, high food grain productivity states (CAGR > 2.50), moderate food grain productivity states (CAGR between 1.90 and 2.50) and low food grain productivity states (CAGR < 1.89). Figure 9.2 shows the food grain productivity growth variations across the selected states of the study. Hence, it is seen that there are wide fluctuations in food grain productivity across the states during the study period.

Non-food Grain Crops

Table 9.2 shows the CAGR productivity trends of majorly cultivated non-food grain crops such as sugarcane, oilseeds and cotton across states. It is seen that sugarcane showed a positive growth rate in the all states except Andhra Pradesh, Himachal Pradesh, Kerala and Maharashtra during mature GR period. Moreover, during early economic reform period (1990–1991 to 1999–2000), sugarcane revealed

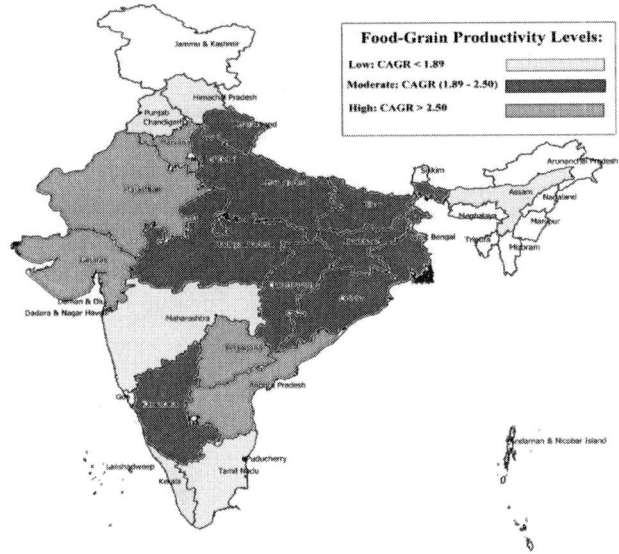

Food-Grain Productivity Levels:

Low: CAGR < 1.89

Moderate: CAGR (1.89 - 2.50)

High: CAGR > 2.50

Figure 9.2 State-Wise Growth Rate of Food Grain Productivity Levels: 1980–1981 to 2014–2015

Source: Based on author's calculations.

This figure has been redrawn by Sanjeev Kumar and is not to scale. It does not represent any authentic national or international boundaries and is used for illustrative purposes only.

Table 9.2 Trends of Productivity (Yield) of Major Non-food Grain Crops at State Level

State	Year	Sugarcane	Oilseeds	Cotton
Andhra Pradesh	1980–1981 to 1989–1990	−1.60	2.77	−5.10
	1990–1991 to 1999–2000	0.91	−2.32	−2.33
	2000–2001 to 2014–2015	0.03	−0.08	4.87
	1980–1981 to 2014–2015	0.28	0.17	2.17
Assam	1980–1981 to 1989–1990	1.16	0.01	−0.21
	1990–1991 to 1999–2000	0.12	−1.08	0.65
	2000–2001 to 2014–2015	0.00	1.72	−1.55
	1980–1981 to 2014–2015	−0.54	0.68	0.56

(Continued)

Table 9.2 *Continued*

State	Year	Sugarcane	Oilseeds	Cotton
Bihar	1980–1981 to 1989–1990	4.55	2.88	2.53
	1990–1991 to 1999–2000	−0.93	2.40	2.53
	2000–2001 to 2014–2015	1.77	2.54	−0.50
	1980–1981 to 2014–2015	1.02	2.75	−0.34
Gujarat	1980–1981 to 1989–1990	3.88	−0.81	−1.68
	1990–1991 to 1999–2000	−3.04	4.38	4.09
	2000–2001 to 2014–2015	−0.15	5.54	11.05
	1980–1981 to 2014–2015	−0.09	2.81	4.36
Haryana	1980–1981 to 1989–1990	2.33	6.26	1.12
	1990–1991 to 1999–2000	0.41	−0.31	−3.35
	2000–2001 to 2014–2015	2.16	1.83	6.20
	1980–1981 to 2014–2015	1.78	2.34	2.22
Himachal Pradesh	1980–1981 to 1989–1990	−6.35	−3.74	−9.51
	1990–1991 to 1999–2000	12.48	8.20	−0.64
	2000–2001 to 2014–2015	0.67	−0.79	1.81
	1980–1981 to 2014–2015	2.26	2.65	2.76
Karnataka	1980–1981 to 1989–1990	0.34	0.57	12.25
	1990–1991 to 1999–2000	2.27	1.11	0.99
	2000–2001 to 2014–2015	0.57	1.64	8.12
	1980–1981 to 2014–2015	0.34	0.24	3.44
Kerala	1980–1981 to 1989–1990	−1.74	−1.26	0.35
	1990–1991 to 1999–2000	3.68	3.36	0.41
	2000–2001 to 2014–2015	1.34	4.97	−1.25
	1980–1981 to 2014–2015	1.57	2.36	−0.66
Madhya Pradesh	1980–1981 to 1989–1990	3.30	5.51	3.64
	1990–1991 to 1999–2000	3.26	3.05	5.30
	2000–2001 to 2014–2015	1.77	2.86	14.4
	1980–1981 to 2014–2015	1.11	2.77	5.54
Maharashtra	1980–1981 to 1989–1990	−1.4	0.75	3.2
	1990–1991 to 1999–2000	0.90	5.13	3.76
	2000–2001 to 2014–2015	1.03	1.34	7.78
	1980–1981 to 2014–2015	−0.51	2.52	4.63

State	Year	Sugarcane	Oilseeds	Cotton
Odisha	1980–1981 to 1989–1990	0.81	1.38	4.48
	1990–1991 to 1999–2000	−0.94	−5.42	6.96
	2000–2001 to 2014–2015	1.41	4.26	6.14
	1980–1981 to 2014–2015	−0.08	−0.77	3.76
Punjab	1980–1981 to 1989–1990	0.65	2.97	9.00
	1990–1991 to 1999–2000	0.12	−0.34	−9.35
	2000–2001 to 2014–2015	1.40	2.57	3.83
	1980–1981 to 2014–2015	0.29	1.38	2.27
Rajasthan	1980–1981 to 1989–1990	0.98	7.01	4.84
	1990–1991 to 1999–2000	−0.78	2.27	−2.92
	2000–2001 to 2014–2015	3.99	2.52	9.79
	1980–1981 to 2014–2015	1.66	2.89	2.08
Tamil Nadu	1980–1981 to 1989–1990	1.33	2.33	5.85
	1990–1991 to 1999–2000	0.48	1.06	0.04
	2000–2001 to 2014–2015	0.51	3.78	7.69
	1980–1981 to 2014–2015	0.14	2.82	1.87
Uttar Pradesh	1980–1981 to 1989–1990	1.81	4.40	3.44
	1990–1991 to 1999–2000	0.77	−0.41	−10.99
	2000–2001 to 2014–2015	0.51	−0.37	0.32
	1980–1981 to 2014–2015	0.70	1.83	0.32
West Bengal	1980–1981 to 1989–1990	2.28	7.5	4.43
	1990–1991 to 1999–2000	3.00	−0.53	−2.83
	2000–2001 to 2014–2015	3.45	2.08	−2.39
	1980–1981 to 2014–2015	1.69	2.07	1.44
All India	1980–1981 to 1989–1990	1.21	2.95	4.10
	1990–1991 to 1999–2000	1.05	2.01	−0.40
	2000–2001 to 2014–2015	0.69	2.62	7.54
	1980–1981 to 2014–2015	0.56	2.01	3.46

Source: Author's calculation based on Directorate of Economics and Statistics, Department of Agriculture, Cooperation and Farmer's Welfare, Ministry of Agriculture and Farmer's Welfare, Government of India.

a positive trend among all the states except in states such as Bihar, Gujarat and Rajasthan. Similarly, sugarcane showed a positive growth rate in major states except Gujarat from 2000–2001 to 2014–2015. For the entire study period, that is, from 1980–1981 to 2014–2015, sugarcane showed positive growth rate in Andhra Pradesh, Bihar, Haryana, Himachal Pradesh, Karnataka, Kerala, Madhya Pradesh, Punjab, Rajasthan, Tamil Nadu, Uttar Pradesh and West Bengal, whereas states such as Assam, Gujarat, Maharashtra and Odisha revealed negative trends in the same period of the study. Moreover, at national level, sugarcane growth rate rose at 1.21 per cent per annum during mature GR period, declined to 1.05 per cent in early economic reform period, 0.69 per cent in economic reform period and become 0.56 per cent per annum during the study period.

The CAGR of the oilseeds productivity was observed to be notice-ably positive in almost all of the selected states for the study except during the study period. In case of national level, the growth rate of oilseeds was 2.01 per cent during the same period. It was also found that oilseeds grew at a mixed rate and fluctuated during mature GR period, early economic reform period and economic reform period. The performance of oilseed productivity sharply declined during 1990–1991 to 1999–2000 as compared to 1980–1981 to 1989–1990 in all selected states except Himachal Pradesh, Karnataka, Kerala and Maharashtra.

The CAGR of cotton productivity is found to be 3.46 per cent per annum during the study period at national level. At state level, it increased in case of the selected states except Bihar and Kerala during the study period. The sub-period analysis of CAGR of cotton produc-tivity shows that there are sharp variations at inter-state level as well as sub-period level of study. Karnataka, Madhya Pradesh, Maharashtra, Odisha and Tamil Nadu are the states that have positive CAGR of cotton productivity during the study period as well as its sub-periods.

From the above analysis, it is observed that the growth rate of non-food grain crops, that is, sugarcane, oilseeds and cotton fluctu-ated with mixed trends at state level during the study period and all its sub-phases. However, widespread variation in terms of growth rate of non-food grain crops is the major concern. In the recent era, as we know that non-food grain crops are also very important for food and nutrition security at national level as well as state level, policymakers should emphasize on these crops to sustain growth rate of non-food grain productivity.

Trends of Value of Output at State Level

Agriculture and allied activities (livestock, forestry and fisheries) play a vital role in the economy of India. Over the years there have been important developments in this sector particularly after the Green revolution. Value of output includes both production and prices received by the producers. Against this background, information on state-wise value of output from the agriculture sector assumes considerable importance. With this in view, a brochure containing state-wise value of output from agriculture and allied activities is disseminated by CSO at regular intervals. The present section discusses the trends of value of output from agriculture and its components, that is, rice and wheat during 1990–1991 to 2014–1205 at state level in India. The result of state level CAGR of value of output from agriculture and its components are presented in Table 9.3. The study period is divided into two sub-periods, that is, from 1990–1991 to 1999–2000 (early economic reforms) and from 2000–2001 to 2014–2015 (economic reforms period).

The results indicate that value of output from wheat grew at positive rate in major states such as Andhra Pradesh, Bihar, Gujarat, Haryana, Himachal Pradesh, Karnataka, Madhya Pradesh, Maharashtra, Odisha, Punjab, Rajasthan, Uttar Pradesh and West Bengal, whereas Assam showed negative growth rate during the study period. It was also found that the growth rate of value of output from wheat in Gujarat was the highest during the study period.

On the other hand, states such as Kerala and Tamil Nadu showed negligible growth rate in terms of value of output of wheat during the study period. At national level, value of output from wheat grew at positive rate of 3.64 per cent during early economic reform,

Table 9.3 *Trends of Value of Output by Agriculture Sector at State Level*

States	Year	Wheat	Rice	Agriculture
Andhra Pradesh	1990–1991 to 1999–2000	–0.49	1.69	1.13
	2000–2001 to 2014–2015	3.35	2.86	3.64
	1990–1991 to 2014–2015	1.49	1.72	3.03
Assam	1990–1991 to 1999–2000	0.03	1.24	0.9
	2000–2001 to 2014–2015	–7.07	3.62	2.78
	1990–1991 to 2014–2015	–4.82	2.20	1.28
Bihar	1990–1991 to 1999–2000	3.56	4.54	–3.33
	2000–2001 to 2014–2015	4.59	0.90	3.12
	1990–1991 to 2014–2015	2.19	–0.84	1.98
Gujarat	1990–1991 to 1999–2000	1.73	3.73	8.74
	2000–2001 to 2014–2015	9.17	1.30	6.77
	1990–1991 to 2014–2015	4.67	0.04	5.23
Haryana	1990–1991 to 1999–2000	3.79	4.30	1.53
	2000–2001 to 2014–2015	2.45	–0.35	2.97
	1990–1991 to 2014–2015	2.72	0.97	2.49
Himachal Pradesh	1990–1991 to 1999–2000	0.80	1.62	0.06
	2000–2001 to 2014–2015	8.44	–0.67	3.01
	1990–1991 to 2014–2015	3.75	–0.18	3.27
Karnataka	1990–1991 to 1999–2000	3.98	3.64	4.83
	2000–2001 to 2014–2015	4.75	4.53	3.29
	1990–1991 to 2014–2015	3.15	3.27	2.16
Kerala	1990–1991 to 1999–2000	–	–4.84	2.70
	2000–2001 to 2014–2015	–	–5.39	–0.95
	1990–1991 to 2014–2015	–	–4.49	0.56
Madhya Pradesh	1990–1991 to 1999–2000	5.47	0.18	1.31
	2000–2001 to 2014–2015	1.39	3.72	6.76
	1990–1991 to 2014–2015	0.22	–6.32	3.02
Maharashtra	1990–1991 to 1999–2000	5.26	1.40	3.45
	2000–2001 to 2014–2015	5.02	0.65	4.22
	1990–1991 to 2014–2015	3.46	–0.17	3.77

States	Year	Wheat	Rice	Agriculture
Orissa	1990–1991 to 1999–2000	0.82	−1.30	0.27
	2000–2001 to 2014–2015	−3.48	4.79	4.63
	1990–1991 to 2014–2015	0.07	1.94	2.14
Punjab	1990–1991 to 1999–2000	2.28	2.34	2.69
	2000–2001 to 2014–2015	1.50	3.18	1.65
	1990–1991 to 2014–2015	1.51	2.99	2.03
Rajasthan	1990–1991 to 1999–2000	6.33	5.93	5.89
	2000–2001 to 2014–2015	1.45	12.62	5.89
	1990–1991 to 2014–2015	1.61	5.68	4.26
Tamil Nadu	1990–1991 to 1999–2000	–	1.87	2.73
	2000–2001 to 2014–2015	–	−7.32	3.34
	1990–1991 to 2014–2015	–	−4.40	2.00
Uttar Pradesh	1990–1991 to 1999–2000	3.19	3.18	1.97
	2000–2001 to 2014–2015	2.09	2.91	2.22
	1990–1991 to 2014–2015	1.88	1.74	2.09
West Bengal	1990–1991 to 1999–2000	5.65	2.67	5.16
	2000–2001 to 2014–2015	−1.91	1.16	1.68
	1990–1991 to 2014–2015	0.74	1.53	2.56
All India	1990–1991 to 1999–2000	3.64	2.05	3.07
	2000–2001 to 2014–2015	2.42	1.58	3.04
	1990–1991 to 2014–2015	1.94	1.23	2.62

Source: Authors own calculation based on MOSPI Database.

2.42 per cent in economic reform period and 1.94 per cent during the entire study period.

Regarding the value of output from rice, it grew at a positive rate in Andhra Pradesh, Assam, Gujarat, Haryana, Karnataka, Odisha, Punjab, Rajasthan, Uttar Pradesh and West Bengal, whereas states such as Bihar, Himachal Pradesh, Kerala, Madhya Pradesh, Maharashtra and Tamil Nadu were showed negative growth rate during the study period. Considering the national level, the growth rate of value of output of rice was 2.05 per cent during early economic reform, 1.58 per cent in economic reform period and 1.23 per cent during the study period.

The CAGR of value of output from agriculture sector grew at a positive rate in the major states such as Andhra Pradesh, Assam, Bihar, Gujarat, Haryana, Himachal Pradesh, Karnataka, Kerala, Madhya Pradesh, Maharashtra, Odisha, Punjab, Rajasthan, Tamil Nadu, Uttar Pradesh and West Bengal during the study period. Regarding at national level, the value of output from agriculture grew at the rate of 3.07 per cent in early economic reform period, followed by 3.04 per cent in economic reform period and decreased to 2.62 per cent per annum during the study period. The CAGR of value of output from agriculture increased in Andhra Pradesh, Assam, Bihar, Haryana, Himachal Pradesh, Madhya Pradesh, Maharashtra, Odisha, Rajasthan, Tamil Nadu and Uttar Pradesh during 2000–2001 to 2014–15 as compared to 1990–1991 to 1999–2000, while CAGR of value of output from agriculture decreased in case of Gujarat, Karnataka, Kerala, Punjab and West Bengal.

From the above analysis it is concluded that the CAGR of value of output from agriculture and its sub-components have been found mostly positive with widespread variation at state level and study sub-phases. There is need to focus on area and region-specific programmes to increase the growth rate of value of output from agriculture in different states of India.

Figure 9.3 shows the levels of state-wise growth rate of value of output from agriculture during the study period.

The state level growth trends of value of output during the study period can be divided into three categories such as high value of output states (CAGR > 3.02), moderate value of output states (CAGR between 2.03 to 3.00) and low value of output states (CAGR < 2.00). Figure 9.3 reveals that the growth rate of value of output from agriculture had widespread variations across the selected states during the study period. It is observed that the variations were highly fluctuated across the states during the study period.

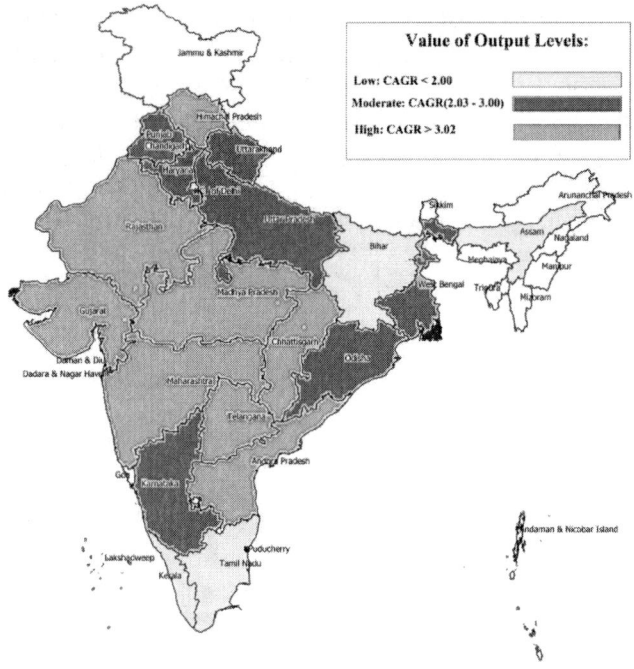

Figure 9.3 *State-Wise Growth Rate of Value of Output from Agriculture: 1990–1991 to 2014–2015*

Source: Based on author's calculations.

This figure has been redrawn by Sanjeev Kumar and is not to scale. It does not represent any authentic national or international boundaries and is used for illustrative purposes only.

Conclusion of the Chapter

The agriculture sector in India is the mainstay for the economic development across the major states in the country. It is an important source of generating employment, raising income and ensuring food security in different states of India. However, the variability in land holdings, agricultural inputs, credit, irrigation facility, marketing system, storage infrastructure, technology and climatic factors is the main cause of widespread variation in agricultural productivity and food security in different states.

Despite the fact that growth rates of food grain crops are fluctuating in different states, food grain crops play a very significant role in food security at state and national level. Similarly, the growth rates in case of non-food grain crops are found impressive despite widespread variations in different states of the country. Values of output from food grain and non-food grain crops are diverse at state and national level.

CHAPTER 10

State-Level Trends of Food Security and Its Components

Innovations that are guided by smallholder farmers, adapted to local circumstances, and sustainable for the economy and environment will be necessary to ensure food security in the future.

—Bill Gates

Introduction

The concept of food security takes into consideration that everyone has physical and economic accessibility to basic food at all times. According to the United Nations, it is not the overall availability of food that is a problem; rather the problem often lies in the poor distribution of food and a lack of purchasing power. In the past, food security problems have been dealt with at both national and global levels. Food security is an important factor that not only ensures human security but is also one of the seven pillars of the United Nation Development Programme's (UNDP) unique concept of human security, along with economic, health, environmental, personal, community and political security. More than 50 per cent of the population of India directly or indirectly depends on the agriculture sector, while most of the land of the agriculture sector is dependent on monsoon. It is witnessed that climate change affects agriculture directly. The main objective of this chapter is to examine the trends of food security and its components at state level.

State-Level Trends of Food Security and Its Components

In order to incorporate different components, food security has continuously undergone significant changes over time in the different states of the country. Due to varying agricultural conditions across states, of late food security has become one of the greatest challenges in the country. The present section analyses the trends of FAI, IFA, IFS and FSI at state level during 1980–1981 to 2014–2015 and its sub-periods. For calculating FSI and its components, the technique of Z-score has been used. The procedure of estimating the FSI and its components has been discussed in Chapter 4. This section is divided into the following four sub-sections:

Food Availability Index

One of the important dimensions of food security is food availability. It means having enough food available to sustain human life. To construct FAI, we have taken variables such as PCFA, per hectare arable land availability and food grain production index. The techniques of Z-score have been used to estimate FAI. The state-level trends of FAI and state ranks during the study period, that is, 1980–1981 to 2014–2015 are shown by Table 10.1 and Figure 10.1. The results indicate that the trends of FAI in Andhra Pradesh, Assam, Bihar, Gujarat, Haryana, Himachal Pradesh, Karnataka, Kerala, Madhya Pradesh, Maharashtra, Orissa, Punjab, Rajasthan, Tamil Nadu, Uttar Pradesh and West Bengal were positive and impressive during the study period.

On the other hand, major states ranked in the following order in terms of FAI: Punjab, Maharashtra, Haryana, Madhya Pradesh and Gujarat followed by Rajasthan, Andhra Pradesh, Orissa, Himachal

Table 10.1 Trends of Food Availability Index of Selected Indian States: Z-Score and Rank

| | Food Availability Index | | | | | | | | | State Rank | |
| | 1980–1981 | | 1989–1990 | 1999–2000 | 2009–2010 | 2014–2015 | | | | | |
States	Z-value	Score/100				Z-value	Score/100			1980–1981	2014–2015
Andhra Pradesh	0.398	39.75	0.345	0.312	0.338	0.295	29.51			7	11
Assam	0.296	29.62	0.190	0.245	0.267	0.387	38.65			10	6
Bihar	0.238	23.84	0.263	0.242	0.153	0.285	28.54			13	13
Gujarat	0.404	40.39	0.221	0.191	0.265	0.356	35.55			5	9
Haryana	0.490	49.04	0.454	0.546	0.601	0.618	61.83			3	3
Himachal Pradesh	0.341	34.13	0.253	0.229	0.162	0.288	28.83			9	12
Karnataka	0.282	28.22	0.257	0.320	0.345	0.423	42.25			12	5
Kerala	0.086	8.62	0.001	0.001	0.000	0.064	6.44			16	16
Madhya Pradesh	0.427	42.69	0.389	0.531	0.412	0.643	64.26			4	2
Maharashtra	0.511	51.06	0.466	0.362	0.348	0.365	36.47			2	7
Orissa	0.358	35.78	0.350	0.221	0.259	0.356	35.61			8	8
Punjab	0.731	73.08	0.755	0.755	0.754	0.808	80.83			1	1
Rajasthan	0.404	40.36	0.415	0.460	0.492	0.611	61.14			6	4
Tamil Nadu	0.101	10.12	0.144	0.164	0.139	0.244	24.38			15	14
Uttar Pradesh	0.284	28.44	0.268	0.332	0.303	0.236	23.58			11	15
West Bengal	0.181	18.14	0.193	0.216	0.224	0.298	29.85			14	10
All states	0.346	34.58	0.310	0.320	0.316	0.392	39.23				

Source: Estimated by author's calculations.

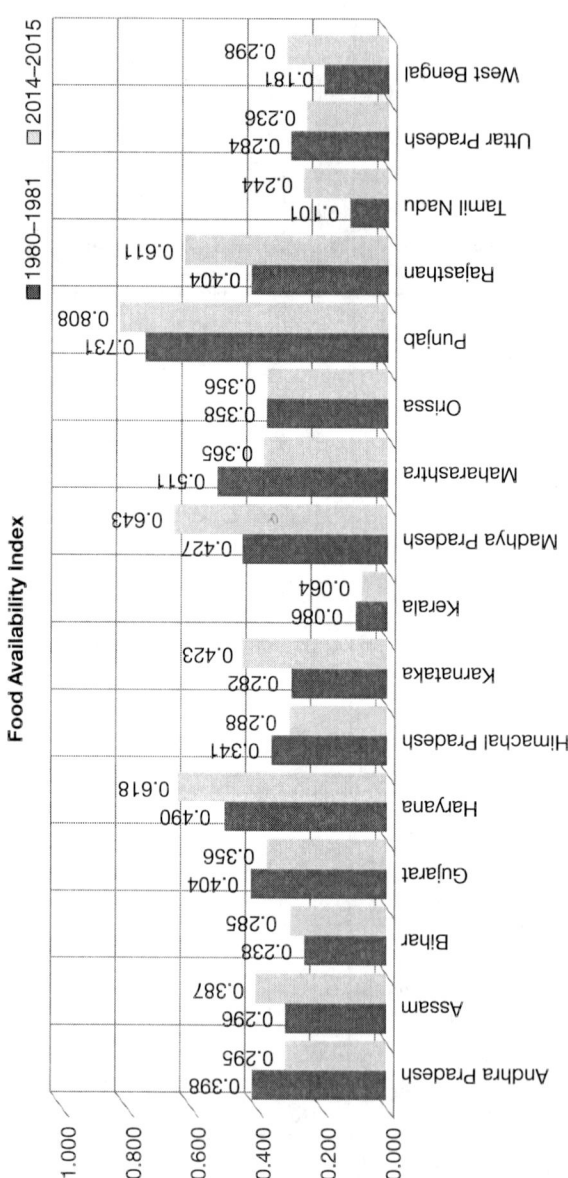

Figure 10.1 Trends of Food Availability Index of Selected Indian States

Source: Estimated by author's calculations.

Pradesh, Assam, Uttar Pradesh, Karnataka, Bihar, West Bengal, Tamil Nadu and Kerala during 1980–1981.

However, during the study period there was no change in the rank of Punjab, Haryana, Orissa and Kerala. Overall, from the result it was found that states such as Punjab and Haryana occupied the highest rank, whereas Kerala had the lowest rank in term of FAI during the study period. It is clear from the analysis that the states which had better land conditions and socio-economic conditions had the highest food availability and those states which had low fertility of land and poor socio-economic conditions had the lowest food availability in the country.

Food Stability Index

IFS is another important dimension of FSI. The analysis of IFS is constructed with five indicators at state level, that is, food grain productivity, per hectare consumption of fertilizer, ratio of gross irrigated area to net sown area, cropping intensity and ratio of forest area to gross sown area. IFS is calculated based on the value of standardized Z-score. The trends of the IFS of selected major Indian states during 1980–1981 to 2014–2015 are presented in Table 10.2 and Figure 10.2.

It has been found that IFS in Andhra Pradesh, Assam, Bihar, Haryana, Himachal Pradesh, Kerala, Madhya Pradesh, Orissa, Punjab, Tamil Nadu, Uttar Pradesh and West Bengal showed a positive trend during the study period, while Gujarat, Karnataka, Maharashtra and Rajasthan did not. IFS of all states increased from 0.157 in 1980–1981 to 0.242 in 2014–2015. On the other hand, states such as Punjab, Haryana, Uttar Pradesh, Kerala and Tamil Nadu ranked better in terms of IFS than Himachal Pradesh, West Bengal, Andhra Pradesh, Orissa, Bihar, Assam, Madhya Pradesh, Karnataka, Maharashtra, Gujarat and Rajasthan during 1980–1981. Further, Punjab ranked first in terms of IFS in 2014–2015 followed by Haryana, West Bengal and Andhra Pradesh. On the other hand, the situation of other states such as Rajasthan, Gujarat, Orissa and Maharashtra was worse in 2014–2015 in case of IFS.

Table 10.2 Trends of Food Stability Index of Selected Indian States: Z-Score and Rank

| | Food Stability Index | | | | | | | State Rank | |
| | 1980–1981 | | 1989–1990 | 1999–2000 | 2009–2010 | 2014–2015 | | 1980–1981 | 2014–2015 |
States	Z-value	Score/100				Z-value	Score/100		
Andhra Pradesh	0.188	18.77	0.196	0.258	0.292	0.354	35.36	8	4
Assam	0.097	9.71	0.061	0.063	0.080	0.137	13.70	11	11
Bihar	0.132	13.22	0.109	0.148	0.149	0.251	25.10	10	7
Gujarat	−0.020	−2.03	−0.032	−0.024	0.035	0.121	12.09	15	13
Haryana	0.285	28.54	0.306	0.407	0.465	0.472	47.19	2	2
Himachal Pradesh	0.216	21.56	0.175	0.163	0.128	0.169	16.92	6	10
Karnataka	0.013	1.32	−0.010	0.051	0.103	0.127	12.72	13	12
Kerala	0.221	22.10	0.170	0.154	0.161	0.252	25.16	4	6
Madhya Pradesh	0.051	5.10	0.050	0.110	0.138	0.245	24.45	12	8
Maharashtra	−0.018	−1.81	−0.023	0.020	0.061	0.071	7.08	14	15
Orissa	0.179	17.85	0.192	0.139	0.088	0.111	11.10	9	14
Punjab	0.601	60.08	0.605	0.618	0.627	0.617	61.71	1	1
Rajasthan	−0.131	−13.08	−0.138	−0.080	−0.072	0.043	4.28	16	16
Tamil Nadu	0.220	21.97	0.162	0.234	0.229	0.228	22.77	5	9
Uttar Pradesh	0.271	27.05	0.258	0.308	0.278	0.283	28.30	3	5
West Bengal	0.203	20.31	0.232	0.348	0.384	0.385	38.48	7	3
All states	0.157	15.66	0.145	0.182	0.197	0.242	24.15		

Source: Estimated by author's calculations.

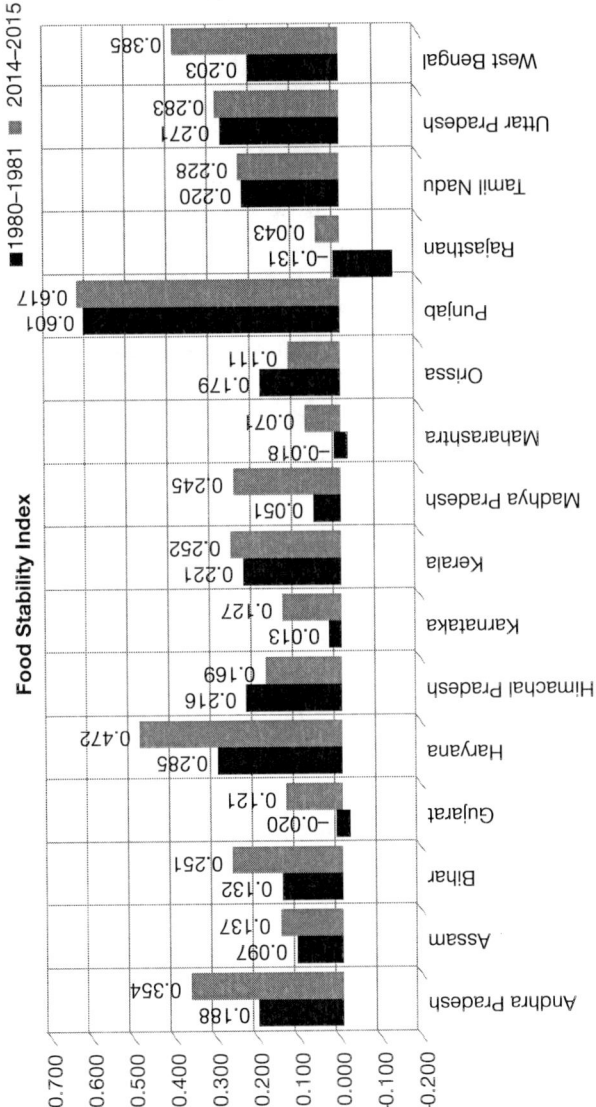

Figure 10.2 Trends of Food Stability Index of Selected Indian States

Source: Estimated by author's calculations.

It is clear that in terms of IFS, Punjab had the highest rank and Rajasthan had the lowest rank during the study period. The data shows Punjab occupied the top rank due to high development in the area of agricultural inputs, technology and productivity.

Food Accessibility Index

As per the World Bank, (1986), access to adequate food for all people at all times is defined as food security. Food security is not only dependent on the food availability and stability but also upon food accessibility. The estimation of IFA has been worked out with six indicators, that is, road length per thousand population, ratio of rural population to total population, urbanization in per cent, population density, literacy rate and credit–deposit ratio. IFA is estimated through standardized Z-score. Table 10.3 and Figure 10.3 present IFA of major Indian states during the study period, that is, 1980–1981 to 2014–2015.

IFA has been found positive in several states such as Andhra Pradesh, Assam, Bihar, Gujarat, Haryana, Himachal Pradesh, Karnataka, Kerala, Madhya Pradesh, Maharashtra, Orissa, Punjab, Rajasthan, Tamil Nadu, Uttar Pradesh and West Bengal during the study period. The value of IFA of all states together increased marginally from 0.399 in 1980–1981 to 0.424 in 2014–2015.

On the other hand, Kerala had the highest rank in term of IFA whereas Bihar occupied the lowest rank in IFA during the study period. There is widespread variation in terms of having food accessibility among the states during the study period. In this regard, the government should be focused on the determinants of the IFA and make effective programmes and policies for securing food accessibility across the major states.

Food Security Index

Food security is the backbone of the states as well as national prosperity and well-being. At the state level, food security is the biggest challenge in ensuring food and nutritional security to masses. In this context,

Table 10.3 Trends of Food Accessibility Index of Major Indian States: Z-Score and Rank

| States | Food Accessibility Index | | | | | | | State Rank | |
| | 1980–1981 | | 1989–1990 | 1999–2000 | 2009–2010 | 2014–2015 | | 1980–1981 | 2014–2015 |
	Z-value	Score/100				Z-value	Score/100		
Andhra Pradesh	0.383	38.260	0.406	0.389	0.415	0.400	39.96	7	10
Assam	0.351	35.10	0.374	0.381	0.452	0.437	43.75	11	6
Bihar	0.262	26.21	0.323	0.327	0.333	0.340	33.95	16	16
Gujarat	0.328	32.84	0.362	0.403	0.389	0.401	40.12	13	9
Haryana	0.328	32.76	0.372	0.384	0.390	0.395	39.51	14	11
Himachal Pradesh	0.374	37.35	0.369	0.402	0.432	0.425	42.52	9	7
Karnataka	0.444	44.42	0.469	0.436	0.450	0.424	42.36	5	8
Kerala	0.638	63.82	0.694	0.644	0.622	0.584	58.41	1	1
Madhya Pradesh	0.337	33.66	0.346	0.370	0.326	0.343	34.25	12	15
Maharashtra	0.490	49.00	0.466	0.544	0.480	0.453	45.27	3	5
Orissa	0.444	44.45	0.512	0.466	0.404	0.386	38.64	4	12
Punjab	0.364	36.44	0.382	0.421	0.437	0.454	45.43	10	4
Rajasthan	0.314	31.36	0.295	0.335	0.379	0.365	36.54	15	13
Tamil Nadu	0.550	55.05	0.580	0.562	0.534	0.524	52.43	2	2
Uttar Pradesh	0.381	38.10	0.339	0.351	0.357	0.358	35.76	8	14
West Bengal	0.398	39.75	0.442	0.476	0.511	0.495	49.46	6	3
All states	0.399	39.91	0.421	0.431	0.432	0.424	42.40		

Source: Estimated by author's calculations.

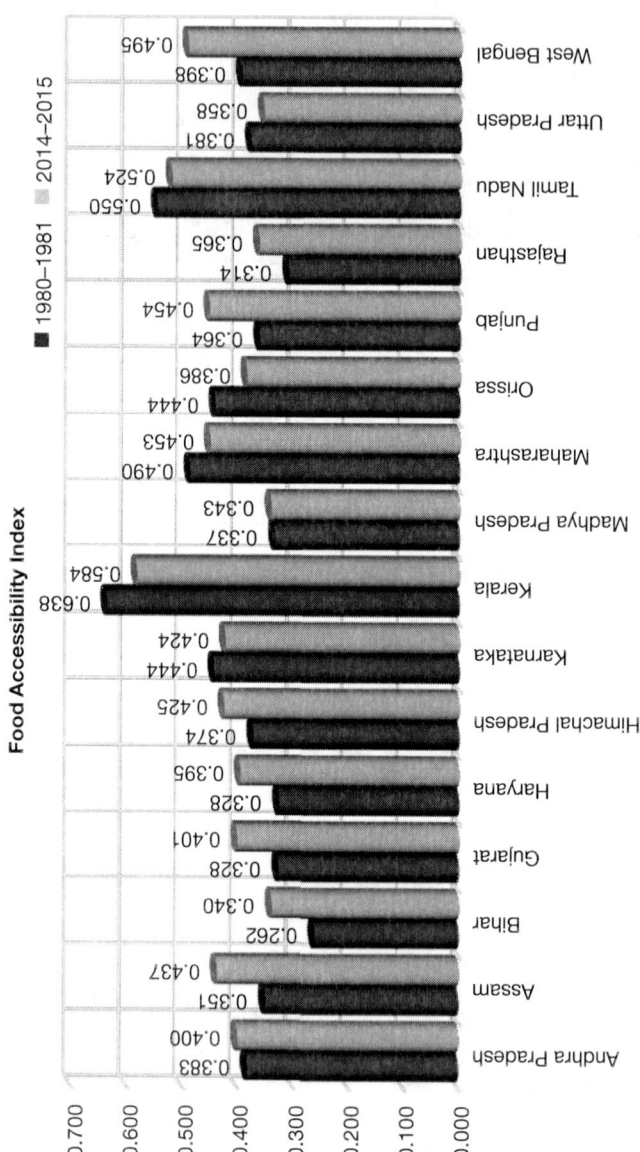

Figure 10.3 Trends of Food Accessibility Index of Major Indian States

Source: Estimated by author's calculation.

the Father of the Nation, Mahatma Gandhi, rightly remarked back in 1946, 'To the hungry, God is bread.' It is sad but true that even after 70 years of our developmental journey, food insecurity continues to exist at national level. Trends of FSI of the selected Indian states during the study period, that is, from 1980–1981 to 2014–2015 are presented in Table 10.4 and Figure 10.4. FSI has been estimated with the help of its components, that is, FAI, IFA and IFS. The details of methodology have been already discussed in Chapter 4.

The trends of FSI show that all selected states, namely, Andhra Pradesh, Assam, Bihar, Gujarat, Haryana, Himachal Pradesh, Karnataka, Kerala, Madhya Pradesh, Maharashtra, Orissa, Punjab, Rajasthan, Tamil Nadu, Uttar Pradesh and West Bengal had positive trends with fluctuations during the study period. Punjab and Haryana had the first and second rank, whereas Orissa and Bihar had the lowest ranks in term of FSI during the study period. The Z-score varied from 20 to 56 in 1980–1981 and from 28 to 63 in 2014–2015. The variations among the states decreased according to time. It is clear from the above analysis that Punjab and Haryana are the most food secure states as they are highly developed agricultural states. These states have sufficient amount of food grain production, consumption expenditure, calories availability and government expenditure on per hectare cultivated land (Shakeel et al. 2012).

Further, state-wise level of food security (measured by Z-score) was divided into three broad categories, namely high level, moderate level and low level of food security in 2014–2015. Figure 10.5 shows the three levels. Punjab, Haryana and Madhya Pradesh fall under the category of high level food security states category, while Uttar Pradesh, Bihar, Orissa, Gujarat, Maharashtra and Himachal Pradesh fall into the low level of food security states category. There were sharp disparities of food security level across the states.

It can be noticed that there are fluctuations and widespread variations in FSI across the states due to the socio-economic and climatic factors. In this context, the government should raise farmer's awareness, make inputs available, encourage better farm practices, provide climatic adaptability seeds, encourage rural entrepreneurship, develop

Table 10.4 Trends of Food Security Index at States Level: Z-Score and Rank

	Food Security Index							State Rank	
	1980–1981		1989–1990	1999–2000	2009–2010	2014–2015			
States	Z-value	Score/100				Z-value	Score/100	1980–1981	2014–2015
Andhra Pradesh	0.323	32.26	0.316	0.320	0.348	0.349	34.95	5	5
Assam	0.248	24.81	0.208	0.230	0.266	0.320	32.04	12	9
Bihar	0.211	21.09	0.232	0.239	0.212	0.292	29.20	15	15
Gujarat	0.237	23.73	0.184	0.190	0.230	0.293	29.25	14	13
Haryana	0.368	36.78	0.377	0.446	0.485	0.495	49.51	2	2
Himachal Pradesh	0.310	31.02	0.265	0.265	0.241	0.294	29.42	8	12
Karnataka	0.247	24.65	0.239	0.269	0.299	0.324	32.44	13	8
Kerala	0.315	31.51	0.288	0.267	0.261	0.300	30.00	6	10
Madhya Pradesh	0.272	27.15	0.262	0.337	0.292	0.410	40.99	10	3
Maharashtra	0.328	32.75	0.303	0.309	0.296	0.296	29.61	3	11
Orissa	0.327	32.69	0.351	0.275	0.250	0.285	28.45	4	16
Punjab	0.565	56.53	0.580	0.598	0.606	0.627	62.66	1	1
Rajasthan	0.195	19.55	0.191	0.238	0.267	0.340	33.97	16	6
Tamil Nadu	0.290	29.05	0.295	0.320	0.301	0.332	33.19	9	7
Uttar Pradesh	0.312	31.18	0.288	0.330	0.313	0.292	29.21	7	14
West Bengal	0.261	26.07	0.289	0.347	0.373	0.393	39.27	11	4
All States	**0.301**	**30.05**	**0.292**	**0.311**	**0.315**	**0.353**	**35.26**		

Source: Estimated by author's calculations.

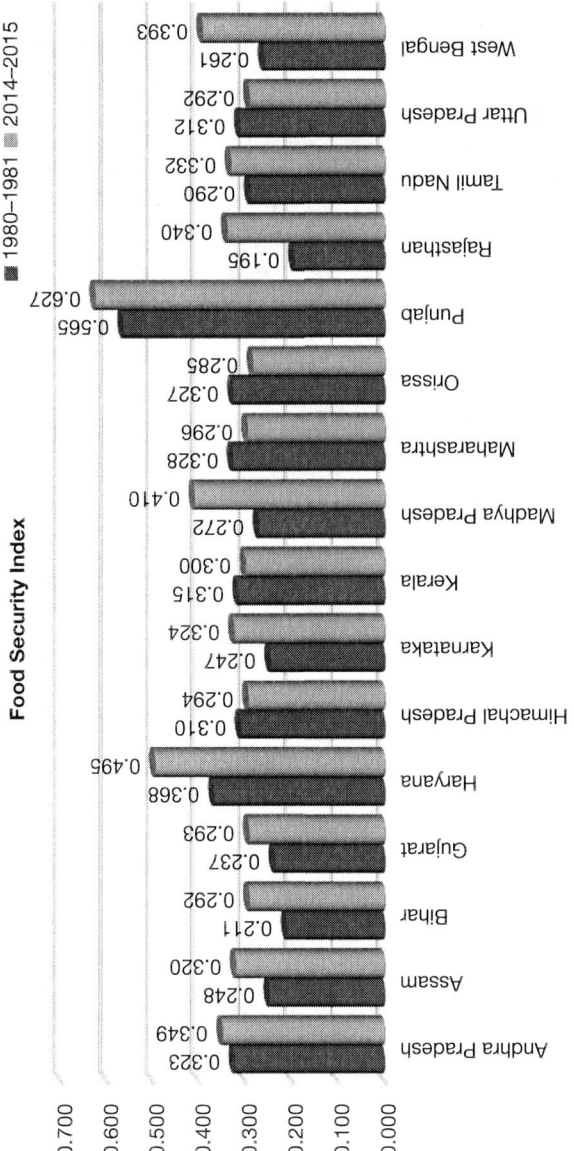

Figure 10.4. *Trends of Food Security Index at State Level*

Source: Estimated by author's calculations.

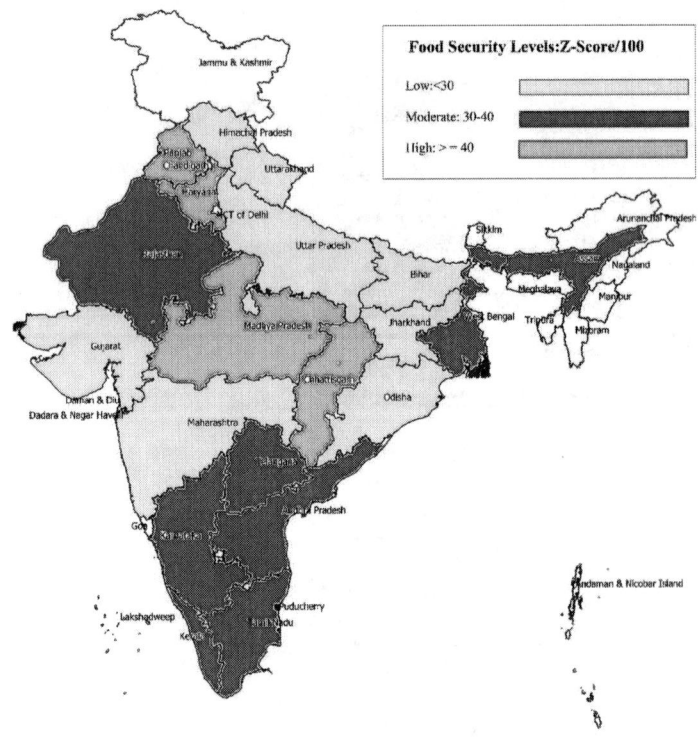

Figure 10.5 *State-Wise Food Security Levels in India: 2014–2015*

Source: Author's calculations.

This figure has been redrawn by Sanjeev Kumar and is not to scale. It does not represent any authentic national or international boundaries and is used for illustrative purposes only.

infrastructure and introduce new technology in different regions of the states in the country.

Conclusion of the Chapter

Performance of the agriculture sector of India in terms of productivity of food grain crops plays a very significant role in food security at state level. In terms of food security, it is found from the above analysis that Punjab and Haryana occupied the highest rank while Kerala had the lowest rank in terms of FAI among all the states in the country. On the other hand, Punjab had the highest rank, whereas Rajasthan occupied the lowest rank in terms of IFS during the study period. With regards to IFA, Kerala had the highest rank whereas Bihar occupied the lowest rank among all the states during the study period. In case of FSI, Punjab and Haryana had the first and second positions, whereas Bihar had the lowest position among all the states at national level. It is seen that high development in the area of agricultural inputs, irrigation, infrastructure, socio-economic factors, climatic factors, research and technology have positive impact on FSI at state level and national level. Overall from the data it is found that there is widespread variation and instability in terms of having food availability, food stability and food accessibility among all the states.

CHAPTER 11

Agricultural Productivity, Food Security and Climate Change
A State-Level Analysis

Sustainable Energy + Food Security + Healthy Environment = Full
Employment + Better Future

—**Phil Harding**

Introduction

Climatic variables also have an impact on food security per se in
different states of the country as they influence the growth of the
agriculture sector and make farm operations difficult, mainly due
to the unpredictability of weather and climate conditions. Change
in the climatic factors results in drying of rivers, loss in biodiversity,
declining water resources, falling water tables, decreasing agricultural
productivity and largely influencing the socio-economic conditions
of the human society. Similarly, high rainfall situations also cause

decline in agricultural land and agricultural productivity, and adversely affect human health which leads to decrease in labour productivity in agriculture, loss of biodiversity and socio-economic conditions of the human society are affected. Therefore, studying the aspect of climate variability in different states of the country is pivotal.

Climate change also has an economic impact on agriculture in terms of changes in crop productivity, profitability and value of output. In this case, the magnitude of climate-induced changes across geographical distribution may impact the ability to increase food production in order to meet the demands of the population. Climate change could thus have far-reaching impact on the patterns of trade among nations, development and food security (Chatterjee 2010).

The fluctuations in agricultural development arise due to huge regional diversities in agro-climatic environment, resource endowment and growth of the population. These regional disparities have widened over the years and significantly across the economy at state-level. Therefore, it is very important to deeply look into the impact of climate change on agricultural productivity and food security across different states. The main objective of the present chapter is to examine the impact of climate change as well as non-climatic variables on agricultural productivity, value of output and food security at state-level.

State-Level Regression Results

Impact of Climatic and Non-climatic Variables on Agricultural Productivity

The impact of the climatic and non-climatic variables on major food grain crops productivity as well as non-food grain crops productivity in the selected states during the study period from 1980–1981 to 2014–2015 has been analysed by using the state-level panel data. The state-level panel data regression model is as follows:

$$(\text{CSP})_{it} = \beta_0 + \beta_1(\text{RAIN})_{it} + \beta_2(\text{MINT})_{it} + \beta_3(\text{MAXT})_{it} +$$
$$\beta_4(\text{FERC})_{it} + \beta_5(\text{GIA/NSA})_{it} + \beta_6(\text{CI})_{it} + \beta_7(\text{FAGSA})_{it} + \quad (1)$$
$$\beta_8(\text{RL})_{it} + \beta_9(\text{PD})_{it} + \beta_{10}(\text{LR})_{it} + Ui,$$

where CSP is crop specific/crop sector productivity; i = state, t = time; RAIN, MINT and MAXT are average annual rainfall, average annual minimum and annual maximum temperature; FERC, GIA/NSA, CI, FAGSA, RL, PD and LR are per hectare consumption of fertilizer, ratio of gross irrigated area to net sown area, cropping intensity, ratio of forest area to gross sown area, road length per 1,000 population, population density and literacy rate respectively; β_0 is constant coefficient term; β_1 to β_{10} are regression coefficients for respective independent variables; and Ui is stochastic error term.

Productivity of Food Grain Crops

The regression results of above equation (1) in case of food grain productivity and its component crops during the study period, that is, from 1980–1981 to 2014–2015 are presented in Table 11.1. The regression results highlight that the factors such as maximum temperature, cropping intensity, population density and literacy rate had positive and statistically significant impact on productivity of wheat whereas rainfall and per hectare gross irrigated area had positive but insignificant impact on wheat productivity. On the other hand, productivity of wheat was negatively affected by minimum temperature, per hectare consumption of fertilizers and forest area during the study period. The value of R-square was 0.7048 which means that around 70 per cent variation in productivity of wheat is explained by the climatic and non-climatic factors during the study period. The magnitude of F-value indicates that the given model is a good fit for wheat productivity. VIF between independent variables is 3.88, which implies that there is absence of multicollinearity in the regression model.

Minimum temperature, annual rainfall, per hectare consumption of fertilizers, gross irrigated area, road length and literacy rate had positive and significant impact on rice productivity, while cropping intensity had positive but insignificant impact on rice productivity during the study period. On the other hand, maximum temperature, forest area and population density had negative and statistically significant impact on rice productivity during the study period. The model explained more than 65 per cent variation in case of rice productivity by the climatic and non-climatic factors during the study period. The F-test

Table 11.1 Regression Results of Productivity of Food Grain and Its Component Crops

Dependent Variables	Regression Values	Independent Variables										
		MAXT	MINT	RAIN	FERC	GIA/NSA	CI	FA_GSA	RL	PD	LR	Constant
Wheat	Coefficient	6.231	−2.8592	0.0204	−0.2594	0.0585	1.5079	−0.1304	−0.0001	0.1597	0.4237	−14.5000
	t-value	13.33	−10.1200	0.4200	−7.8900	1.5800	8.3500	−5.7100	0.0000	3.2700	4.8300	−7.4100
	p-value	0.000	0.0000	0.6730	0.0000	0.1140	0.0000	0.0000	0.9980	0.0010	0.0000	0.0000
	R-squared = 0.7048	Adj. R-squared =0.6990				$F_{(10, 514)} =$ 122.70	Prob. $> F = 0.000$		No. of obs. = 525		Mean VIF = 3.88	
Rice	Coefficient	−2.5329	1.7207	0.1450	0.3299	0.1288	0.1409	−0.1775	0.1887	−0.131	0.1326	8.0388
	t-value	−6.5900	7.4000	3.6400	12.1900	4.1800	0.9300	−9.2900	4.7100	−3.320	1.8400	4.9700
	p-value	0.0000	0.0000	0.0000	0.0000	0.0000	0.3510	0.0000	0.0000	0.0010	0.0660	0.0000
	R-squared = 0.6506	Adj. R-squared = 0.6442				$F_{(10,549)} =$ 102.21	Prob. $> F = 0.000$		No. of obs. = 560		Mean VIF = 3.88	
Cereals	Coefficient	−1.0924	0.4959	0.0896	0.2461	0.2401	0.6197	−0.0399	0.1441	0.0127	0.2277	3.0377
	t-value	−3.9000	2.9300	3.0900	12.4900	10.700	5.6300	−2.8700	4.9400	0.4400	4.3400	2.5800
	p-value	0.0000	0.0040	0.0020	0.0000	0.0000	0.0000	0.0040	0.0000	0.6590	0.0000	0.0100
	R-squared = 0.7921	Adj. R-squared =0.7883				$F_{(10,549)} =$ 209.19	Prob. $> F = 0.0000$		No. of obs. = 560		Mean VIF = 3.88	

(Continued)

Table 11.1 Continued

Dependent Variables	Regression Values	MAXT	MINT	RAIN	FERC	GIA/NSA	CI	FA_GSA	RL	PD	LR	Constant
Coarse cereals	Coefficient	-0.1717	-1.7518	0.0509	0.3624	0.3418	0.0395	0.2087	-0.0338	0.0971	0.6539	5.6564
	t-value	-0.3300	-5.5000	0.9300	9.7800	8.1000	0.1900	7.9700	-0.6200	1.8000	6.6200	2.5500
	p-value	0.7440	0.0000	0.3500	0.0000	0.0000	0.8490	0.0000	0.5380	0.0730	0.0000	0.0110
	R-squared = 0.6062	Adj. R-squared = 0.5991				$F(10, 549) = 84.52$	Prob. > F = 0.000			No. of obs. = 560		Mean VIF = 3.88	
Pulses	Coefficient	2.6749	-1.2620	0.0875	0.0584	-0.026	0.6377	0.0396	0.0248	0.3201	0.1464	-5.6149
	t-value	6.8900	-5.3700	2.1800	2.1400	-0.830	4.1800	2.0500	0.6100	8.0300	2.0100	-3.4400
	p-value	0.0000	0.0000	0.0300	0.0330	0.4080	0.0000	0.0410	0.5400	0.0000	0.0450	0.0010
	R-squared = 0.4593	Adj. R-squared = 0.4495				$F(10, 549) = 46.64$	Prob. > F = 0.000			No. of obs. = 560		Mean VIF = 3.88	
Food grain	Coefficient	-1.3005	0.3380	0.0798	0.2310	0.2004	0.8408	-0.0464	0.1367	0.0879	0.2419	2.8374
	t-value	-4.6300	1.9900	2.7400	11.6800	8.9000	7.6200	-3.3200	4.6700	3.0400	4.5900	2.4000
	p-value	0.0000	0.0470	0.0060	0.0000	0.0000	0.0000	0.0010	0.0000	0.0020	0.0000	0.0170
	R-squared = 0.8128	Adj. R-squared = 0.8094				$F(10, 549) = 238.40$	Prob. > F = 0.000			No. of obs. = 560		Mean VIF = 3.88	

Source: Author's calculation.

value indicates that the given model is a good fit for productivity in case of rice crop. VIF between independent variables is 3.88, which implies that there is absence of multicollinearity in the regression model.

The values of R-square is 0.7921 which means that the explanation power of model is around 79 per cent in cereals productivity during the study period by the climatic and non-climatic factors. The magnitude of F-value indicates that the given model is a good fit for cereals productivity. The result shows that the climatic variables, that is, minimum temperature and rainfall, and the non-climatic variables, that is, consumption of fertilizer, gross irrigated area, cropping intensity, road length and literacy rate had positive and significant impact on cereals productivity whereas population density had positive impact on productivity of cereal crops during the study period. Maximum temperature and forest are negatively associated with cereals productivity.

The regression results also highlight that per hectare consumption of fertilizers, gross irrigated area, forest area and literacy rate had positively and statistically significant impact on coarse cereals productivity, whereas rainfall, cropping intensity and population density had positive but insignificant impact on the coarse cereals productivity. Minimum temperature had negative and significant impact on coarse cereals productivity. On the other hand, maximum temperature and road length had negative but insignificant impact on the coarse cereals productivity. The value of R-square was 0.6062 means that around 61 per cent variation in coarse cereals productivity is explained by the variation in climatic and non-climatic factors during the study period. The magnitude of F-value indicates that the given model is a good fit for coarse cereals productivity. VIF between independent variables is 3.88, which implies that there is absence of multicollinearity in the regression model.

In case of pulses, maximum temperature, rainfall, consumption of fertilizer, cropping intensity, forest area, population density and literacy rate had positive and significant impact on productivity of pulses, whereas road length had positive impact at insignificant level. Minimum temperature had negative and significant impact on pulses productivity, whereas gross irrigated area had negative impact on productivity of pulses at the low level of significance. The explanation power of the model (value of R-square) is around 0.46 during the study period in case pulses productivity.

The panel data regression results regarding food grain productivity at state-level indicate that the factors such as fertilizer consumption, gross irrigated area, cropping intensity, road length, population density, literacy rate, annual rainfall and minimum temperature had positive and statistically significant impact on the food grain productivity during the study period. Similarly, maximum temperature and forest area had negative and significant impact on the food grain productivity during the study period. The value of R-square is very high, that is, 0.8128 which means that the model describes more than 81 per cent variation in food grain productivity by the variation in climatic and non-climatic factors during the study period. In other words, the impact of climatic and non-climatic factors on food grain productivity is highly significant during the study period. Overall, it can be concluded that climatic and non-climatic factors affect the crop-wise productivity across major states during the study period. F-value indicates that the given model is a good fit for food grain productivity and VIF value implies the absence of multicollinearity in the regression model.

Productivity of Non-food Grain Crops

In the case of non-food grain crops, it is seen that the performance of non-food grain crops is directly related to climatic and non-climatic variables at state-level. Table 11.2 shows the results of panel data multiple regression equation (1) for non-food grain crop productivity. The result reveals that factors such as fertilizers consumption, road length, literacy rate, rainfall and minimum temperature have positive and statistically significant impact on sugarcane productivity during the study period. Similarly, population density and maximum temperature had negative but insignificant impact, whereas cropping intensity and area under forest had negative and significant impact on the sugarcane productivity during the study period. The value of R-square is 0.7657, which implies that more than 76 per cent variation in sugarcane productivity is explained by the variation in climatic and non-climatic factors during the study period. The F-value reveals that

Table 11.2 Regression Results of Non-food Grain Crops Productivity

Dependent Variables	Regression Values	MAXT	MINT	RAIN	FERC	GIA/NSA	CI	FA_NSA	RL	PD	LR	Constant
						Independent Variables						
Sugarcane	Coefficient	-0.3375	2.5603	0.1182	0.0638	0.1305	-0.8683	-0.166	0.0840	-0.0553	0.2222	6.9964
	t-value	-1.0700	13.3700	3.6100	2.8600	5.1500	-6.9800	-10.540	2.5500	-1.7000	3.7400	5.2500
	p-value	0.2870	0.0000	0.0000	0.0040	0.0000	0.0000	0.0000	0.0110	0.0890	0.0000	0.0000
	R-squared = 0.7657		Adj. R-squared = 0.7614		$F_{(10, 549)}$ = 179.40		Prob. > F = 0.000		No. of obs. = 560		Mean VIF = 3.88	
Oilseeds	Coefficient	0.9039	0.6731	-0.0552	0.0021	0.2355	-0.4883	-0.1032	-0.0030	-0.0425	0.5696	1.6285
	t-value	2.3600	2.9100	-1.3900	0.0800	7.6700	-3.2400	-5.4200	-0.0800	-1.0800	7.9300	1.0100
	p-value	0.0190	0.0040	0.1640	0.9360	0.0000	0.0010	0.0000	0.9390	0.2800	0.0000	0.3130
	R-squared = 0.5902		Adj. R-squared =0.5827		$F_{(10,549)}$ = 79.07		Prob. > F = 0.0000		No. of obs. = 560		Mean VIF = 3.88	
Cotton	Coefficient	-1.0170	0.9827	0.0262	0.1915	0.4592	0.0757	-0.0362	0.0510	-0.3293	0.5816	2.5564
	t-value	-1.7200	2.7400	0.4300	4.5900	9.6700	0.3300	-1.2300	0.8300	-5.4100	5.2400	1.0300
	p-value	0.0860	0.0060	0.6690	0.0000	0.0000	0.7450	0.2190	0.4090	0.0000	0.0000	0.3060
	R-squared = 0.4896		Adj. R-squared =0.4803		$F_{(10,549)}$ = 52.66		Prob. > F = 0.0000		No. of obs. = 560		Mean VIF = 3.88	

Source: Author's calculation.

the given model is a good fit for sugarcane productivity and the VIF value implies the absence of multicollinearity in the regression model.

For oilseeds productivity, it is seen that the factors such as gross irrigated area, literacy rate, minimum and maximum temperature had positive and statistically significant impact during the study period. Oilseeds productivity was positively affected by per hectare of consumption of fertilizers but it was not significant during the same period. It is also negatively affected by rainfall, road length and population density. On the other hand, cropping intensity had negative and significant impact on oilseeds productivity during the study period. However, around 59 per cent variation in oilseeds productivity is explained by the climatic and non-climatic factors during the study period. The F-value shows that the given model is a good fit for oilseeds productivity.

Regarding cotton productivity, the determinants such as per hectare consumption of fertilizers, gross irrigated area, literacy rate and minimum temperature had positive and statistically significant impact on cotton productivity whereas rainfall, cropping intensity and road length had positive but insignificant impact on cotton productivity during the study period. The variables such as maximum temperature and forest area had negative but insignificant impact on cotton productivity during the same period. It is also observed by the value of R-square that nearly 49 per cent variation in cotton productivity is explained by the variation in climatic and non-climatic factors during the study period. From the above analysis, it is concluded that the climatic and non-climatic factors had crop-specific effects on the non-food grain crops productivity.

Impact of Climatic and Non-climatic Variables on Value of Output by Agriculture

The impact of climatic and non-climatic variables on state-wise value of output by the agricultural sector and its crop components during the study period from 1990–1991 to 2014–2015 has been discussed using the following regression equation by using panel data:

$$(VAO)_{it} = \beta_0 + \beta_1(CI)_{it} + \beta_2(FERC)_{it} + \beta_3(GIA/NSA)_{it} +$$
$$\beta_4(FAGSA)_{it} + \beta_5(RL)_{it} + \beta_6(LR)_{it} + \beta_7(RAIN)_{it} + \beta_8(MINT)_{it} + (2)$$
$$\beta_9(MAXT)_{it} + Ui,$$

where VAO is per hectare value of output by agricultural sector and its crop sector, and other independent variables are as same as discussed above. To avoid multicollinearity, we have changed the form of all variables, that is, dependent as well as independent variables. The regression results of equation (2) are given in Table 11.3.

The results reveal that the factors such as per hectare consumption of fertilizers and maximum temperature had positive and statistically significant impact, while literacy rate and rainfall had positive but insignificant impact on value of output from agriculture during the study period. On the other hand, road length, literacy rate and minimum temperature had negative and significant impact on value of output from agriculture. However, the variables such as gross irrigated area, forest area and cropping intensity had negative but insignificant impact on the value of output from agriculture during the study period. The value of R-square shows that more than 65 per cent variation in value of output of agriculture is explained by the climatic and non-climatic factors during the study period. A high F-value for value of output from agriculture indicates that the given model is a good fit. Moreover, VIF value of 3.47 indicates absence of multicollinearity in the regression model.

In case of value of output of wheat, it was found that increasing literacy rate, rainfall and maximum temperature had positive and statistically significant impact whereas cropping intensity had positive but insignificant impact on wheat value of output during the study period. On the other hand, the factors such as per hectare consumption of fertilizer, forest area and road length had negative and statistically significant impact on value of output of wheat, whereas gross irrigated area had negative impact but statistically insignificant impact on value of output of wheat. Around 65 per cent variation in value of output from wheat is explained by the climatic and non-climatic factors during the study period.

Table 11.3 Regression Results of Value of Output from Agriculture during 1990–1991 to 2014–2015

Dependent Variables	Regression Values	Independent Variables									
		CI	FERC	GIA/NSA	FAGSA	RL	LR	RAIN	MINT	MAXT	Constant
VO Agriculture	Coefficient	-0.2533	0.2460	-0.0826	-0.0396	-0.1455	0.2992	0.0603	-0.7726	7.4282	-9.1490
	t-value	-1.1300	5.0200	-1.5400	-1.2300	-2.2200	1.8500	0.9600	-2.1900	11.4100	-3.5100
	p-value	0.2590	0.0000	0.1240	0.2190	0.0270	0.0650	0.3390	0.0290	0.0000	0.0000
	R-squared = 0.6504			Adj. R-squared = 0.6423			F (9, 390) = 80.62	Prob. > F = 0.000		No. of obs. = 400	Mean VIF = 3.47
VO Wheat	Coefficient	0.3236	-1.2167	-0.5112	-1.0956	-2.2802	4.8905	0.7347	-25.1565	29.6670	-30.1788
	t-value	0.2700	-4.7500	-1.8100	-6.6700	-6.7900	5.3000	2.0300	-12.0900	7.7000	-2.0200
	p-value	0.7870	0.0000	0.0710	0.0000	0.0000	0.0000	0.0440	0.0000	0.0000	0.0440
	R-squared = 0.653			Adj. R-squared = 0.644			F (9, 390) = 59.06	Prob. > F = 0.000		No. of obs. = 400	Mean VIF = 3.47
VO Rice	Coefficient	3.0961	1.1910	-0.0549	0.1187	-0.2141	-2.732	0.4869	4.0954	1.3301	-16.1743
	t-value	6.3700	11.2100	-0.4700	1.6000	-1.5100	-7.790	3.5600	5.3500	0.9400	-2.8600
	p-value	0.0000	0.0000	0.6370	0.1890	0.1330	0.0000	0.0000	0.0000	0.3470	0.0040
	R-squared = 0.5768			Adj. R-squared = 0.5670			F (9, 390) = 59.06	Prob. > F = 0.000		No. of obs. = 400	Mean VIF = 3.47

Source: Author's calculation.

Concerning the value of output from rice crop, the factors such as per hectare consumption of fertilizer, cropping intensity, annual rainfall and minimum temperature had positive and significant impact, whereas forest area and maximum temperature had positive but insignificant impact on value of output of rice. On the other hand, literacy rate had negative and statistically significant impact on value of output of rice whereas forest area and road length had negative but insignificant impact on the value of output of rice during the study period. The value of R-square is 0.5768, which means that around 57 per cent variation in value of output of rice is explained by the climatic and non-climatic variables during the study period. The magnitude of the F-value implies that the model is good fit for value of output of rice and VIF value indicates the absence of multicollinearity in the regression model.

Overall, the above analysis has shown that the climatic variables, that is, annual rainfall, average minimum temperature and average maximum temperature as well as non-climatic variables such as cropping intensity, per hectare consumption of fertilizers, gross irrigated area, forest area, road length and literacy rate have influenced the value of output from wheat, rice and value of output from agriculture during the study period.

Impact of Climatic and Non-climatic Variables on FSI

The impact of climatic factors and non-climatic factors on FSI and its components, FAI, IFS and IFA has been estimated by the following panel data multiple regression equations during the study period 1980–1981 to 2014–2015:

$$(\text{FSI})_{it} = \beta_0 + \beta_1(\text{CI})_{it} + \beta_2(\text{RL})_{it} + \beta_3(\text{GIA/NSA})_{it} + \beta_4(\text{FAGSA})_{it} + \beta_5(\text{FERC})_{it}$$

$$+ \beta_6(\text{LR})_{it} + \beta_7(\text{UR})_{it} + \beta_8(\text{PD})_{it} + \beta_9(\text{RAIN})_{it} + \beta_{10}(\text{MINT})_{it} + \beta_{11}(\text{MAXT})_{it} + Ui$$

$$(\text{FAI})_{it} = \beta_0 + \beta_1(\text{CI})_{it} + \beta_2(\text{RL})_{it} + \beta_3(\text{GIA/NSA})_{it} + \beta_4(\text{FAGSA})_{it} + \beta_5(\text{FERC})_{it}$$

$$+\beta_6(LR)_{it}+\beta_7(UR)_{it}+\beta_8(PD)_{it}+\beta_9\,(RAIN)_{it}$$
$$+\beta_{10}(MINT)_{it}+\beta_{11}(MAXT)_{it}+\,Ui$$

$$(IFS)_{it}=\beta_0+\beta_1(CI)_{it}+\beta_2(RL)_{it}+\beta_3(GIA/NSA)_{it}+\beta_4(FAGSA)_{it}$$
$$+\beta_5(FERC)_{it}$$

$$+\beta_6(LR)_{it}+\beta_7(UR)_{it}+\beta_8(PD)_{it}+\beta_9(RAIN)_{it}+\beta_{10}(MINT)_{it}+\beta_{11}$$
$$(MAXT)_{it}+\,Ui\,(3)$$

$$(IFA)_{it}=\beta_0+\beta_1(CI)_{it}+\beta_2(RL)_{it}+\beta_3(GIA/NSA)_{it}+\beta_4(FAGSA)_{it}$$
$$+\beta_5(FERC)_{it}$$

$$+\beta_6(LR)_{it}+\beta_7(UR)_{it}+\beta_8(PD)_{it}+\beta_9(RAIN)_{it}+\beta_{10}(MINT)_{it}+\beta_{11}$$
$$(MAXT)_{it}+\,Ui,$$

where FSI, FAI, IFS, IFA are food security index, food availability index, index of food stability and index of food accessibility respectively; RAIN, MAXT and MINT are average annual rainfall, annual maximum temperature and annual minimum temperature respectively; CI, GIA/NSA and FERC are cropping intensity, gross irrigated area as per cent of net sown area and per hectare fertilizer consumption respectively; RL, LR, UR and PD are road length per thousand population, literacy rate, urbanization and population density respectively. The form of dependent and independent variable has been transformed to avoid the problem of multicollinearity.

Table 11.4 presents the results of regression equation (3). The regression results reveal that the factors such as cropping intensity, road length, gross irrigated area, forest area, per hectare consumption of fertilizer and literacy rate had positive and statistically significant impact on FSI during the study period, while, average annual maximum temperature had negative and significant impact on FSI. Population density and minimum temperature had positive but insignificant impact on FSI during the same period. Urbanization had negative and statistically significant impact while rainfall had negative but insignificant impact on FSI. From the results it is perceived that any increment in rainfall had negative but insignificant impact on FSI during the study period. The value of R-square is 0.6012, which denotes that more than 60 per cent variation in FSI is explained by the climatic and non-climatic factors during the study period. On the

Table 11.4 *Regression Results of Food Security Index and Its Components Index*

		Independent Variables											
D V	*Regression Values*	*CI*	*RL*	*GIANSA*	*FAGSA*	*FERC*	*L R*	*UR*	*PD*	*RAIN*	*MINT*	*MAXT*	*Constant*
Food Security Index	Coefficient	0.315	0.072	0.730	0.041	0.032	0.737	–0.188	0.046	–0.033	0.046	–0.996	–8.964
	t-value	3.120	2.640	3.570	2.980	1.670	13.870	–6.200	1.620	–1.240	0.280	–3.880	–8.310
	P-value	0.002	0.009	0.000	0.003	0.095	0.000	0.000	0.105	0.214	0.776	0.000	0.000
	R-squared = 0.6012		Adj. R-squared = 0.5932		F (11,548) = 75.1		Prob. > F = 0.0000		No. of obs. = 560		Mean VIF = 4.71		
Food Stability Index	Coefficient	0.450	–0.004	0.156	0.103	0.003	1.477	–0.277	0.130	–0.100	–0.289	1.608	–13.970
	t-value	2.770	–0.080	4.750	4.670	0.090	17.320	–5.700	2.840	–2.370	–1.110	3.910	–8.080
	p-value	0.006	0.934	0.000	0.000	0.925	0.000	0.000	0.005	0.018	0.268	0.000	0.000
	R-squared = 0.648		Adj. R-squared = 0.6409		F (11,548) = 91.72		Prob. > F = 0.0000		No. of obs. = 560		Mean VIF = 4.71		
Food Availability Index	Coefficient	0.863	–0.002	0.000	–0.003	0.054	0.029	–0.036	–0.101	0.073	0.916	–0.330	–6.641
	t-value	3.990	–0.030	0.010	–0.120	1.320	0.260	–0.560	–1.650	1.290	2.640	–0.600	–2.880
	p-value	0.000	0.978	0.992	0.907	0.000	0.796	0.577	0.099	0.199	0.009	0.548	0.004
	R-squared = 0.082		Adj. R-squared = 0.0639		F (11,548) = 4.47		Prob. > F = 0.0000		No. of obs. = 560		Mean VIF = 4.71		
Food Accessibility Index	Coefficient	–0.369	0.253	0.091	0.002	0.014	0.860	–0.304	0.129	–0.052	–0.631	2.028	–7.727
	t-value	–3.860	9.830	4.720	0.120	0.810	17.140	–10.650	4.790	–2.070	–4.120	8.380	–7.590
	p-value	0.000	0.000	0.000	0.907	0.421	0.000	0.000	0.000	0.039	0.000	0.000	0.000
	R-squared = 0.7066		Adj. R-squared = 0.7008		F (11,548) = 120.01		Prob. > F = 0.0000		No. of obs. = 560		Mean VIF = 4.71		

Sources: Author's calculation.

other hand, the value of F-statistics implies that the model is good fit for regression result. Similarly, VIF value is 4.71 which reveals that there is absence of multicollinearity in regression model.

Considering FAI, it is found that cropping intensity, per hectare consumption of fertilizer and average minimum temperature had positive and significant impact, whereas gross irrigated area, literacy rate and rainfall had positive but insignificant impact on IFA during the study period. The variables such as road length, forest area, urbanization and maximum temperature had negative but insignificant impact on FAI, whereas population density had negative but significant on FAI during the same period.

Concerning IFS, the regression result describes that cropping intensity, gross irrigated area, forest area, literacy rate, population density and maximum temperature had positive and significant impact whereas per hectare consumption fertilizer had positive but insignificant impact on IFS during the study period. Urbanization and rainfall had negative and significant impact, whereas road length and minimum temperature had negative but insignificant impact on IFS during the study period. The regression model also highlights that around 65 per cent variation in IFS is explained by the climatic and non-climatic factors during the study period.

Regarding IFA, the variables road length, gross irrigated area, literacy rate, population density, and maximum temperature had positive and significant impact, whereas forest area, per hectare consumption of fertilizer had positive but insignificant impact on IFA during the study period. Cropping intensity, urbanization, rainfall and minimum temperature had negative but significant impact on IFA during the study period. The value of R-square is 0.7066, which means that more than 70 per cent variation in IFA is explained by the climatic and non-climatic factors during the study period. The magnitude of F-value implies that the given model is a good fit for food accessibility index and the VIF (4.17) indicates that absence of multicollinearity in the regression model.

The regression result indicates that the effects of climatic variables and non-climatic variables on FSI as well as its components have mixed trends, but most of the parameters impact food security as expected during the study period.

Conclusion of the Chapter

The state-level regression results indicate that food grain and non-food grain productivity has been affected by the climatic variables as well as non-climatic variables during the entire study period. However, the regression results vary across specific crops because every crop has its own climatic conditions. The panel data regression indicates that climatic variables, that is, annual rainfall, average minimum temperature and average maximum temperature as well as non-climatic variables such as cropping intensity, per hectare consumption of fertilizers, gross irrigated area, forest area, road length and literacy rate have influenced positively as well as negatively the value of output from agriculture during the study period.

Most of the variables, namely cropping intensity, road length, gross irrigated area, forest area, fertilizer consumption and literacy rate in the regression model were found to have a positive and significant impact on food security index, whereas urbanization was found to have a negative impact on FSI at a low level of significance in selected different states during the study period in India. The impact of maximum temperature on FSI was found negative and significant. This indicates the serious implications of food security. In sum, it is seen that impact of the climatic variables and non-climatic variables on FSI and it component index varied across the selected major 16 states during the study period.

CHAPTER 12

Concluding Synthesis

Indian agriculture is the most vulnerable to climate changes. The variability of climate have serious implications on agricultural productivity at crop level and food security of the nation as a whole. Due to changes in some environmental factors such as temperature and rainfall, crop growth is affected immensely. These factors can affect crop growth and agricultural productivity, and in turn, food security situation in the economy, positively as well as negatively, depending on regional or geographical location and status of socio-economic development (Greg et al. 2011).

Therefore, this book analyses the emerging trends of agriculture, food security and climatic variables at national as well as state level in India. Moreover, it explores the impact of climatic and non-climatic variables on agricultural/crop productivity and value of output from agriculture. It also touches upon the aspect of food security and its components at national and state level in the last 35 years. The present chapter aims to synthesize the work that has been done in the preceding chapters and present the conclusions obtained from the empirical analysis.

Agricultural/Crop Productivity and Climate Change

The performance of the agriculture sector has not been very impressive in the country since its independence. The share of agriculture in the total GDP was 52 per cent in 1951–1952 which sharply decreased to 17.6 per cent in 2014–2015 at national level. It has been experienced that growth rate of non-agriculture sector is always higher than the growth rate of the agriculture sector at national level. It is found that growth rates of food grain crops (i.e., rice, wheat, coarse cereals, pulses) and non-food grain crops (i.e., oilseeds, sugarcane, cotton, tobacco, jute and mesta) have widespread variations in terms of area, production and productivity in the country. Moreover, majority of farmers in India are small and marginal, having small size of land holdings. These small sizes of land holdings are operationally non-viable because the high division of land restricts and hinders the diffusion of modern technology in agriculture. As a result, agricultural productivity decreases and disguised unemployment increases due to overmanning at national level. In case of climatic variables at national level, it is observed that the annual rainfall decreased during the study period. The trend value of annual rainfall have shown declining trends with a magnitude of –1.366 during the study period. The annual minimum temperature increased by about 1 °C during 1950–1951 to 2014–2015 in India. It is also observed that the annual maximum temperature increased at the rate of 0.016 per year during the entire study period at national level. Climatic variables have directly affected the productivity of various crops in Indian agriculture. It is estimated by Ranuzzi and Srivastava (2012) that if the temperature goes up to 20 °C, then rice production will be decreased by almost one tonne/hectare. Similarly, with 10 °C rise in mean temperature, wheat yield will decrease by 7MT or around $1.5 billion at current prices per year in India.

The regression results also revealed a similar pattern whereby climatic as well as non-climatic factors influenced the agriculture sector in India in terms of crop-specific productivity, production and value of output from agriculture during the study period. The effect of climatic variables as well as non-climatic variables had been mixed during the study period. However, the national level regression results showed that the effect of climatic factors such as annual rainfall and maximum temperature had a positive impact, whereas minimum temperature had negative and significant impact on food grain production during the pre-reform and study periods at national level. It is clear that high fluctuations in rainfall and temperature have affected food grain production during recent years in the country. Further, factors such as size of average land holdings, direct institutional credit for agriculture, improved irrigation facilities, consumption of fertilizers, cropping intensity, education and climatic variables have been found as the main determinants of agricultural development at national level.

Regarding productivity of food grain crops, the regression results revealed that annual rainfall had positive and significant impact on productivity of food grain crops whereas minimum temperature had negative but significant impact on productivity of food grain crops during the study period at national level. During pre-reform period, the climatic factors such as rainfall and maximum temperature had positive and significant impact on productivity of food grain crops whereas minimum temperature had negative but significant impact on productivity of food grain at national level. During the post-reform period, it was found that rainfall had positive and significant impact whereas minimum temperature had negative but significant impact on productivity of food grains. On the other hand, the impact of average maximum temperature on food grain productivity during the economic reform period was found negative and significant. Moreover, other empirical result findings of food grain crops productivity also showed that any increment in maximum temperature had negative impact on rice, cereals, coarse cereals, food grain and cotton productivity during the study period and the impact was also statistically significant (Geethalakshmi et al. 2011; Kalra et al. 2008), while productivity of wheat, pulses, oilseeds, sugarcane, jute and mesta was positively affected due to increase in maximum temperature. However, wheat, coarse cereals, pulses, oilseeds, sugarcane, jute and mesta productivity was negatively affected due to increase in minimum temperature (Kumar & Parikh 2001), while rice, cereals, food grain and cotton productivity was affected positively due to changes in minimum temperature. Any increment in rainfall had a positive relationship with productivity of all crops.

Considering non-climatic variables, the regression results highlighted that the capital formation in agriculture and gross irrigated area had positive and significant impact on productivity of food grains.

Variables such as number of tractors, agricultural labour and literacy rate had positive impact but forest area and fertilizer consumption had negative and insignificant impact on food grain productivity throughout the study period at national level. The result also showed that the non-climatic variables such as gross capital formation, literacy rate and consumption of fertilizer had negative and insignificant impact on productivity of rice whereas agricultural labour, number of tractors, gross irrigated area had positive but insignificant impact on rice productivity at national level. Forest area had negative and significant impact on the productivity of rice crop at national level. Further, the variables namely, gross capital formation in agriculture, literacy rate, agricultural labour, number of tractors, consumption of fertilizers and gross irrigated area had positive and insignificant impact, whereas forest area had negative impact on the wheat productivity during the study period at national level.

Gross capital formation in agriculture and gross irrigated area had positive and significant impact on pulses productivity during the study period at national level. The regression results also show that good rainfall condition had a positive impact whereas consumption of fertilizers and forest area had negative impact on oilseeds productivity during study period at national level. Maximum temperature, agricultural labour, number of tractors and gross irrigated area had positive and insignificant whereas minimum temperature, gross capital formation in agriculture, literacy rate had negative and insignificant impact on oilseeds productivity during the study period at national level. In case of sugarcane, variable such as consumption of fertilizers had positive impact on productivity of sugarcane during 1980–1981 to 2014–2015. Variables such as rainfall, maximum temperature, tractors, forest area and gross irrigated area had positive and insignificant impact, whereas minimum temperature, government expenditure, literacy rate and agricultural labour had negative and insignificant impact on the sugarcane productivity at national level. On the other hand, maximum temperature had positive impact whereas minimum temperature had negative and significant impact on the jute and mesta productivity at national level. Similarly, rainfall, agricultural labour, consumption of fertilizers had positive and insignificant impact, whereas gross capital formation, literacy rate, tractors, forest area gross irrigated area had negative and insignificant impact on jute and mesta productivity at national level. Productivity of cotton was affected positively by rainfall, minimum temperature, agricultural labour, number of tractors and gross irrigated during the study period. On the other hand, maximum temperature, expenditure on agriculture, literacy rate, consumption of fertilizers and forest area had negative and insignificant impact on cotton productivity in India during the study period.

Value of Output from Agriculture and Climate Change

The impact of rainfall when regressed on value of output revealed a positive and statistically significant relationship between value of output from agriculture sector and its major components, namely, rice, cereals, food grain, pulses, oilseeds and cotton during the study period. Further in case of wheat and coarse cereals, it had positive impact although statistically insignificant. On the other hand, annual rainfall had a negative and insignificant impact on value of output of sugarcane and jute and mesta during the entire study period. Average minimum temperature had negative and significant impact on value of output from the agriculture sector across its crop sectors except rice, cotton, coarse cereals, jute and mesta. Further, the impact of maximum temperature on value of output from rice and cotton was found negative and significant at national level during the study period while it has positive impact in case of other crops.

In case of value of output from coarse cereals, jute and mesta, rainfall had a negative and insignificant impact. The results indicate that average annual maximum temperature had a statistically significant and positive impact on value of output from the agriculture sector and its components except cotton. These regression results on climatic factors indicate that the value of output from the agriculture sector is being affected by climatic factors in both ways; most of the factors have positive impact and some have negative impact in case of food grain crops, non-food grain crops and on value of output by agriculture sector during the study period. However, in case of non-climatic factors, it was found that gross irrigated area and gross capital formation in agriculture had positive and statistically significant impact on value of output from agriculture during the study period. On the other hand, consumption of fertilizers and area under forest had positive but insignificant impact, whereas number of tractor had negative but statistically significant impact on the value of output from agriculture. In the case of value of output from cereals, gross irrigated area had positive and significant impact on this crop. On the other hand, forest area had negative and statistically significant impact on the value of cereals. Other variables had an insignificant impact. Gross irrigated area and gross capital formation in the agriculture sector had positive impact on value of output in food grain during the study period, whereas forest area had negative and significant impact on value of food grain output. In the case of value of output from oilseeds, gross irrigated area had positive and statistically significant impact, whereas forest area had negative and statistically significant impact on value of oilseeds.

Food Security and Climate Change at National Level

The trends of population and food grains both were positive, but the trends of population were more progressive which has been the major cause of slow growth rate of per capita net availability of food grain production over the years. Moreover, the per capita net availability of nutritious food items such as milk, fish, eggs, fruits and vegetables went up substantially during the study period at national level. On the other hand, the trends of buffer stocks of food grain crops highly fluctuated during the study period at national level. Also, it is a fact that increasing agriculture production can achieve food security as well as improve the overall income of farmers which is in sync with honourable prime minister's vision of doubling farmers' income at national level. Growth in the agriculture sector will improve the level of production and food security and its linkages with other sectors will enhance overall economic growth.

The trend of food security scores in India reveals that it increased from 15 in 1980–1981 to 65 in 2014–2015. Food stability as well as food availability indices are the major contributors towards enhanced food security during the study period. It is found that FSI was 0.218 in 1980–1981 and increased to 0.721 in 2014–2015. CAGR of FSI was 4.8 per cent per annum during the pre-reform period, that is, 1980–1981 to 1990–1991; but during the reform period, 1990–1991 to 2014–2015, it was only 2.37 per cent per annum and increased at the rate of 3.0 per cent per annum at national level. Further, the trends lines indicate that the composite Z-score of FSI and its components had positive and significant at national level during study period. But it is a matter of concern that the growth rate of FSI has been declining during the reform period of the study.

Karl Pearson's correlation coefficient of FSI is positively correlated with FAI, IFS and IFA. FAI is positively correlated with IFS and IFA. Similarly, IFS is positively correlated with IFA. It is observed that all components of FSI are highly correlated to each other. The value of correlation coefficient among food security and its dimension is found to be positive and significant at 1 per cent level of significance. The regression results regarding food security indicate that climatic variability in terms of rainfall, minimum and maximum temperature affected FSI and its components during the study period at national level. In the case of climatic variables, the result indicates that annual rainfall and maximum temperature had a negative and significant impact on FSI during 1980–1981 to 2014–2015 at national level, whereas the impact of minimum temperature on FSI is found negative during the study period. The model shows that value of R-square is 0.6976; which means that about 70 per cent variation in FSI is explained by the climatic and non-climatic variables.

Moreover, in case of non-climatic variables, the regression result shows that cropping intensity, livestock as ratio of gross sown area, road length network as ratio of gross sown area and gross capital formation in agriculture sector as ratio of gross sown area had positive and statistically significant impact on the FSI during study period at national level. On the other hand, number of tractors as ratio of gross sown area, fertilizer consumption as ratio of gross sown area, gross irrigated area as ratio of gross sown area and poverty ratio had positive and insignificant impact on the FSI, while urbanization had negative impact on FSI at national level.

The State Level Synthesis

The state level results indicate that CAGR of food grains productivity during the study period was found highest in Rajasthan followed by Andhra Pradesh, Gujarat Haryana, Karnataka, West Bengal, Madhya Pradesh and Bihar in that order. On the other hand, the other states such as Kerala, Assam, Maharashtra, Uttar Pradesh, Himachal Pradesh, Orissa, Tamil Nadu and Punjab's food grain productivity growth rate was lower than the national average, that is, 2.06 per cent per annum during the study period. The growth rate of food grain, viz, wheat, rice, cereals, coarse cereals, pulses and total food grains is found fluctuated and mixed growth rate during the early economic reforms period in the different states of the country. Overall from the above analysis the results reveal that productivity of food grain crops grew at positive rate but with quite fluctuating trends across the states during the study periods. In case of non-food grains, CAGR of oilseeds productivity was observed noticeably to be positive in almost all of the selected states except during the study period. The results reveal that sugarcane grew at positive rate in all states except Andhra Pradesh, Himachal Pradesh, Kerala and Maharashtra during GR period. It is observed that growth rate of non-food grain crops, that is, sugarcane, oilseeds and cotton fluctuated with mixed trends at state level during the study period and in all sub-phases. However, widespread variations in term of growth rate of non-food grain crops was the major concern. During the recent era, as we know that non-food grain is also very important for food and nutrition security at national level as well as state level, policymakers should emphasize on these crops to sustain growth rate of non-food grain productivity. CAGR of value of output from agriculture sector grew at positive rate in the major states such as Andhra Pradesh, Assam, Bihar, Gujarat, Haryana, Himachal Pradesh, Karnataka, Kerala, Madhya Pradesh, Maharashtra, Orissa, Punjab, Rajasthan, Tamil Nadu, Uttar Pradesh and West Bengal during the study period. CAGR of value of output from agriculture increased in Andhra Pradesh, Assam, Bihar, Haryana, Himachal Pradesh, Madhya Pradesh, Maharashtra, Orissa, Rajasthan, Tamil Nadu and Uttar Pradesh during 2000–2001 to 2014–2015 as compared to 1990–1991 to 1999–2000. While, CAGR of value of output from agriculture decreased in case of Gujarat, Karnataka, Kerala, Punjab and West Bengal during 2000–2001 to 2014–2015 as compares to 1990–1991 to 1999–2000.

The state level trends of FAI in Andhra Pradesh, Assam, Bihar, Gujarat, Haryana, Himachal Pradesh, Karnataka, Kerala, Madhya Pradesh, Maharashtra, Orissa, Punjab, Rajasthan, Tamil Nadu, Uttar Pradesh and West Bengal were found to be positive and impressive during the study period. On the other hand, rank of the major states in terms of FAI was found to be in the following order: Punjab, Maharashtra, Haryana, Madhya Pradesh and Gujarat. These states were comparatively better than the other states such as Rajasthan, Andhra Pradesh, Orissa, Himachal Pradesh, Assam, Uttar Pradesh, Karnataka, Bihar, West Bengal, Tamil Nadu and Kerala. In terms of IFS Punjab had the highest rank and Rajasthan had the lowest during the study period. The data shows that in terms of IFA Punjab occupied the top rank due to high development in the area of agricultural inputs, technology and productivity. IFA has been found positive in several states such as Andhra Pradesh, Assam, Bihar, Gujarat, Haryana, Himachal Pradesh, Karnataka, Kerala, Madhya Pradesh, Maharashtra, Orissa, Punjab, Rajasthan, Tamil Nadu, Uttar Pradesh and West Bengal during the study period. The value of IFA of all states together has marginally increased from 0.399 in 1980–1981 to 0.424 in 2014–2015. FSI in all selected states, namely, Andhra Pradesh, Assam, Bihar, Gujarat, Haryana, Himachal Pradesh, Karnataka, Kerala, Madhya Pradesh, Maharashtra, Orissa, Punjab, Rajasthan, Tamil Nadu, Uttar Pradesh and West Bengal showed positive trends with fluctuations during the study period. Punjab and Haryana had the first and second ranks, whereas Orissa and Bihar had the lowest first and second ranks in term of FSI during the study period. The Z-score varied from 20 to 56 in 1980–1981 and from 28 to 63 in 2014–2015. The variations among the states decreased according to time. It is clear from the above analysis that Punjab and Haryana are the most food secure states as they are highly developed agriculturally. These states have sufficient amount of food grain production, consumption expenditure, calories availability and government expenditure on per hectare-cultivated land (Shakeel et al. 2012).

The state level trends of climatic variables, namely, annual rainfall, average annual maximum and minimum temperatures show high level variability during the study period. The state level growth rate of temperature difference during the study period can be divided into three categories, namely, high growth rate in temperature difference states (CAGR > 0.12%), moderate growth rate in temperature difference states (CAGR between –0.11% and 0.11%) and low growth rate in temperature difference states (CAGR < –0.11%). The figure 5.11 reveals that the growth rate of temperature difference states has widespread fluctuations across the selected states during the study period. It is observed that the variations highly fluctuated across the states during the study period in terms of annual rainfall as well as temperature. The state level panel data regression result regarding food grain productivity indicate that the factors such as per hectare consumption of fertilizers, gross irrigated area, cropping intensity, road length, population density, literacy rate, annual rainfall and minimum temperature had positive and statistically significant impact on the food grain productivity during the study period. On the other hand, maximum temperature and forest area had negative and significant impact on the food grain productivity during the study period. The value of R-square was very high, that is, 81.26 which means that the model described more than 81 per cent variation in food grain productivity by the variation in climatic and non-climatic factors during the study period. Overall, it is concluded that climatic and non-climatic factors affected the food grain productivity and its components crops' productivity across the major states during the study period.

In case of non-food grain crops, the result revealed that that the factors such as per hectare consumption of fertilizers, road length, literacy rate, rainfall and minimum temperature had positive and statistically significant impact on sugarcane productivity during the study period. On the other hand, population density and maximum temperature had negative impact during the study period. In the case of oilseeds productivity, factors such as gross irrigated area, literacy rate, minimum temperature and maximum temperature had positive and statistically significant impact during the study period. It was negatively affected by rainfall, road length and population density. Regarding cotton productivity, the determinants such as per hectare consumption of fertilizers, gross irrigated area, literacy rate and minimum temperature had positive and statistically significant impact on cotton productivity whereas rainfall, cropping intensity and road length had positive but insignificant impact on cotton productivity during the study period. The variables such as maximum temperature and forest area had negative but insignificant impact on cotton productivity during the same period. The state level regression results regarding value of output from agriculture reveal that factors such as per hectare consumption of fertilizers and maximum temperature had positive and statistically significant impact while literacy rate and rainfall had positive but insignificant impact on value of output from agriculture during the study period. On the other hand, road length, literacy rate and minimum temperature had negative and significant impact on value of output from agriculture. However, the variables such as gross irrigated area, forest area and cropping intensity had negative but insignificant impact on the value of output from agriculture during the study period.

The panel data regression result regarding food security reveals that factors such as cropping intensity, road length, gross irrigated area, forest area, per hectare consumption of fertilizer and literacy rate had positive and statistically significant impact on FSI during the study period, while the impact of maximum temperature on FSI was found negative and significant during the study period. On the other hand, population density and minimum temperature had positive but insignificant impact on FSI during the same period. Urbanization had negative and statistically significant impact while rainfall had negative but insignificant impact on FSI during the study period. From the results, it is perceived that any increment in rainfall had negative but insignificant impact on FSI during the study period. The value of R-square is 0.6012, which denotes that more than 60 per cent variation in FSI is explained by the climatic and non-climatic factors during the study period.

Policy Suggestions from the Study

In the light of the above stated empirical results, it is witnessed that there is a need to intervene, which can help farmers to adopt climate changes and reduce the loss of agricultural production and value of output from agriculture. Farmers should particularly change the cropping pattern with changes in rainfall and temperature. Similarly, huge financial support for efficient land management, balanced fertilizers use and enhanced irrigated area as well as capital formation in agriculture need to be promoted. Hence, programmes and policies focused on reducing GHGs emission through raising the forest coverage areas, improving conservation mechanisms, efficient management and development of scientific instruments, and more allocation of funds on agricultural research and development for the overall development of the agriculture sector. The government should focus towards the changing the type of crops which are grown to better match the changed pattern of temperature and rainfall. Effective adaptation strategies, involving technological innovation and intuitional development are the key factors which would help to improve agricultural productivity as well as food security of the nation. Climate variability in terms of rainfall and temperature has become an emerging issue of the agriculture sector and food security in India. It is obvious that majority of India's population depends on climate-sensitive sectors such as agriculture, forestry and fishery for their livelihood. Due to the adverse impact of climatic variability, rainfall is declining and temperatures are increasing. Thus, droughts and floods are increasing and these are affecting food security and livelihoods of the people in the country. This delineates the need to change the national level policymaking, planning and public–private partnerships, thus laying out a global vision for modifying longer time trends for sustainable development and reducing the food security problems in India. At state level, there is a need to focus on area- and region-specific programmes in order to increase the growth rate of value of output from agriculture in different states of India.

Agricultural intensification will further strain natural resources. Increasing competition for land and water will entail increase in the demands for housing and industrialization; and thus it is highly likely that this would result in a diversion from agriculture. The impact of climate change on agricultural production is not just limited to crops. The changes in climatic factors will also affect food grain production and food security via its direct or indirect impact on other components of the agriculture sector, especially livestock and fisheries production which is closely linked with crop production. In order to address the impact of climate change on agriculture sector, careful management of resources such as soil, water and biodiversity is required. Sustainable agriculture is possible only through production systems with the efficient use of environmental goods and services without damaging these assets. There is also a requirement to reduce pollution of water, air, land, less use of chemical fertilizers, insecticides and pesticides, forestation, plantation and biodiversity at state and national level. There is a need to focus in the areas of changing cropping pattern, agriculture credit facilities, price stability, better irrigation facilities, providing bio-fertilizers, better infrastructure facilities, crop insurance facility, modern techniques to farmers, extension of technology and more government expenditure on agriculture, rural development and flood control, and promote public–private sector partnerships to overcome the adverse effects of climate variability and value of productivity.

The government should focus on soil health, water conservation management and pest management. For achieving a diversified nutritious food basket, the production model should be diversified to crops, livestock, fisheries, poultry, agro-forestry and homestead gardens supported by nurseries. These nurseries can make-up for deficits in food and nutrition from climate-related productivity (yield) losses of crops. Farm ponds, fertilizer trees and biogas plants must be promoted in all semi-arid rainfed areas at state and national level. In order to improve food security at state level and national level, the Government of India need to adopt strategies such as to increase food grain production, intervention in the grain markets, institutions of public distribution system and maintenance of stocks for major food grains. The government may also decide to limit exports in order to preserve national supply and the stability of domestic prices. Pro-poor policy, basically small and marginal farms oriented agricultural growth policy should be adopted since small and marginal farms are predominant at states and national and farm sizes are decreasing. The productivity of small holder's agriculture is the key for promoting agricultural growth. It is crucial to expand small holder access to finances for agriculture, risk management strategies, inputs efficiency, services and extension and increase investment in rural infrastructure at states level and national level. Cropping intensity, agricultural labour division and literate farmers may be better idea for improvement in food security. Cropping intensity may increase the rotation of crops resulting in more food production and this may increase employment opportunities and generate the higher level income. Moreover, a large scale climate literacy programme or climatic information, namely, information-related cyclone, floods, and droughts as well as short-term training to farmers is necessary to prepare farmers from rapid fluctuations in weather conditions and to take precautionary actions and to avoid loss of land productivity at crop level. At state level, the region specific strategies must be needed to avoid the impact of climatic variability. Network of meteorological observatories should be increased up to farm level. Currently, IMD temperature stations networks across the states is insufficient, though it has a good number of rain gauge stations. Thus, there is a pressing need to record surface air temperature across the states. This will provide a better picture of temperature variability over the states under the projected climate change scenario in India. Crop-specific and location-specific crop weather relationships are to be worked out based on long period experimental data. There is an urgent need to build the capacity of different stakeholders on climate resilient agriculture; structured training programmes need to be designed and implemented at all levels with a time frame. Climate resilient agriculture should become an important component of farmer's training programmes, organized by primary extension service providers. There is a need to utilize the indigenous knowledge of farmers in coping with climatic variability. Strengthen international cooperation and integrate climate change dimensions into the relevant international policies and programmes is need of the day in order to build capacities in developing countries to conserve and sustainably use genetic resources for food and agriculture system of the nation. Adaptive capacity of the nation should be strengthened by providing public goods and services such as better climate information, research and development on heat-resistant crop variety, early warning systems. Further some innovative risk sharing instruments such as index-based insurance schemes and implement aggressive public-private partnerships for reforestation and aforestation at state level, national level should be explored. During the recent era, food security not only requires conventional agricultural policies focusing towards stability but also policies oriented towards procuring healthy and environmentally sustainable food for the population. Now it is high time to formulate an indicator that pursues both 'food security' in the conventional sense, as well as current concerns like sustainability and conservation of food. In the 21st century, food security must be achieved in the context of food availability; food stability and food safety at aggregate level as well as disaggregate level in India. Hence, in a nutshell it can be argued that Indian agriculture is sensitive to climate variations and changing precipitation levels. Some of the crops, namely wheat, sugarcane, paddy etc. are the most affected by meteorological changes. Further, correlating the changes in the climate with food security, it can be inferred that adverse effects on agricultural productivity of main stable crops like wheat and paddy has led to food insecurity in India. Policy implications and adaptations have been recommended to mitigate the impacts of climate change on agricultural productivity of specific crops and food security.

References

Ahlawat, Savita, and Dhian Kaur. 2013. 'Food Security in India: A Case Study of Kandi Region of Punjab'. *International Journal of Humanities and Social Sciences* 7(4): 622–626.

Ahmad, J., A. Dastgir and S. Haseen. 2011. 'Impact of Climate Change on Agriculture and Food Security in India'. *International Journal of Agricultural Environmental and Biotechnology* 4(2): 129–137.

Asha Latha, K. V., M. Gopinath and A. R. S. Bhat. 2012. 'Impact of Climate Change on Rain Fed Agriculture in India: A Case Study of Dharward'. *International Journal of Environmental Science and Development* 3(4): 368–371.

Asian Development Bank. 2012. *Food Security and Poverty in Asia and the Pacific: Key Challenge and Policy Issues*. Mandaluyong City: Asian Development Bank.

Auffhammer, Maximilian, Veerabhadran Ramanathan and Jeffrey R. Vincent. 2012. 'Climate Change, the Monsoon, and Rice Yield in India'. *Climate Change* 111(2): 411–424. doi: 10. 1007/s 10584-011-0208-4

Banday, U. J., and R. A. Ranjan. 2014. 'Deterioration of Agricultural Productivity due to Climate Change in Haryana' (MPRA, Paper No. 72654). Available at: https://mpra.ub.uni-muenchen.de/72654/8/MPRA_paper_72654.pdf

Beg, Noreen, Jan Corfee Morlot, Ogunlade Davidson, Yaw Afrane-Okesse, Lwazikazi Tyani, Fatma Denton, Youba Sokona, Jean Philippe Thomas, Emilio Lèbre La Rovere, Jyoti K. Parikh, Kirit Parikh and A. Atiq Rahman. 2002. 'Linkages between Climate Change and Sustainable Development'. *Climate Policy* 2(2–3): 129–144.

Bhalla, G. S., and G. Singh. 1997. 'Economic Liberalization and Indian Agriculture: A State-wise Analysis'. *Economic and Political Weekly* 32(13): A2–A18.

Bhandari, H., S. Pandey, R. Sharan, D. Naik, I. Hirway, S. K. Taunk and A. S. R. A. S. Sastri. 2007. 'Economic Costs of Drought and Rice Farmers' Coping Mechanisms'. In *Economic Costs of Drought and Rice Farmers' Coping Mechanisms: A Cross-country Comparative Analysis*, edited by S. Pandey, H. Bhandari and B. Hardy, 43–112. Los Baños: International Rice Research Institute.

Birthal, Pratap S., Tajuddin Khan, Digvijay S. Negi and Shaily Agarwal. 2014. 'Impact of Climate Change on Yields of Major Food Crops in India: Implication for Food Security'. *Agricultural Economic Research Review* 27(2): 145–155.

Bocchiola, D., L. Brunetti, A. Soncini, F. Polinelli and M. Gianinetto. 2017. 'Agriculture and Food Security under Climate Change in Nepal'. *Advances in Plants and Agriculture Research* 6(6): 194–199.

Brahmanand, P. S., A. Kumar, S. Ghosh, S. Roy Chowdhury, R. B. Singandhupe, Rajbir Singh, P. Nanda, H. Chakraborthy, S. K. Srivastava and M. S. Behera. 2013. 'Challenges to Food Security in India'. *Current Science* 104(7): 841–846.

Breisinger, Clemens, Olivier Ecker, Perrihan Al-Riffai, Richard Robertson, Rainer Thiele, and Manfred Wiebelt. 2011. 'Climate Change, Agricultural Production and Food Security' (Germany Kiel Working Paper No. 1747). Kiel: Kiel Institute for the World Economy.

Brown, M. E., and Funk, C. C. 2008. 'Food Security under Climate Change'. *Science, New Series* 319(5863): 580–581.

Bush, L., and W. B. Lacy, eds. 1984. 'Introduction, What Does Food Security Mean?' In *Food* Security *in the United States*. Total Population series 1, part 11 B(1). Boulder, CO: Westview Press.

Chakraborty, S., A. V. Tiedemann and P. S. Teng. 2000. 'Climate Change: Potential Impact on Plant Diseases'. *Environment Pollution* 108(3): 317–326.

Charles, S. 2011. 'Climate Changes: Impacts on Food Safety'. *Natural Resources and Environment* 26(1): 44–47.

Chatterjee, B. and M. Khadka. 2011. Climate Change and Food Security in South Asia. Jaipur (India): CUTS International.

Chaturvedi, V. 2015. 'The Cost of Climate Change Impacts for India' (Working Paper No. 11). New Delhi: Council on Energy, Environment and Water.

Ching-Cheng, Chang. 2002. 'The Potential Impact of Climate Change on Taiwan's Agriculture'. *Agricultural Economics* 27(1): 51–64.

Corfee-Morlot, J., and S. Agrawal. 2004. 'The Benefits of Climate Policy'. *Global Environment Change*, 14 (2004): 197–199. Available at: https://www.oecd.org/env/cc/40132932.pdf

Cook, J. T., and D. A. Frank. 2008. 'Food Security, Poverty and Human Development in the United States'. *Annals of the New York Academy of Sciences* 1136: 193–209.

Dagar, J. C., A. K. Singh, R. Singh and A. Arunachalum. 2012. 'Climate Change vis-a-vis Indian Agriculture'. *Annals of Agricultural Research* 33(4): 189–203.

Das, Haripada. 2015. *Global Climate Change and Agriculture Implications for Food Security*. Hyderabad: BS Publication, 18–19.

Data, M., D. Daschaudhuri and N. P. Singh, eds. 2008. 'Effect of Climate Variability on Crop Productivity in North East India'. In *Climate Change and Food Security*, 103–117. New Delhi: New India Publishing Agency.

Decker, W. L. 1975. 'The Impact of Climate on World Food Production'. *The American Biology Teacher* 36(9): 334–338.

Demeke, A. B., A. Keil and M. Zeller. 2011. 'Using Panel Data to Estimate the Effect of Rainfall Shock on Smallholders Food Security and Vulnerability in Rural Ethiopia'. *Climate Change* 108(1–2): 185–206.

Dev, S. M., and A. N. Sharma. 2010. 'Food Security in India: Performance, Challenges and Policies' (Oxfam India Working Paper Series 08). New Delhi: Oxfam India.

Downing T.E., O.J. Kuik, and J.B. Smith, 2004. 'Distributional Aspects of Climate Change Impacts'. *Global Environmental Change: Human and Policy Dimensions* 14(3), 259–272.

EPA 2014. Climate change indicators in the United States, Third Edition, EPA 430-R-14-004, U.S. Environmental Protection Agency. www.epa.gov/climatechange/indicators.

FAO. 1989. 'Sustainable Agricultural Production: Implications for International Agricultural Research'. FAO Research and Technology Paper No. 4. Rome, Italy. p. 5.

———. 1996. 'Rome Declaration on World Food Security and World Food Summit Plan of Action' (World Food Summit, 13–17 November, Rome). Available at: http://www.fao.org/3/w3613e/w3613e00.htm

———. 2006 (June). *Food Security* (Policy Brief, Issues 2). Rome: FAO.

———. 2008a. Climate Change and Disaster Risk Management: Technical Background Document from the Expert Consultation on 28 to 29 February 2008, Rome: Food and Agriculture Organisation. ftp://ftp.fao.org/docrep/fao/meeting/013/ai786e.pdf

———. 2009. *Food Security and Agricultural Mitigation in Developing Countries: Options for Capturing Synergies*. Rome: FAO.

———. 2010. *Climate Change Mitigation and Adaptation in Agriculture, Forestry and Fisheries*. Rome: FAO.

FAO, IFAD and WFP 2012. The State of Food Insecurity in the World 2012, Economic growth is necessary but not sufficient to accelerate reduction of hunger and malnutrition. Rome, FAO.

Felkner, John, Kamilya Tazhibayeva and Robert Townsend. 2009. 'Impact of Climate Change on Rice Production in Thailand'. *The American Economic Review* 99(2): 205–210.

Fischer, G., M. Shah, F. N. Tubiello and H. Velhuizen. 2005. 'Socio-economic and Climate Change Impacts on Agriculture: An Integrated Assessment, 1990–2080'. *Philosophical Transactions of the Royal Society* 360(1463): 2067–2083.

Foley, J. A., R. DeFries, G. P. Asner, C. Barford, G. Bonan, S. R. Carpenter, F. S. Chapin, M. T. Coe, G. C. Daily, H. K. Gibbs, J. H. Helkowski, T. Holloway, E. A. Howard, C. J. Kucharik, C. Monfreda, J. A. Patz, C. Prentice, N. Ramankutty and P. K. Snyder. 2005. 'Global Consequences of Land Use'. *Science* 309: 570–574. Available at: http://www.fao.org/fileadmin/user_upload/rome2007/docs/Global_Consequences_of_Land_Use.pdf

Food and Agriculture Organization. 2016. 'State of Food and Agriculture: Climate Change'. Agriculture and Food Security (Rome: FAO, 2016), (http://www.fao.org/3/a-i6030e.pdf.)

Futang, W., and Zhao Zong-ci. 1995. 'Impact of Climate Change on Natural Vegetation in China and its Implication for Agriculture'. *Journal of Biogeography* 22(4–5): 657–664.

Gaiha, R. 2003. 'Does Right to Food Matter?' *Economic and Political Weekly* 38(40): 4269–4276.

Goswami, B. N., V. Venugopal, D. Sengupta, M. S. Madhusoodanan and K. Xavier Prince. 2006. 'Increasing Trend of Extreme Rain Events over India in a Warming Environment'. *Science* 314(5804): 1442–1445.

Goswami, P. K., and B. Chatterjee. 2010. 'Linkage between Rural Poverty and Agricultural Productivity across the Districts of Uttar Pradesh in India'. *Journal of Development and Agricultural Economics* 2(2): 26–40.

Government of India. 2011. *Agriculture Census 2010–11*. New Delhi: Agriculture Census Division, Department of Agriculture and Cooperation, Ministry of Agriculture.

———. 2015. *Agricultural Statistics at a Glance*. New Delhi: Department of Agriculture and Cooperation, Ministry of Agriculture.

———. 2016a. *Agricultural Statistics at a Glance*. New Delhi: Department of Agriculture and Cooperation, Ministry of Agriculture.

———. 2016b. *Economic Survey 2015–16*. New Delhi: Ministry of Finance.

Greg, E. E., B. E. Anam, M. F. William and E. J. C. Duru. 2011. 'Climate Change, Food Security and Agricultural Productivity in Africa: Issues and Policy Directions'. *International Journal of Humanities and Social Science* 1(21): 205–223.

Guiteras, Raymond. 2009. *The Impact of Climate Change on Indian Agriculture*. College Park, MD: University of Maryland [mimeo]. Available at: http://econdse.org/wp-content/uploads/2014/04/guiteras_climate_change_indian_agriculture_sep_2009.pdf

Gupta, S., P. Sen and S. Srinivasan. 2012. 'Impact of Climate Change on Indian Economy: Evidence from Food Grain Yields' (Working Paper No. 218). New Delhi: Centre for Development Economics.

Hadke, P., and Surendra Jichkar. 2006. 'Food Security: The Indian Scenario'. *Indian Journal of Agricultural Economics* 61 (3): 469–480.

Hay, J. 2007. 'Extreme Weather and Climate Events and Farming Risks'. In *Managing Weather and Climate Risks in Agriculture*, edited by Sivakumar, M. V. K. and R. Motha, 1–19. Berlin: Springer.

Hollaender, M. 2010. 'Human Right to Adequate Food: NGOs have to Make the Difference'. *CATALYST*, Newsletter of Cyriac Elias Voluntary Association (CEVA) 8(1): 5–6.

IPCC 2007. Fourth Assessment Report, Climate Change 2007: Synthesis Report, Summary for Policy Makers. Geneva: Intergovernmental Panel on Climate Change.

Iqbal, K., and A. Siddique. 2012. 'The Impact of Climate Change on Agricultural Productivity: Evidence from Panel Data of Bangladesh' (Discussion Paper 14.29). University of Western Australia, 14–29. Available at: http://www.business.uwa.edu.au/__data/assets/

pdf_file/0012/2655894/14-29-The-Impact-of-Climate-Change-on-Agricultural-Productivity-Evidence-From-Panel-Data-of-Bangladesh.pdf

Jaswal, S. S. 2014. 'Challenges to Food Security in India'. *Journal of Humanities and Social Science* 19(4): 93–100.

Javeed, S., and A. Manuhaar. 2013. 'Climate Change and Its impact on Productivity of Indian Agriculture'. *Journal of Economics & Social Development* 9(1): 146–151.

Joshi, K., and P. Chaturvedi. 2013. 'Impact of Climate Change on Agriculture'. *Octa Journal of Environment Research* 1(1): 39–42.

Joshi, P.K., Suneetha Kadiyala and S. Mahendra Dev 2011. 'India's Economy Roars Ahead but Nutritional Improvement is Stalled', Global Food Policy Report, International Food Policy Research Institute, Washington, D.C., U.S.A.

Kannan, E., and S. Sundaram. 2011. 'Analysis of Trends in India's Agricultural Growth' (Working Paper No. 276). Available at: http://www.environmentportal.in/files/file/Analysis%20of%20Trends%20in%20India%E2%80%99s%20Agricultural%20Growth.pdf

Kapur, D., R. Khosla and P. B. Mehta. 2009. 'Climate Change: India's Options'. *Economic and Political Weekly* 36(31): 34–42.

Kaul, S., and G. Ram. 2009. 'Impact of Global Warming on Production of Jowar in India' (Special issue: Sustainable agriculture in the context of climate change). *Agricultural Situation in India* 66(5): 253–256.

Khatkar, R. K., V. K. Singh and D. Suthar. 2006. 'Consumption Pattern and Food Security in Haryana and Rajasthan'. *Indian Journal of Agricultural Economics* 61(3): 404–443.

Krishna, Nishanth, Rashmi Kundapur, N Udaya Kiran and Sanjeev Badige. 2015. 'Food Security and Nutrition Consumption among Households in the Semi-Urban Field Practice Area of K.S. Hedge Medical Academy, Mangalore: A Pilot Study'. *Journal of Health Science* 5(2): 31–37.

Kumar, A., and A. Sharma. 2014. 'Climate Change and Sugarcane Productivity in India: An Econometric Analysis'. *Journal of Social and Development Science* 5(2): 111–122.

Kumar, Anjani, M. C. S. Bantilan, Praduman Kumar, Sant Kumar and Shiv Jee. 2012. 'Food Security in India: Trends, Patterns and Determinants'. *Indian Journal of Agriculture Economics* 67(3): 445–463.

Kumar, A., and P. Sharma. 2013. 'Impact of Climate Variation on Agricultural Productivity and Food Security in Rural India' (Discussion Paper, Economics the Open-Access, Open–Assessment E-Journal, No. 2013-43). Available at: http://www.economics-ejournal.org/economics/discussionpapers/2013-43/file

Kumar, Ajay, Pritee Sharma and Sunil Kumar Ambrammal. 2014. 'Climate Effects on Food Grain Productivity in India'. *Journal of Studies in Dynamics and Change* 1(1): 38–48.

Kumar, K. S. K. 2007. 'Climate Change Studies in Indian Agriculture'. *Economic and Political Weekly* 42(42–46): 13, 15–18.

Kumar, K. S. K., and J. Parikh. 2001. 'Socio-Economic Impacts of Climate Change on Indian Agriculture'. *International Review for Environmental Strategies* 2(2): 277–293.

Krishnan, R., V. Kumar, M. Sugi and J. Yoshimura. 2009. 'Internal Feedbacks from Monsoon-Midlatitude Interactions during Droughts in the Indian Summer Monsoon'. *Journal of Atmospheric Science* 66(3): 553–578.

Kumar, Rohitashw, and H. R. Gautam. 2014. 'Climate Change and Its Impact on Agricultural Productivity in India'. *Climate Weather Forecasting* 2(1). doi: 10.4172/2332-2594.1000109

Kumar, S., and S. Gupta. 2015. 'Crop Diversification in India: Emerging Trends and Determinants and Policy Implications'. *International Journal of Current Research* 7(6): 40.

Kumar, S. N., P. K. Aggarwal, S. Rani, S. Jain, R. Saxena and N. Chauhan. 2011. 'Impact of Climate Change on Crop Productivity in Western Ghats, Coastal and Northeastern Regions of India' (Special section: Climate change: projections and impact for India). *Current Science* 101(3): 332–341.

Lambrou, Y. and S. Nelson. 2010. Farmers in a changing climate – Does gender matter?, Food Security in Andhra Pradesh, India, FAO, Rome Italy. (Also available at: www.fao.org/docrep/013/i1721e/i1721e00.htm)

Lee, H. L. 2009. 'The Impact of Climate Change on Global Food Supply and Demand, Food Prices, and Land Use'. *Paddy Water Environmental* 7(4): 321–331.

Lekhi, R. K., and J. Singh. 2016. *Agricultural Economics*. New Delhi, Kalyani Publishers.

Lobell, David B., and Sharon M. Gourdji. 2012. 'The Influence of Climate Change on Global Crop Productivity'. *Plant Physiology* 160(4): 1686–1697.

Maan, V. K., and S. Kumar. 2012. 'State Wise Agricultural Sector Growth and Performance'. *International Journal of Application or Innovation in Engineering and Management (IJAIEM)* 1(2): 18–25.

Mahato, A. 2014. 'Climate Change and Its impact on Agriculture'. *International Journal of Scientific and Research Publication* 4(4): 1–6.

Mahmood, N., B. Ahmad, S. Hassan and K. Bakhsh. 2012. 'Impact of Temperature and Precipitation on Rice Productivity in Rice—Wheat Cropping System of Punjab Province'. *The Journal of Animal and Plant Sciences* 22(4): 993–997.

Mall, R. K., and P. K. Agarwal. 2002. 'Climate Change and Rice Yields in Diverse Agro-Environments of India: Evaluation of Impact Assessment Models'. *Climate Change* 52(3): 315–330.

Masters, G., P. Baker and J. Flood. 2010. 'Climate Change and Agricultural Commodities' (CABI Working Paper 02). Available at: https://www.cabi.

org/Uploads/CABI/expertise/climate-change-and-agricultural-commodities-working-paper.pdf

Mendelsohn, Robert, Ariel Dinar and Larry Williams. 2006. 'The Distribution Impact of Climate Change on Rich and Poor Countries'. *Environment and Development Economics* 11(2): 159–178.

Mendelsohn, R., and A. Dinar. 2001. 'The Effect of Development on the Climate Sensitivity of Agriculture'. *Environment and Development Economics* 6(1): 85–101.

Modgal, S. C. 2012. *Food Security of India: An Overview*. New Delhi: National Book Trust Publication.

Nastis, S. A., A. Michailidis and F. Chatzitheodoridis. 2012. 'Climate Change and Agricultural Productivity'. *African Journal of Agricultural Research* 7(35): 4885–4893.

Neenu, S., A. K. Biswas and A. Subba Rao. 2013. 'Impact of Climate Factors on Crop Production—A Review'. *Agriculture Review* 34(2): 97–106.

Nelson, Gerald C., Mark W. Rosegrant, Jawoo Koo, Richard Robertson, Timothy Sulser, Tingju Zhu, Claudia Ringler, Siwa Msangi, Amanda Palazzo, Miroslav Batka, Marilia Magalhaes, Rowena Valmonte-Santos, Mandy Ewing and David Lee. 2009. *Climate Change: Impact on Agriculture and Costs of Adaptation* (Food Policy Report, 19). Washington, DC: IFPRI.

Oluoko-Odingo, A. A. 2009. 'Determinants of Poverty: Lessons from Kenya'. *Geo Journal* 74(4): 311–331.

Panda, Architesh. 2009. 'Assessing Vulnerability to Climate Change in India'. *Economic and Political Weekly* 44(16): 105–107.

Pandey, A. 2015. 'Food Security in India and States: Key Challenges and Policy Option'. *Journal of Agricultural Economics and Rural Development* 2(1): 012-021.

Parnell, W. R., and C. Smith. 2008. 'Food Security: Current Research Initiatives Globally and in New Zealand'. Paper presented at Nutrition Society of New Zealand Conference, Christchurch, 8–9 December.

Parry, Martin L., Cynthia Rosenzweig, Ana Iglesias, Matthew Livermore and Gunther Fischer. 2004. 'Effect of Climate Change on Global Food Production under SRES Emissions and Socio-Economic Scenarios'. *Global Environment Change* 14(1): 53–67.

Pathania, S., and G. D. Vashist. 2006. 'Food Security: Present Scenario and Future Strategies'. *Indian Journal of Agricultural Economics* 61(3): 412–413.

Porter, J.R., L. Xie, A.J. Challinor, K. Cochrane, S.M. Howden, M.M. Iqbal, D.B. Lobell and M.I. Travasso 2014. 'Food Security and Food Production Systems'. In C.B. Field, V.R. Barros, D.J. Dokken, K.J. Mach, M.D. Mastrandrea, T.E. Bilir, M. Chatterjee, K.L. Ebi, Y.O. Estrada, R.C. Genova, B. Girma, E.S. Kissel, A.N. Levy, S. MacCracken, P.R. Mastrandrea & L.L. White, eds. *Climate Change: Impacts, Adaptation, and Vulnerability*, pp. 485–533, Contribution of Working Group II to the Fifth Assessment

Report of the Intergovernmental Panel on Climate Change. Cambridge, UK, and New York, USA, Cambridge University Press.

Prajapati, R., S. Singh and R. Gangwar. 2015. 'Effect of Climate Change on Plant Diseases in Bundelkhand Zone Leading to Changing in Cropping Pattern'. *Agriways* 3(2): 120–138.

Rajeevan, Madhaven, Jyoti Bhate and Ashok K. Jaswal. 2008. 'Analysis of Variability and Trends of Extreme Rainfall Events over India Using 104 Years of Gridded Daily Rainfall Data'. *Geographical Resources Letters*, 35(18). doi:10.1029/2008GL035143

Raman, R., and R. Kumari. 2012. 'Regional Disparity in Agricultural Development: a District Level Analysis for Uttar Pradesh'. *Journal of Regional Development and Planning* 1(2): 71–90.

Ranuzzi, A., and R. Srivastava. 2012. 'Impact of Climate Change on Agriculture and Food Security'. *ICRIER, policy series 16*. New Delhi. Available at: http://www.icrier.org/pdf/Policy_Series_No_16.pdf

Reilly, J. 1995. 'Climate Change and Global Agriculture: Recent Findings and Issues'. *American Journal of Agricultural Economics* 77(3): 727–733.

Rukhsana. 2011. 'Dimension of Food Security in a Selected State Uttar Pradesh'. *Journal of Agricultural Extension and Rural Development* 3(2): 29–41.

Shakeel, A., A. Jamal and N. Zaidy 2012. 'A Regional Analysis of Food Security in Bundelkhand Region (Uttar Pradesh, India). *Journal of Geography and Regional Planning*, 5(9): 252–262.

Singh, A. P. 2015. 'Ensuring Food Security of Rural People: Some Policy Interventions'. *Management Insight* 11(2): 11–24.

Singh, Gurbachan. 2016. 'Climate Change and Food Security in India: Challenges and Opportunities'. *Irrigation and Drainage* 65(S1): 5–10.

Singh, K. 2014. 'Food Security in India: Performance and Concerns'. *Journal of Humanities and Social Science (IOSR-JHSS)* 19(7): 106–119.

Sinha, A. 2006. 'Trends in Food Consumption and Nutrition: Food Security Concerns'. *Indian Journal of Agricultural Economics* 61(3): 415–416.

Sinha, S. K., and M. S. Swaminathan. 1991. 'Deforestation, Climate Change and Sustainable Nutrition Security: A Case Study of India'. Climatic Change 19: 201–209.

Slingo, Julia M., Andrew J. Challinor, Brian J. Hoskins and Timothy R. Wheeler. 2005. 'Introduction: Food Crops in a Changing Climate'. *Philosophical Transaction: Biological Science* 360(1463): 1983–1989.

Solomon, S., D. Qin, M. Manning, R. B. Alley, T. Berntsen, N. L. Bindoff, Z. Chen, A. Chidthaisong, J. M. Gregory, G. C. Hegerl, M. Heimann, B. Hewitson, B. J. Hoskins, F. Joos, J. Jouzel, V. Kattsov, U. Lohmann, T. Matsuno, M. Molina, N. Nicholls, J. Overpeck, G. Raga, V. Ramaswamy, J. Ren, M. Rusticucci, R. Somerville, T. F. Stocker, P. Whetton, R. A. Wood, and D. Wratt. 2007. Technical summary. In Climate Change 2007: The Physical Science Basis. Contribution of Working Group I to the Fourth Assessment Report of the Intergovernmental Panel on Climate Change, S.

Solomon, D. Qin, M. Manning, Z. Chen, M. Marquis, K. B. Averyt, M. Tignor, and H. L. Miller, (eds.) Cambridge, U.K., and New York: Cambridge University Press.

Srinivasan, J. 2008. 'Climate Change, Greenhouse Gases and Aerosols'. *Resonance* 89: 1147–1155.

Srivastava, A., S. N. Kumar and P. K. Aggarwal. 2010. 'Assessment on Vulnerability of Sorghum to Climate Changes in India'. *Agriculture Ecosystem and Environment* 138(3–4): 160–169.

State of Indian Agriculture 2015–16. Report on Indian Agriculture, Ministry of Agriculture & Farmers Welfare, Government of India (GoI), https://eands.dacnet.nic.in/PDF/State_of_Indian_Agriculture,2015-16.pdf

Tripathi, A. 2016. 'How to Encourage Farmers to Adopt to Climate Change?' (IEG Working Paper No. 369). http://www.iegindia.org/upload/profile_publication/doc-130616_190752IEG%20WP%20369%20AT.pdf

Unninayar S. 1989. Basic Data Requirements of an Agro-climatic System, in Climate and Food Security. International Rice Research Institute, Manila: Philippines.

Varghese, K. A., A. Mordia and M. L. Gurjar. 2006. 'Inter-State Assessment of Food Security'. *Indian Journal of Agricultural Economics* 61(3): 423–424.

Vermeulen, Sonja J., Bruce M. Campbell and John S. I. Ingram. 2012. 'Climate Change and Food System' *The Annual Review of Environment and Resources* 37: 195–222.

Wagh, R. M. 2013. 'Global Warming and Its Impact on Agriculture'. *Review of Research*, 2(11): 11–22.

Wang, Jinxia, Robert Mendelsohn, Ariel Dinar, Jikun Huang, Scott Rozelle and Lijuan Zhang. 2009. 'The Impact of Climate Change on China's Agriculture'. *Agricultural Economics* 40(3): 323–337.

World Bank. 1986. Poverty and Hunger: Issues and Options for Food Security in Developing Countries. Washington DC.

World Bank. 2007. 'Population Issues in the 21st Century: The Role of the World Bank. Health, Nutrition and Population (HNP)' (discussion paper). Washington, DC: World Bank.

———. 2008. *World Development Report, Agriculture for Development*. Washington, DC: World Bank.

———. 2013a. 'Warming Climate in India to Pose Significant Risk to Agriculture, Water Resources, Health' (press release). New Delhi.

World Economic Forum. 2008. *Global Risks 2008: A Global Risk Network Report*. Geneva: WEF. Available at: https://www.stat.berkeley.edu/~aldous/157/Papers/WEF_GlobalRisks_Report_2008.pdf

Zhai, F., T. Lin and E. Byambadori. 2009. 'A General Equilibrium Analysis of the Impact of Climate Change on Agriculture in the People's Republic of China'. *Asian Development Review* 26(1): 206–225.

About the Author

Sanjeev Kumar is working in the Department of Economics, University of Lucknow. He was previously working at Dyal Singh College (DSC), University of Delhi. He obtained his doctorate (Ph.D) in Economics from Chaudhary Charan Singh University, Meerut. He also qualified UGC NET-JRF and SLET and was awarded junior and senior research fellowship from University Grants Commission, New Delhi, for his doctoral work. He has published several books and research papers in refereed journals and has done more than six major research projects from ICSSR, MHRD, NIAP-ICAR and Delhi University. His research interests are in the field of agricultural and rural development.

Index

33/41